CRIMINAL CONVERSATIONS

THE SOCIAL FOUNDATIONS OF AESTHETIC FORMS
JONATHAN ARAC, EDITOR

THE SOCIAL FOUNDATIONS OF AESTHETIC FORMS

A SERIES OF COLUMBIA UNIVERSITY PRESS
JONATHAN ARAC, EDITOR

Critical Genealogies: Historical Situations for Postmodern Literary Studies
Jonathan Arac
Advertising Fictions: Literature, Advertisement, and Social Reading
Jennifer Wicke
Masks of Conquest: Literary Study and British Rule in India
Gauri Viswanathan
Left Politics and the Literary Profession
Lennard J. Davis and M. Bella Mirabella, editors
The Vietnam War and American Culture
John Carlos Rowe and Rick Berg, editors
Authors and Authority: English and American Criticism, 1750–1990
Patrick Parrinder
Reaches of Empire: The English Novel from Edgeworth to Dickens
Suvendrini Perera
Radical Parody: American Culture and Critical Agency After Foucault
Daniel T. O'Hara
The Profession of Authorship in America, 1800–1870
William Charvat
Narrating Discovery: The Romantic Explorer in American Literature, 1790–1855
Bruce Greenfield
The Author, Art, and the Market: Rereading the History of Aesthetics
Martha Woodmansee
Rethinking Class: Literary Studies and Social Formations
Wai Chee Dimock and Michael T. Gilmore, editors
Cities of the Dead: Circum-Atlantic Performance
Joseph Roach

CRIMINAL CONVERSATIONS

Sentimentality and Nineteenth-Century Legal Stories of Adultery

Laura Hanft Korobkin

COLUMBIA UNIVERSITY PRESS

NEW YORK

The author and the Press wish to thank the Department of English, Boston University for its contribution toward the cost of reproducing the cover illustration.

Columbia University Press
Publishers Since 1893
New York   Chichester, West Sussex

Library of Congress Cataloging-in-Publication Data
Korobkin, Laura Hanft.

Criminal conversations : sentimentality and nineteenth-century legal stories of adultery / Laura Hanft Korobkin. — Casebook ed.

p. cm. — (The social foundations of aesthetic forms)

Includes bibliographical references (p. 223) and index.

ISBN 0–231–10508–8 (cloth : acid-free paper). — ISBN 0–231–10509–6 (paper : acid-free paper)

1. American fiction—19th century—History and criticism. 2. Adultery in literature. 3. Literature and society—United States—History—19th century. 4. Trials (Adultery)—United States—History—19th century. 5. Legal stories, American—History and criticism. 6. Law and literature—History—19th century. 7. Sentimentalism in literature. I. Title. II. Series: Social foundations of aesthetic forms series.

PS374.A34K67 1998
813.'309353—dc21   98-3018
CIP

Casebound editions of Columbia University Press books are printed on permanent and durable acid-free paper.

Printed in the United States of America
c 10 9 8 7 6 5 4 3 2 1
p 10 9 8 7 6 5 4 3 2 1

Contents

Acknowledgments

I have been supported at every stage of writing this book by extraordinary advisers, critics, and friends. It began as a dissertation in the English department at Harvard, where Sacvan Bercovitch and Elaine Scarry were the ideal thesis directors, generous with their time, insightful with their comments and suggestions, patient and helpful in every way. I would like to thank the Whiting Foundation for a dissertation-finishing fellowship, the Pembroke Center for Teaching and Research on Women at Brown University for a postdoctoral fellowship, and the Bunting Institute of Radcliffe College for a Bunting Institute Fellowship. I was lucky to have the intellectual and personal support of a year at the Pembroke Center and a year at the Bunting Institute. Earlier versions of the chapters about the Henry Ward Beecher trial were published in the *Yale Journal of Law and the Humanities* and in *The New Nineteenth Century: Feminist Readings of Underread Victorian Texts.* I would also like to thank my colleagues at Boston University for their interest and support.

I want to express my thanks to the many people who have read and commented helpfully on drafts of various chapters, including Nancy Armstrong, Lawrence Buell, Lynda Bundtzen, Carolyn Dever, Wai Chee Dimock, Leo Damrosch, Philip Fisher, Richard Fox, Margery Garber, Virginia Jackson, Nancy Jones, Helena Meyer-Knapp, Martha Minow, Susan Mizruchi, Janaki Nair, Allison Pingree, Ellen Rooney, Susan Staves, James Wexler, and Elizabeth Weed. Audiences at the Center for Interdisciplinary Studies at the College of Holy Cross, at the Bunting Institute, and at the University of Washington in Seattle, and especially the Columbia University Press readers, all offered provocative and useful suggestions. Mary Lou Kete deserves special thanks for her critical acuity, cheerfulness, and friendship. Saki Bercovitch has also been a continuing source of friendship and advice.

Most of all, I want to thank my family, whose love and energy are the foundations of my life. This book is for my husband Barry and for my children, Rachel and Rob.

CRIMINAL CONVERSATIONS

PART I

Introduction and Historical Foundation

PROLOGUE

Telling Stories in the Courtroom

Near the end of E.D.E.N. Southworth's novel *Ishmael* (1863–64), Judge Merlin proudly offers Southworth's eponymous hero his first law case, one that he assures him will be "easy": representing a husband who seeks custody of his children from the wife he has abused and abandoned. When the husband tried "to get possession of their children, in order to coerce her through her affection for them," the judge explains to Ishmael, the wife removed them "to a place of secrecy" (440). The husband has now served her with a writ of habeas corpus, which everyone expects will be granted as a matter of course. "You cannot do better than take this brief," Judge Merlin assures his idealistic, self-made protégé. "It is the very neatest little case that ever a lawyer had; all the plain law on your side; a dash of the sentimental too, in the injured father's affection for the children that have been torn from him, the injured husband for the wife that repudiates him. Now you are good at law, but you are great at sentiment" (441–42).

The judge is more perceptive than he realizes. Ishmael's feelings are immediately engaged, and he sees in the domestic conflict a potentially moving story of parental affection and tragic family rupture. To him, however, the story is not about an affectionate father, but about a poor, virtuous, and loving mother who has struggled long and hard to support and maintain her family in the face of neglect and abandonment. Refusing to represent the husband, Ishmael seeks out the deserted wife, Mrs. Walsh, and defends her without charge.

When the day of the trial comes, three "giants of the law" represent the husband. Each shapes the facts of the case using his own principle of rhetorical logic. The first sets out the law in "sledge-hammer style, sonorously striking the anvil and ringing all the changes upon law, custom, precedent and so forth that always gave the children into the custody of the father" (467).[1] The second "had charge of the eloquence 'business' of that stage, and dealt in pathos, tears, white pocket handkerchiefs and poetical quotations. He drew a most heart-rending picture of the broken-spirited husband and father, rejected by an unforgiving wife and ill-conditioned children, becoming a friendless and houseless wanderer over the wide world; in danger of being driven, by despair, to madness and suicide! He compared the plaintiff to Byron, whose poetry he liberally quoted" (467). The third "did up the genteel comedy" with "a supply of 'little jokes' gleaned from Joe Miller, current comic literature, dinner tables, clubs, etc. . . . He was very witty on the subject of matrimonial disputes in particular, which reminded him of another 'little joke,' which he also told; but most of all he was amused at the caprice of womankind, who very often rather like to be compelled to do as they pleased, which reminded him of a third 'little joke' . . ." (468).

When Ishmael finally rises to speak, he is indeed "great at sentiment." For two impassioned hours, he paints the poor wife's miseries in heart-wrenching detail. In addition to "the minor advantages of youth, manly beauty, a commanding presence, a gracious smile and a sweet, deep sonorous voice," Ishmael is "no paid attorney; it was not his pocket that was interested, but his sympathies; his whole heart and soul were in the cause that he had embraced, and he brought to bear upon it all the genius of his powerful mind" (470). "The giants attempted to answer him," Southworth writes, "but it was of no use. After the freshness, the fire, the force . . . in Ishmael's utterances, their old, familiar, well-worn styles, in which the same arguments, pathos, wit that had done duty in so many other cases was paraded again, only bored their hearers. . . . The triumvirate of the Washington bar were dethroned, and Prince Ishmael reigned in their stead" (472). Mrs. Walsh's little family is preserved, and the abusive husband ordered not only to give up custody but also to pay her a separate support allowance.

I begin with Southworth's fictional courtroom because its complex interweaving of the harsh facts of women's legal status with various genres of forensic storytelling captures many of the central questions this book addresses. One set of questions interrogates the relationship between trial process and narration in real life. Who is authorized to speak, and who sits silent in the courtroom? What *kinds* of stories win cases, and why? Is the power of certain litigative stories rooted in their familiarity, their appropriation of well-known literary genres, characters, and rhetorical strategies? Does trial structure favor certain ways of telling a party's story? Ishmael's courtroom success derives as much from the superiority of his narrative approach as from the inherent justness of his cause. But it also accomplishes more. In contrast to the "well-worn styles" of his opponents,

Ishmael's rhetoric aims at making an abused wife vividly sympathetic to a panel of male judges. Southworth's gender-conscious depiction raises a second set of questions I will be asking about how real courtrooms work. Do women come to court as active, empowered speakers, or do they figure primarily as objects in stories told by and to men? Does the law itself—its procedural rules, precedents, assumptions, and customary logic—make it difficult for women's experience to be fully articulated, heard, or responded to? How have the past century's changes in America's images of women, sexuality, and marriage, particularly as those images are discursively embodied in its literary narratives, changed women's relation to the law?

I want to begin by looking more closely at Ishmael's fictional triumph. Southworth's courtroom scene privileges Ishmael's strategic use of sentimentality, the rhetorical genre I will be exploring in greatest detail. Until quite recently, E.D.E.N. Southworth was critically dismissed as one of the many female scribblers whose emotional excesses and mindless escapism constituted the ignoble field against which such "serious" writers as Hawthorne, Melville, and, eventually, Howells and James, rebelled.[2] In the past decade, Nina Baym and Mary Kelley have rediscovered her for modern readers; excellent critical work has been done on several of her novels; and one of her most popular works, *The Hidden Hand*, has been reissued.[3] Yet while critics have praised the feisty independence and frank passion of Southworth's many heroines, and at least one has noted Ishmael's role as "counsel for womanhood to the world" (Kelley 324), none has, to my knowledge, commented on Southworth's sophistication about the workings of public institutions in general and the narrative structure of trial process in particular.

One of the best-selling novelists of the nineteenth century, Southworth obviously knew how to move readers deeply.[4] It is no coincidence that her description of Mrs. Walsh's trial accords victory not to powerful logic or legal expertise, but to the homely details that elicit sympathy, to the storyteller wise in the techniques Southworth herself perfected. My point is not simply that Ishmael is a Southworth-like storyteller, but that Southworth's sophistication about how emotionally effective storytelling *works* enabled her to read courtroom interaction in ways that her contemporaries, both legal and literary, could not.

Significantly, Southworth represents Ishmael's courtroom contest as a battle among genres. His victory is the triumph of engaging sentimentality over cold logic, Romantic pathos, and farcical humor, of a fresh new form over genres that have lost their effectiveness. Ishmael's cause is surely just, but he is able to win because his rhetorical framing of that cause maximizes its authenticity and impact. Ishmael operates, of course, in a universe that runs according to Southworth's rules. The judges immediately recognize her hero's superiority and reject the artificial presentations of his opponents because Southworth structures the novel to vindicate the "truth" of Ishmael's forensic sentimentality and to reject as inadequate the genres of storytelling set against it. However, Southworth is also being faithful to what often worked—and works—in real courtrooms. As I will discuss in more detail below, while "sentimentality" labels a recognizable literary genre, it is also a set of rhetorical strategies used by narrators in any storytelling situation to construct a bond of sympathetic intimacy. Though it is often associated with female authors and female readers, in the nineteenth century courtroom sentimentality was often the rhetorical tool of choice for male lawyers who, like Southworth's Ishmael, argued their cases to all-male juries and judges.[5] If novelists use sentimentality to elicit deeply emotional, personal responses from readers, lawyers use it to elicit the same kind of responses from jurors. Just as we, the readers, have legitimated Ishmael Worth's heroic virtue by suffering—perhaps even weeping—with him through the impoverished, abandoned childhood that constitutes the first half of the novel, so the judges legitimate Mrs. Walsh's virtuous sufferings by being made to *feel* them through Ishmael's evocative descriptions. It is also important that while Southworth's packed courtroom responds to a traditionally acceptable legal speaker, an educated and articulate young man, it also bends to what is unmistakably a "female voice," in the sense that Ishmael's forensic powers are wholly dedicated to articulating the often painful realities of contemporary women's domestic lives.[6] Ishmael's challenge is to present Mrs. Walsh's plight in a mode and manner that will elicit sympathetic action from empowered male listeners. Yet Ishmael's victory does not represent a simple fantasy of female empowerment, nor is it merely an argument for legal reform grounded in Southworth's own harsh experience.[7] In narrative terms, the seeming rationality of patriarchal law is triumphantly opposed and conquered by the "heart's truth" of the sentimental story genre. In the real courtrooms I will be looking at, the same intersections of gender, genre, law, and story occupy a central position. Southworth deftly solves the difficulty by authorial fiat: in her world, the discourse of law responds to the discourse of female experience through the mediation of sentimental narrative. In actual cases, the generic interplay is neither so straightforward nor so clearly resolved.

In this context, the defeat of Ishmael's opponents becomes a critique of the genres they deploy. None of them adopts a narrative mode adequate to the emotional complexities of marital relationships. Instead, each frames the case in a way that distances the audience from the events and actors described, a strategy antithetical to sentimentality's emphasis on the forging of emotional bonds. The "objective" lawyer presents the case as an open-and-shut problem in logic and law, requiring only the coldly rational application of law to fact, but omitting the range of evocative personal circumstances that are, for Southworth, the heart of the case. Neither his own nor his hearers' sympathies are implicated. The "objective" lawyer is imaged as a bludgeoning blacksmith, "striking the anvil" with a "peculiar sledge-hammer style," wielding "the law" in heavy, unresponsive strokes as he mechanically raises and lowers his hammer with stern detachment.

The "pathetic" lawyer is equally ineffective. His forensic Romanticism—tagged for readers by references to Byron, madness, suicide, and wandering—represents a genre that has lost its authenticity and become merely an affectation. He seems to suffer agonies, yet touches no one because he is so clearly untouched himself. Mrs. Walsh is dismayed when he ends his oration "with tears in his eyes" and then sinks to his seat "utterly overwhelmed by his feelings and holding a drift of white cambric to his face" (468). Smiling, Ishmael reassures her that "everybody knows Berners—his 'madness' and 'suicide,' his 'gulf of perdition' and his white cambric handkerchief are recognized institutions. See! the judge is actually smiling over it" (468). As the courtroom regulars know, neither the lawyer's exaggerated and unrealistic characterization of events nor his displays of seeming emotion have been triggered by the particulars of Mr. Walsh's case. His melodramatic tears and phrases are merely his stock-in-trade: generic, insincere, and therefore unaffecting.

Because Mrs. Walsh cannot win her case unless the judges believe her narrative of spousal abuse, the greatest danger she faces is from the insinuating, farcical style of the "comic" lawyer. Not only does his approach trivialize the destruction of Mrs. Walsh's family, it invites dismissive, knowing laughter at her stance of resistance. The lawyer's amusement "at the caprice of womankind, who very often rather like to be compelled to do as they please," and the "little jokes" he tells as proof, invoke the genres of farce and pastourelle, in which women "really" want whatever men want them to, and in which refusals of sex or submission can be confidently ignored as mere playacting.[8] In such tales, women's words are, virtually by definition, not to be trusted; their cries for help are appropriately met with laughter.[9] By making Mrs. Walsh a character in the kind of story in which women are by nature deceitful, pleasure-loving, and inconsequential, the "comedy" lawyer assures the judges that nothing she says need be listened to with respect. Southworth, well aware of the operation of such comedy in the courtroom, has Ishmael tell Mrs. Walsh that this lawyer "is the most serious opponent we have. I would rather encounter half a dozen each of Wisemans and Berners than one Vivian. Take human nature in general, it can be more easily laughed than reasoned or persuaded in or out of any measure. People would rather laugh than reflect" (468). Despite his youth, Ishmael knows how to analyze forensic approaches in terms of the responses they elicit, and he therefore realizes that success may be won by those who make jurors happy and comfortable as well as those who engage them emotionally.

Even more important, Southworth demonstrates the subtle way that literary logic can control legal outcomes. Had heroic Ishmael not appeared to save the day, the power of a familiar *literary* story about "the caprice of womankind" might well have operated to rob Mrs. Walsh of the credibility she needed to win her case. Were the court to allow Mrs. Walsh to keep her children, the "comedy" lawyer Vivian argues, she would probably "take the first opportunity of voluntarily reconciling herself to her husband and giving him back herself, her home, and her children, which would be equal to any 'little joke' he had ever heard in his life" (468). Vivian is suggesting to the judges that they can predict Mrs. Walsh's future behavior not from her testimony or past actions, but from the predictable plot and punchline of "little jokes" about wandering wives, to which it is "equal." If they make the mistake of believing her to be sincere, he implies, the joke will be on them. They will look like fools for failing to recognize that she can be best understood very simply: not as an individual but as a literary stereotype whose shallow capriciousness can be confidently inferred.

By recognizing that literary stories and styles can win cases and influence judicial assessments, Southworth refuses to relegate literature to a sphere of entertainment, pleasure, or art distinct from the worldly arenas of law and power. Even the lightest comedy, the amusing "little jokes" that circulate from club to courtroom and back, she suggests, can control the way that legally empowered men "read" women's narratives of personal injury, and consequently can discredit women's testimony in court. Such stories are not trivial, nor are they merely aesthetic; they exert enormous and very real power. In the chapters that follow I will explore this suggestive equality between the stories people tell in court and the stories their listeners already know.

CHAPTER I

Criminal Conversation and the Conversational Process of the Law

Introduction

At a conference on law and narrative at Yale in February 1995, Alan M. Dershowitz spoke about the O. J. Simpson trial, then in its second month. The prosecution team was cheating, Dershowitz insisted, by using "the power of storytelling" when they argued that Simpson's history of domestic battering was persuasive evidence that he murdered his ex-wife, Nicole. This "literary logic" encouraged jurors to make inferences about O. J.'s conduct based on the way wife-battering had preceded murder in other highly publicized cases and seemingly similar fictional stories. When the defense's turn came, Dershowitz promised, things would be different. Instead of telling stories, the defense would present the jury with "hard data."[1]

But after the prosecution rested, things were not different. Jurors were harangued at mind-numbing length with a new set of stories, this time about race prejudice, police misconduct, and an elaborate frame-up worthy of the most abstruse detective novels. Scarce bits of "hard data" were woven into a story about a racist cop's instant vendetta against a rich African American, a story aimed directly at jurors' justifiable anger at white police based on a history of other incidents and a familiarity with other stories. Yet Dershowitz's comments are hardly surprising. Every advocate wants the jury to believe that he is the trial's sole purveyor of unconstructed truth while his opponents are mouthing nothing but lies. At the same time, he *must* shape his client's case into a coherent story. Because the story I'm telling you is true, the lawyer will argue, it's not a "story" at all. The other guys may sound persuasive, but that just shows how carefully they've had to work on their story to make it so realistic. You'll find that it's not so hard to fill in the blanks left by the evidence, to put together the real story of what happened. Because what happened here is lot like what happens everywhere, a lot like stories you already know. Because, ladies and gentlemen of the jury, it's your story too.

Storytelling in the courtroom is not optional. It cannot be disentangled from the "real" job of proving a case or arguing it to the jury. To win, a party must present credible testimony and persuasive forensic argument, each of which requires that the events triggering the lawsuit be represented to the fact finder through verbal narrative. The narratives, moreover, must be consistent, coherent, persuasive, and unambiguously moral. That takes work. A good final argument, for instance, must demonstrate that party's entitlement to win. It must explain testimonial inconsistencies, refute expected counterstories, cast characters as heros and villains. Above all, it must successfully achieve what Riffaterre has called in another context the "textual effect" of realism.[2] Indeed, from the filing of the legal complaint to the examination of witnesses and arguments of counsel at trial to the issuance of an appeals court opinion, lawyers, litigants, and judges engage in a continual process of narrative shaping and presentation. To have one's "day in court" signifies not winning or losing, but having the opportunity to tell one's story to an empowered listener in a public forum. Litigation, in short, is essentially conducted by constructing, delivering, and interpreting stories.

But to say that litigants write—or perform—stories for jurors to "read," or even to declare that such narratives are the constitutive elements of all litigation, is to say little that is not self-evident. Scholars in the burgeoning field of law and literature have made this point in a variety of ways. They have proffered a "storytelling model" of trial process and its "narrative coherence," identified "the storytelling strategy" as the "underlying genre of trial discourse," and explained that stories are the vehicles through which trial conflicts are presented and anterior reality "reconstructed."[3] Valuable as this work is—in some cases it is very sophisticated indeed—it tends to leave out the very aspects of storytelling that, for me, make it most interesting: genre, literature, culture, and history. Instead, such scholarship has treated the category of "story" as a unitary genre, essentialist and transhistorical. This book, in contrast, is part of the recent interdisciplinary effort to analyze the *kinds* of stories told in courtrooms.[4] My analysis of courtroom storytelling is based on the recognition that such stories function as critical cultural forms. Just as with a novel or a poem, we can look at the organizing logic, rhetorical features, plots, and stereotypical characters that constitute a lawyer's "story of the case" and find the crucial links between that story and the culture that produces it. Seen in this light, litigative stories naturally change as their cultural context changes; like literary stories, they are both reflectors of and catalysts for larger cultural shifts.

In referring to litigative discourse as both "narrative" and "story," I have in mind primarily the uninterrupted statements and arguments of trial counsel and the finished essays delivered as appellate court decisions. A witness's answers under questioning also form a narrative, particularly when, taken together, they constitute a connected, shaped version of anterior events. Both terms are important. "Narrative" suggests the authorial process of selection and shaping, inclusion and exclusion, inflection and style that make final arguments crafted literary products. It also implies the existence of a narrator who is himself in some sense a literary construct. "Story," a less technical term, suggests fictionality and a kinship with other narratives about human experience: the stories we tell each other about what happened yesterday, the literary stories we read, the human interest stories we follow breathlessly on the evening news.

Significantly, it is often impossible to tell from the text alone whether a story or narrative is fictional or factual. A person can describe plausible events in a believable way although the events may never have happened, or may have happened quite differently. How then to persuade listeners that the story should be believed? The narrative can be shaped to increase its credibility and the narrator trained in the body language of sincerity, but what do we do when another person comes along and describes the same events in a sharply conflicting way? The clearer the opposing narratives are, the more murky may be our sense of the events referred to. In the courtroom, this referential ambiguity is key; litigants characterize their opponents' narratives as lies, but have little to set against them but their own narratives. Even "real" evidence—the bloody socks or the black bag—must be translated into verbal narrative, introduced through the testimony of one witness and then explained, often through the testimony of another. It is important to remember that the disputed events that triggered a lawsuit are always utterly, inaccessibly gone. All we have to prove them with, to make them real for juror-listeners, are the representational capacity of language and the emotional impact of theater.

The art of persuasive artlessness, of telling a story so that it appears to be more history than fiction, is the central challenge of forensic speaking. Jurors must decide that something did or didn't happen based on the credibility of a live speaker's performed narrative tested against similar but conflicting narratives. Credibility depends on the apparent truthfulness of the speaker, which may have more to do with acting ability, articulateness, and personality traits than with honesty. It also depends on the believability of the narrative itself, and here "literary" qualities like consistency, coherence, and persuasive rendering of detail often carry the day. A central argument of this book is that a critical component in determining a litigative narrative's juridical acceptance will be the degree to which it reminds jurors of other stories, litigative or otherwise, that they accept as true. By using the word "true" I do not mean to suggest that jurors only see truth in narratives about historical events that actually occurred; rather, they may find, as literary readers often do, that even science fiction or sentimental romance novels depict what Hawthorne called "the truth of the human heart": psychological truth about character, behavior, emotions, and relationships.[5]

Jurors must always make inferences from evidence; in doing so, they necessarily construct their own "story of the case," and they do so, as Pennington and Hastie have shown, by positing and revising coherent narratives of "what happened."[6] We know that jurors draw on their own personal experience to construct such stories. What I'm suggesting is that they also draw on their literary experience—indeed, that jury arguments encourage them to do so. A literary mode like sentimentality provides a shared interpretive system that both lawyers and jurors can rely on as lawyers encode past factual experience into forensic narratives and jurors decode those narratives back into facts that now carry strong evaluative inflections. If lawyers have no choice but to turn events into stories, jurors have no choice but to evaluate them as such.

Litigative narratives—particularly the opening and closing arguments of counsel—utilize preexisting components familiar to their constructors from stories they have read, heard, watched, or told. As Robert Ferguson commented in a brilliant study of John Brown's successful self-construction at his murder trial as a "hero of Romance": "We can only tell the stories we know how to tell, and the degree of our understanding—our appreciation—depends on issues of narrative and genre often present but usually missed in our studies of the legal process" (37). In framing their cases for the jury as stories they "know how to tell," lawyers invite jurors, explicitly or implicitly, to make analogies between the case at hand and, say, a movie, novel, or sensationalized story from the tabloids. A primary purpose of such connections is to elicit the same judgmental responses to the witnesses and fact constellations in the case that jurors had earlier to fictional characters and plots. So John Brown becomes a Romantic hero, and O. J. Simpson the victim of a racist police plot, because lawyers assume that jurors already know what they think of each character in such a story, already know how such stories "turn out." The literary referent, even when it is no more than a series of suggestive characterizations or inflections, provides jurors with a coherent guide, a road map for traveling through the welter of evidence in the case and arriving at a judgment.

If Dershowitz—a famously mesmerizing courtroom speaker—was more than a bit disingenuous in asserting his disdain for "the power of storytelling," he was also inevitably implicating his own trial practice when he purported to reject the forensic exploitation of "literary logic." As a criminal defense lawyer, Dershowitz has a strong interest in arguing against the use of storylines that permit inferences of guilt to be drawn from "predictor" facts like spousal abuse. In "Life Is Not a Dramatic Narrative," an article-length version of his talk, Dershowitz argued that life itself is random, a series of unpredictable and unrepeatable coincidences without inherent meaning or consistency, so that any presentation of narrative coherence necessarily becomes an "importation" of narrative into the courtroom, one that will "confuse fact with fiction and endanger the truth-finding function of the adjudication process" (101). This viewpoint reflects a late twentieth-century set of assumptions about science, evolution, and religion, as Dershowitz's citations of Stephen Jay Gould and Richard Feynmann, among others, attest.[7] His assumptions about randomness would have been incomprehensible to earlier Americans, from those of John Winthrop or Mary Rowlandson's generations, who saw every object and event as a manifestation of God's master narrative, to the nineteenth-century lawyers and jurors at Henry Ward Beecher's 1875 adultery trial, who still believed in such meaning-giving ideas as the internal consistency of individual character or the predictability of behavior from earlier behavior. It is precisely such underlying assumptions about the "natural" coherence of events or the relevance of particular kinds of evidentiary facts to inferential predictions about subsequent behavior that reveal the critical connection between legal and other discourses within a particular culture at a particular historical moment.

Once we begin to look at forensic arguments as a form of cultural practice connected to other forms of public discourse such as novels, journalism, or political speeches, the way is opened for a new kind of law and literature analysis that places courtroom storytelling firmly within a historical, cultural, and literary context. It is possible to ask just how litigative process really works in narrative terms. How do culturally powerful stories and strategies circulate from literary to litigative sites and back again? If we look closely at the stories lawyers tell about past events, or the detailed narratives appellate court judges craft to delineate the substance of legal rights, can we identify where and why they appropriate vocabulary, logic, plots, and genres from their literary contexts of origin? Perhaps the most interesting consequence of this approach is that it provides new access to the law's treatment of specific subjects. I mean "subjects" here in both senses of the word: the specific subject matters dealt with in various categories of cases; and the living people who, as litigants and lawyers, are subjects of the law's process and power.

The primary narrative subjects this book explores are gender, marriage, and sexuality, specifically adulterous sexuality, in the late nineteenth and early twentieth centuries in America. I am interested in cases whose subject matter requires the production of narratives about these topics. I am also interested in the larger historical issue of how real women operated as subjects within late nineteenth-century American law, where they were silenced and where they spoke, how the gender-inflected literary logic used in certain cases controlled the cases' outcome, and whether and to what extent American courtrooms became sites of empowerment for women during this period.

This study of courtroom storytelling concentrates on sentimentality, a mode many might consider antithetical to legal analysis. I define sentimentality both as a literary genre with recognizable attributes of form and content, and as a rhetorical strategy used by authors to engage readers' deepest emotions. Sentimentality has long been the critical missing term in American literary histories, receiving only minimal and almost universally dismissive attention. In recent years, literary critics have begun to take it seriously, to argue for the importance of sentimental literature and to explore the significance of sentimentality within nineteenth-century American culture. The legal arena—principles, appellate decisions, the reasoning of judges and advocates—has traditionally been thought of as so characterized by objectivity, logic, and masculine rationality that it would be the last place to find sentimental stories or sentimental storytelling in a position of dominance. Yet as I demonstrate throughout this book, sentimentality permeates legal process in a number of important ways. It provides the controlling mode for jury arguments that strive to convince jurors that their own deepest beliefs and emotions are at stake. Perhaps less obviously, American legal history shows that sentimental fiction has played an important role in providing lawmaking judges with a set of narratives about affectively based marriage that can be used to establish new legal definitions of spousal obligation. Once we recognize the key role sentimentality played in nineteenth-century legal discourse, disparaging associations of sentimentality with an emasculating "feminization" of public discourse or assumptions that it is primarily employed by female authors for a female audience become very hard to sustain. Ann Douglas's "feminization" thesis about late nineteenth-century American, and especially religious, culture has come under a variety of attacks, especially from those who, like Jane Tompkins and Nina Baym, see in sentimental fiction a mode that represents and encourages female empowerment. In the courtroom, I will argue, sentimentality was used by male lawyers and judges to persuade male juries, as part of an arsenal of available rhetorical strategies. It was not perceived as discontinuous with other, more traditionally "masculine" ways of framing narratives; rather, as has been the case since the days of Aristotle, forensic rhetoric relies on emotional impact as a legitimate and fundamental means of effective persuasion.[8]

To focus my exploration of the broad issues outlined above, I have organized this book primarily around a single cause of action: criminal conversation, the civil tort of adultery.[9] It is especially useful for exploring questions about the relation of litigative storytelling to gender because every case presents issues about marital and extramarital sex, about the rights and obligations of husbands and wives, and, less obviously, about the links among gender, property, social relations, and power. In the period I study, the tort experienced a popular vogue and underwent radical changes. Limiting my legal texts to one kind of lawsuit provides a manageable, concentrated glimpse of how nineteenth-century American legal process dealt with a broad range of questions about women and marriage. In addition, though criminal conversation cases are not representative of torts in general and differ in many ways from other kinds of suits, such as those for murder or antitrust, they follow the adversarial storytelling process that characterizes all American litigation and can thus be used, with caution, as paradigms for the culturally linked narrativity of that process.

Criminal Conversations is in three parts. After this introductory chapter, part I provides a historical background for the tort of criminal conversation. Part II looks in detail at a single criminal conversation trial, Theodore Tilton's 1875 case against Henry Ward Beecher. Part III takes up a group of state appellate court decisions from about 1870 to 1920 determining whether or not women could be plaintiffs in criminal conversation and alienation of affection cases. The book's organization is doubly chronological. First, it follows the history of criminal conversation from its origins in thirteenth-century writs of ravishment and trespass, through its American heyday at the Beecher trial, to its disfavor and virtual demise by the end of the twentieth century. Second, it follows the chronological trajectory of a typical lawsuit by looking at three discrete litigative moments: the filing of a legal complaint, the document through which a party defines a wrong and demands "relief" (chapter 2); the drama of the trial, with a special emphasis on the adversarial storytelling process through which lawyers fight to establish the facts of the case (chapters 3 and 4); and the rendering of an appeals court decision, where the focus is on setting out the relevant law so that it can be applied in other cases (chapters 5 and 6).

The historical background detailed in chapter 2 is crucial to understanding the tort's later discursive development. When criminal conversation emerged as a discrete cause of action at the end of the seventeenth century, four hundred years of legal and linguistic history were dragged along with it. This seemingly unshakable past controlled the words a husband had to use to describe his wife's infidelity, excluded her from participating in the lawsuit, and insisted that her adultery be described as the infliction of property damage by one man on another man. The power of the past over the present was exerted in the form of residual counterfactual stories—legal fictions—such as that husband and wife were one person, or that consensual adultery was a rape achieved "by force and arms." Because these legal fictions were so central to the tort's conceptual basis—and consequently to what I call the "law's story" of adultery—later metamorphoses had to struggle against their shaping influence. By the late nineteenth century, the changing status of women began to exert a variety of pressures on the law's ability to continue treating women as silent sexual objects and adultery as a commercial injury against a husband's property rights. While some pressures came from "outside," from female litigants who wanted to avail themselves of a traditional legal remedy, others came from "inside," as judges became increasingly uncomfortable enforcing notions of spousal rights and obligations dating from the seventeenth century. My argument in chapters 5 and 6 is that because the tort's operative concepts of gender were contained in a particular legal "story," the conflict between past and present could be resolved *narratively*, by changing the plot, valence, and vocabulary of the story that appellate law told about what husbands and wives owed to each other. Because law speaks through stories, it can appropriate new literary kinds of stories about marriage and use them to rewrite the legally binding parameters of spousal obligation. In the case of criminal conversation, this resolution turned out to be only a temporary accommodation that ultimately helped bring about the tort's eventual self-destruction. The history of these criminal conversation cases provides a vivid example of the way that literary fiction can weave its way into the very real public power of the law.

A word about the way that I use literary texts. It will be obvious that this book is not "about" nineteenth-century literary fiction in any simple way. Because my primary focus is on understanding the narrativity of litigation, the way it works through creating and appropriating literary forms, my chapters are organized around legal, not literary, texts. And, while the cases I analyze are about adultery and adultery litigation, most of the literary texts I consider are not. *Criminal Conversations* is not a theme study of fictions dealing with sexual infidelity. Yet my analysis is deeply engaged with literary fictions and with literary genres and modes of storytelling.

There are three kinds of literary analysis in this book. In the first, I draw analogies between the rhetorical strategy employed by a lawyer or judge to teach jurors how to "read" the case and similar strategies used in literary fiction to engage readers and teach them how to interpret the story as they read. Thus in chapter 2 I compare the way Beecher's lawyer, William Maxwell Evarts, engaged the emotions of the jury to a parallel strategy employed by Beecher's sister, Harriet Beecher Stowe, in *Uncle Tom's Cabin*. In chapter 3, I explore the ways that Elizabeth Tilton's sentimental reading strategies shaped her interpretation of a very unsentimental novel, Charles Reade's *Griffith Gaunt*, and analyze the extraordinary role her epistolary account of that reading experience played in the Beecher trial.

The second kind of literary analysis turns to literature as a culturally available storehouse of powerful and familiar stories. Here, my focus is on sentimentality as a genre rather than as a mode of rhetorical engagement (though the two are obviously connected). Sentimental fictions share recognizable sets of plots, stereotypical characters, moral inflections, and depictions of domestic life. In chapters 5 and 6, I argue that appeals court judges appropriated stories about domesticity and marriage from literary fictions and used them to instantiate the legal parameters of spousal rights and obligations. While I do not offer extended analyses of specific literary texts, I draw on recent critical work in the field as well as on fictional works like Southworth's *Ishmael* and T. S. Arthur's *Anna Lee*, which created a domestic ideal that could be borrowed by legal writers—indeed, could be borrowed and used long after the heyday of sentimentality as a literary genre had passed.

The third kind of literary analysis is of fictions that deal explicitly with courtroom storytelling. It is not surprising that when novelists like E.D.E.N. Southworth or Mark Twain turned their attention to courtrooms, they understood and represented them as battlegrounds for different modes of storytelling. In championing—or attacking—the power of forensic sentimentality, such novelists give us an important vantage point for understanding what was happening in nineteenth-century courtrooms. Trial scenes within novels often present characters' testimony and lawyers' arguments as compressed, unambiguous narrative versions of the larger complex events that constitute the novel as a whole. In Howells's *A Modern Instance*, for example, the oppositional in-court divorce narratives of Squire Gaylord and Bartley Hubbard—equally melodramatic stories that simply reverse the casting of hero and victim—are counterpointed by the novel's earlier nuanced depiction of the gradual, mutually produced deterioration of the Hubbards' marriage, in which neither spouse is cast as angel or villain. Such fictional trials are important examples of the capacity of narrative to render experience persuasively, the different generic modes through which it does so verbally, and the necessary inadequacy of any particular narrative as a vehicle for fully capturing the complexities of that experience. In *Griffith Gaunt*, Charles Reade depicts a murder trial at which his heroine, by becoming her own defender, gains and vigorously exploits an author's power to control the shape and meaning of a forensic narrative—the narrative of her own life. In *The Gilded Age*, Mark Twain and Charles Dudley Warner attack what they see as the deceptiveness of sentimental rhetoric by depicting a trial at which an emotional appeal to a jury overrides a more just but "merely" rational counterargument.

While my notion of an interactive, borrowing process between literary and legal discourses suggests that the legal changes I trace did in their turn affect literary fiction in turn-of-the-century America, my primary emphasis is on the portion of the interaction that produces legal, not literary, narratives. There is a great deal of interesting research to be done, especially in exploring how the law's changing story of marriage registered in, and produced, the obsession with marriage, adultery, and divorce in the works of James, Chopin, Deland, Wharton, and others. Much of the excellent recent work of such law and literature scholars as Brook Thomas, Wai Chee Dimock, and Alexander Welch has concentrated very productively on readings of law-related literary texts. I focus on how the interactions work in the other direction, from literature into law, using legal arguments, documents, and decisions as primary texts.

Like Twain and Dershowitz, much of American legal culture is deeply suspicious of forensic storytelling yet unable to do without it. Stories are made up, crafted, fictional, false. They are also powerful, moving, disturbing, life-changing. Stories *do* things to readers: they change the ways we think about issues and events, change the way we understand ourselves. Though it distrusts the effect stories have on readers, legal discourse continually uses stories to construct—and change—conclusions about facts and principles of law. This study does not purport to be a treatise on the narrativity of litigation. Rather, by examining the way one cluster of issues—gender, sexuality, marriage, and adultery—wove in and out of legal narratives in late nineteenth-century America, it offers a starting point for understanding the connections among law, narrative, and gender in American culture.

Conversing in the Bedroom and in the Courtroom: The Tort of Criminal Conversation

"Criminal conversation" is the tort of adultery. It is the legal name for the private, civil cause of action that gradually came to succeed writs for abduction, "raptus," and trespass, and it has been part of Anglo-American jurisprudence since the end of the seventeenth century. In the classic case, the husband sued his wife's lover for money damages to compensate him for the injury to his spousal rights caused by her adultery.[10] The "conversation" referred to has nothing to do with the exchange of words, however; it denotes the act of adultery itself. In using the word "conversation" to mean sexual intercourse, English civil law kept alive one of the many meanings that had been packed into the word over the centuries. Between the time of its first appearance in English in the fourteenth century and its current association solely with verbal interaction, "conversation" has referred to, among other things, the place where one lives or dwells, physically or spiritually (holy men "that has theire conversacioun in heven," Hampole 1340); the act of consorting or having dealings with others ("that natural instinct which man hath to live in conversation," Parsons 1594); a manner of conducting oneself in the world or society ("A man of vertuous conversation, and wythoute cryme," *Bk. Com. Prayer* 1552); an occupation or study ("out of long experience in business and much conversation in books" Bacon 1626); as well as to sexual intercourse (an early book "on America" describes New World men who "lyven lyke bestes" and "hath conversacyon with the wymen, who that they ben, or who they fyrst mete," anon. 1511).[11]

Fifty years before the first criminal conversation case, the word reached a kind of apotheosis in John Milton's 1640s divorce tracts, the *Tetrachordon* and the *Doctrine and Discipline of Divorce*, where it became his central, inclusive term for the affirmative possibilities of marital union. "In God's intention a meet and happy conversation is the chiefest and the noblest end of marriage," Milton declares (*Div.* 391, and c.f. 382). In fact, so central is Milton's notion of conversation to his argument that the divorce tracts can be read as keying proposed changes in the divorce laws to the term as he uses it. When is it, he asks, that a marriage is made in God's eyes and is therefore binding? Not when the parties consent, nor when church rites are finished, "for the efficacie of those depends upon the presupposed fitnesse of either party." After carnal knowledge? "Least of all; for that may joyn persons whom neither law nor nature dares joyn: tis left, that only then, when the minds are fitly dispos'd, and enabled to maintain a cheerfull conversation, to the solace and love of each other, according as God intended and promis'd in the very first foundation of matrimony" (*Div.* 479). While successful marital conversation clearly includes joyous sexual union, its primary emphasis is on emotional and spiritual interchange with "a fit conversing soul" (*Div.* 397).

If true marriage is to be established only when the spouses achieve "individual and intimate," "apt and cheerfull," or "cheerfull and agreeable" conversation, Milton argues, then divorce should be permitted when the "unfitness" of the spouses' minds make such comforting communion impossible (*Tet.* 102, *Div.* 382, 393). Why should the law permit divorce for adultery or for impotence, thus stressing the merely physical over the spiritual, yet have "no care about the unconversing inability of mind, so defective to the purest and most sacred end of marriage" (*Div.* 393)? Instead, divorce should be permitted when a spouse is found to be "deficient and unable to performe the best duty of marriage in a cheerfull and agreeable conversation" (*Div.* 393). In his tracts on divorce, then, Milton brings together virtually all the meanings of "conversation" earlier uses had deployed, reformulates the term as an ideal of loving mutual interchange, and then attempts to instantiate it with *legal* meaning, to make it the law's critical marker for both the constitution and the dissolution of marriage.

English law did not adopt Milton's suggestions. Divorce remained virtually unobtainable until the Matrimonial Causes Act of 1857.[12] As for "conversation," the word did come into popular legal parlance a few decades later, but only as half of a two-word phrase denoting adulterous sex. A "criminal conversation" legally included any extramarital conjoining of bodies even where the act was quite perfunctory or, to use Milton's phrase, "but an animal excretion" (*Tet.* 101). To the extent that the law made "conversation" signify, it thus selected precisely the meaning Milton was at greatest pains to discredit. If Milton filled the term with possibility, emotional mutuality and openness, the law's usage reduced it to its narrowest and least resonant aspect, the "merely" physical. Since Milton's time, the richness of meanings available for common usage of the word "conversation" has been thoroughly whittled away. From the 1690s onward, criminal conversation, or "crim. con." as it came to be known, contracted the word's legal meaning to sexual intercourse, while our contemporary vernacular usage limits it to talk, discourse, and verbal communication.[13] So separate are the paths down which the word has traveled that the two narrow surviving meanings do not even overlap, producing understandable confusion when modern speakers first hear the legal phrase "criminal conversation."

That confusion proceeds from difficulty as much with the word "criminal" as with "conversation." The lawsuit is not a criminal case at all, but a civil action for damages between two private litigants. Back in the late seventeenth century, tort law needed to add the descriptive label "criminal" to the word "conversation" to identify the sex at issue in the tort suit as wrongful, for as we've seen, any two bodies, married or unmarried, could have a sexual "conversation." The plaintiff-husband sued his wife's lover for money damages to compensate him for the violation of his spousal right to the exclusive sexual use of his wife's body. Though often emphatically public in impact, all criminal conversation cases are structured as private disputes framed in terms of injury to property. The lovers' sex is "criminal" because it is adulterous and therefore violates the laws (originally canon or religious laws) of marriage; it may or may not also violate the criminal laws of the state. In the Commonwealth of Massachusetts in 1997, adultery is a felony punishable by up to three years in prison (M.G.L. c. 272 sec. 14). Though rarely enforced, criminal adultery statutes are still very much on the books.[14]

Yet the logic of criminal and civil adultery cases is profoundly different, and that difference is important. As a crime, adultery is constituted as a wrong to marriage, to the community, and ultimately to the state. Like all crimes, it is appropriate for punishment because it threatens the stability and security of communal norms; criminal cases are therefore brought not by the particular victim but by the ultimate injured party: the state. The plaintiff in a criminal case is the "Commonwealth of Massachusetts" or "The People of the State of New York."[15] Hawthorne's magistrates and townspeople who gather to witness Hester Prynne's proud shame in *The Scarlet Letter*'s opening scene come not just to see a sinning adulteress punished but to participate in a ritual that warns and heals a community damaged by one who, as one townswoman says, "has brought shame upon us all."

As a civil wrong, however, adultery is essentially a private, commercial matter. The court acts as an official arbiter and redresser of a dispute between an individual plaintiff and an individual defendant. Instead of a civilization-destroying injury, the sexual act is a compensable injury to property, assessed in financial terms. If he loses, the defendant does not face a prison term or a fine to the state. Instead, he pays compensatory (and sometimes exemplary) damages directly to the person who has been injured: the plaintiff.

The tort of criminal conversation thus has little to do with either crime or conversation. By entombing the linguistic past in its terminological present, the law keeps the phrase "criminal conversation" alive, though the sexual meaning of "conversation" is virtually obsolete and the identifier "criminal" is downright misleading. When we hear the phrase today, the gap between the way the law uses the words and the way we ordinarily do creates a space inevitably filled by contemporary associations. "Criminal conversation" is a wonderfully suggestive designation for a lawsuit about illicit sexual activity.

"Criminal conversation." The phrase suggests a crime committed through forbidden speech acts: the treasonous revelations of a Defense Department "mole"; the discreet hiring of a hit man; the conspiratorial plottings of international terrorists. Communications like these are crimes whether or not the contracted-for murder or the skyscraper bombing ever takes place; the law considers the conversation alone enough to jeopardize the continued security of governmental and financial institutions. Where there is a legal obligation to keep silent, conversations about prohibited subjects are themselves crimes. In using the term "criminal conversation" to characterize adultery, the law's phrase-making power links illicit sexual intercourse with these other kinds of stability-threatening verbal exchange, suggesting that adultery is criminal because it represents the "utterance" of something dangerous. By recognizing extramarital "conversations" as profound threats to the institution of marriage, the law may be said to impose on the wife an obligation not merely of chastity but of *muteness*, a duty not to "speak" with anyone but her husband. If a wife's adultery is a necessarily subversive form of self-expression, illicit sexual conversations violate the spousal bond, the law assumes, regardless of what is "said."

Where the subject matter of a criminal conversation lawsuit thus invokes adulterous sexuality as one form of communication, the legal process through which such suits are conducted constitutes another. Litigation is always profoundly conversational, and its alternating exchanges are one of this book's central concerns. The act of initiating a criminal conversation case transforms the intimate domestic conversations originally "spoken" by husband, wife, and lover into the materials from which the adversarial litigative "conversations" between plaintiff and defendant will be constructed in court. Litigation is a dialogic process; all forensic narratives participate in its interactive, responsive movements. Its dialectical format surrounds every assertion with an unspoken, previously spoken, or not-yet-spoken challenge. The insistent rhythm of a trial is its swing from direct examination to cross-examination, from plaintiff to defendant, from defense to rebuttal. Each narrative element as it emerges in testimony must therefore battle for authenticity not only with the explicit alternatives and attacks already mounted, but with the as-yet-invisible challenges so firmly implied by the trial's adversarial imperative that they will be immediately supplied by the minds of attentive listeners. Because trials proceed not by proclamation but by question or assertion and response, juries learn to anticipate, question, and critique arguments even as they are being delivered.

Looked at hopefully, as for instance in the critical works of James Boyd White, the resultant "culture of argument" means that "for the litigant, the lawyer and the observer alike, the central ethical and social meaning of the practice of the adversary hearing is its perpetual lesson that there is always another side to the story, that yours is not the only point of view" (266). It teaches us "over and over again, how little we can foresee, how much we depend on others, and how important to us are the practices we have inherited from the past. It is a way of creating a world in part by imagining what can be said on the other side. In these ways it is a lesson in humility" (266).

But if the conversationality of litigation reminds both speaker and listener of human interdependence and limits, it also creates an atmosphere of deep and structural antagonism. Litigation is often more like mortal combat than polite speech, though it adheres to procedural rules requiring adversaries to listen to each other and to respond with words, not blows.

Forensic speaking is thus much like shadow boxing: every affirmation is also a defense and a preemptive strike. Tellers must anticipate challenges and disempower them before they materialize. Trial narratives are both formed and deformed by these pressures; their twists and turns reflect detours, expansions, reinflections made necessary by the range of explicit and implicit narratives that must be defeated. In chapter 3, for instance, I will consider at length the final arguments in the six-month Beecher-Tilton trial, in which speakers devoted whole days to countering arguments that had not yet been made but that they expected from opposing counsel. Consequently, neither party's version of "what happened" could be presented or can now be read as if, like a Victorian novel, it were a linear, sequential narrative of fictional "truth." The analyses that follow strive to keep in view both the conversationality of litigative narratives and the bundle of invisible shadows that wrap around them, determining in large measure their particular texture and shape.

It is important to remember that procedural and substantive law play a vital role in shaping the narratives through which litigants and lawyers enter the courtroom conversation. As I will discuss in chapter 5, every cause of action has its own set of legal requirements and assumptions, which I call "the law's story," for that kind of case. When the law changes (as for instance when New York law expanded the grounds for divorce from adultery alone to a range of reasons including incompatibility) the stories told in court change too (the marital breakdowns described in New York divorce complaints suddenly ascribed less fault and complained of less infidelity).[16] The law's first story of criminal conversation, as we will see in detail in chapter 2, made the adulterous sexual act something that was "done" not just *by* the man and woman performing it but *to* the absent spouse. By entering the wife's body, the male lover committed an assault, indeed, an actual trespass on the rights of the absent husband. There was nothing the lovers could do either to bring the wife into the legal case or to argue that the sexual act concerned no one but the lovers themselves. The litigative conversation was carried on in the courtroom between the two men, husband and lover, and was therefore always in a gendered, specifically male voice. Moreover, a successful case required the jury to assess what were essentially property damages against the lover. So the story of a wife's adultery—which we might see as being about the urgency of passion or the breakdown of a marriage—is rewritten by the legal system as a "rational" narrative about the financial assessment of injury to male-owned property. The public, adversarial, male-voiced conversation in the courtroom is a litigative reformulation of the private sexual "commerce" that both men have carried on through the woman's body. The mutual sexual activity—the sexual conversation—between the man and woman disappears. Unruliness and passion are contained by the seeming objectivity of legal discourse.

Thus, the heterosexual conversation of adulterous bodies in bed becomes the homosocial conversation of litigative parties in court. The aggressive exclusion of the wife's voice from the courtroom can be read as more than coincidental. If the legal case was triggered by the wife's "speaking out of turn," her illicit sexual communication with a lover, the ensuing criminal conversation litigation enforces wifely silence with a vengeance. This is an important key to understanding how such cases "speak" culturally. The wife's threatening assertion of agency and subjectivity, her adulterous conversation in private, is perceived as dangerous. It is punished by a complete suppression of her voice within the litigation that seems to declare that in court at least, unruly female speech will not be heard, will not disrupt male authority. As chapters 5 and 6 explore, the fixed criminal conversation script generated by several centuries of legal process was deeply gendered, unlike (or at least more than) the scripts for other kinds of lawsuits like breach of contract or murder. When late nineteenth-century American wives, newly freed from the disabilities of coverture by the Married Women's Property Acts, picked up that script, came into court as vocal and demanding plaintiffs, and began to bring criminal conversation cases against other women (their husbands' female lovers), the response was, as might be imagined, anything but simple.

CHAPTER 2

The Transformative Magic of Legal Fictions: The Suppression of Sex in Early English Civil Adultery Cases

Counterfactual Allegations

In 1620, Humphrey Hide brought an action of trespass in the court of the King's Bench against Edmund Cyssell, in which he alleged that on 21 August 1608, in London, Cyssell:

> assaulted Elizabeth, the plaintiff's wife, and beat and ill-treated her, and took and carried away the said Elizabeth together with a gown, a petticoat, a smock and a head-dress valued at 20 pounds, of the plaintiff's goods and chattels, and detained and kept her for five years without the plaintiff's leave, whereby the plaintiff wholly lost the comfort and company and also the advice and help in domestic affairs which the plaintiff could and should have had and enjoyed with his wife during that time.
>
> *Hide v. Cyssell*, Cro. Jac. 538 (1620).
> Baker & Milsom 308. Orig. allegs. in Latin; trans. Baker & Milsom.

Taken at face value, these allegations describe a terrifying attack on Hide's wife, presumably causing her serious bodily injuries, and the theft of numerous valuable goods belonging to Hide, primarily women's clothing. Was the defendant a robber? A violent kidnapper? The allegations seem straightforward enough, but when their legal obscurities are decoded, we find that what is actually being described is a husband's lawsuit for damages against a man with whom his wife has been having an extramarital affair.[1] Yet sex is nowhere mentioned. The story of the adultery has been completely erased from the text of the plaintiff's allegations, and another story has been substituted. The text describes a trespass on property, a theft of clothing, a kidnapping, and a physical assault. In all likelihood, however, no one was hurt, no force was used, and Elizabeth was wearing the gown and petticoat when she left with her lover. Through the use of preestablished legal phrases, and particularly through a series of related "legal fictions" that perform a complex linguistic conjuring act, one kind of narrative has become another kind. A story we would now characterize as being about sexual relationships, adulterous desire, and the betrayal of marriage is discursively represented, in the verbal formulations of legal language, as a narrative about assault and theft.

From its origins in thirteenth-century writs of abduction and ravishment through the development of the tort of criminal conversation in the seventeenth and eighteenth centuries, civil adultery litigation (the husband's suit for money damages against his wife's lover) has employed a startling array of such legal fictions. These obviously artificial verbal formulas controlled how litigants' individual experiences would be brought within the jurisdictional ambit of the legal system. Because these fictions dictated how events had to be described in order to qualify for an award of damages, plaintiffs routinely alleged that their chattels had been stolen, the services of their wives "lost," and their wives forcibly "ravaged," when what had really occurred was a consensual sexual affair between a married woman and her lover. These statements *seemed* to be specific assertions about "what happened" in a particular case. Yet they were understood by all concerned to be blatantly counterfactual, pointedly unmimetic linguistic constructions responsive not to the facts of the case but to the requirements of the law.

Legal fictions can be found in every area of the law: treatises expound them; judges deploy them; students learn to wield them. Corporations are "persons"; contracts are deemed to contain "implied" conditions that none of their parties ever thought about; everyone is assumed to know the law; in an action of trover, a defendant is alleged to have found a chattel he may really have taken by force.[2] These fictions have been part of legal language since its inception, and they have by no means disappeared in the modern era.

Legal fictions are called "fictions" not because they are stories (although, as I will argue, most of them are), but because they are untrue.[3] They have no relation to the unique particularities of a lawsuit; instead, they deploy generic verbal formulas to insert new "facts" into the case, which everyone knows do not "really" belong there. A plaintiff might once have alleged that he resided on the island of Minorca, "to wit in the parish of St. Mary le Bow in the Ward of Cheap," but no one really believed that a Mediterranean island had somehow been transported to the city of London (Barfield 114, Fuller 18). Yet such "false facts" are of great practical use in litigation: they permit the court to act as if they were true. In this example, a London court could take jurisdiction over a dispute arising in a far-flung colony, a case it would otherwise have no power to hear, by accepting without question the plaintiff's allegation that the dispute arose within the court's well-established jurisdictional boundaries. Legal fictions solve problems, particularly procedural ones that develop when something external to the law changes without a corresponding change in the law. In *Ancient Law* (1864), Sir Henry Maine offered this definition:

> I now employ the expression "Legal Fiction" to signify any assumption which conceals, or affects to conceal, the fact that a rule of law has undergone alteration, its letter remaining unchanged, its operation being modified. . . . The *fact* is . . . that the law has been wholly changed; the *fiction* is that it remains what it always was. . . . [Legal fictions] satisfy the desire for improvement, which is not quite wanting, at the same time that they do not offend the superstitious disrelish for change which is always present. (25)

For example, a court that has well-developed ways of dealing with living people may be at a loss for how to exert legal power over the abstract, impersonal entity that is a corporation. Instead of inventing a completely new set of procedures or waiting for major legislative reforms, the court exploits the fictional trope of personification and applies the established notion of "jurisdiction over the person" by declaring that for these purposes a corporation *is* a person.

Similarly, as we will see, a court that can hear only cases involving damage to property affords a remedy to a cuckolded husband by treating the act of adultery as if it were a violent assault or a theft of the husband's property. During the first several hundred years of adultery litigation (thirteenth–eighteenth centuries), the allegations necessary to initiate it were structured by a set of five interrelated legal fictions: of marital unity; of adultery as a trespassory injury to property; of adultery as a theft of the husband's goods; of adultery as a loss of services; and of adultery as a rape of the wife. Working together, these fictions blurred the borders between fact and law, metaphorical and "actual" truth, individual experience and paradigmatic legal narrative.

The transformative work of legal fictions in adultery litigation is the subject of this chapter. By tracing the early history of civil adultery litigation through its affiliated legal fictions, my analysis first demonstrates the crucial role of legal fictions in bringing private sexual behavior within the regulatory purview of the public civil court system. To bring civil adultery claims in the King's courts rather than in ecclesiastical courts, adultery had to be conceptualized as an injury to the husband's property, a financially assessable harm for which an award of money damages could compensate. Over time, the legal fictions invented to solve this essentially procedural problem of limited jurisdiction came to constitute the heart of the tort itself until, as I explore in chapter 5, late Victorian courts found themselves mired in such discussions as whether wives had a "property right" in their husbands' affection. The complex weight of historical and legal baggage that came to burden criminal conversation litigation in the nineteenth century began to accumulate at this crucial founding moment.

Second, this analysis shows that the operation of legal fictions is a subtle but significant instance of the way that literary structures shape both legal discourse and cultural assumptions. Later chapters take up the creative narrativizing function performed by attorneys and appellate courts. I argue that trial lawyers and appellate court judges make the raw data of subjective experience and abstract legal principles into meaningful and coherent narratives by appropriating stories, characters, and strategies developed in literary contexts. While those discussions will emphasize law's crucial openness to creative story writing, this chapter analyzes the law's use of rigidly predetermined formulaic tropes and metonymies. Individual litigants did not invent these tropes and, in most cases, had no control over when or how they could use them. Though denominated "fictions," the formulas did not supply complete or complex stories, but directed litigants to insert or characterize facts in specific ways while omitting others altogether. Yet especially in the context of adultery litigation, legal fictions worked in ways that were profoundly literary, for they exploited the capacity of language to create alternative realities, metaphorical representations of relationships and events that carried substantial cultural power.

My third aim is to demonstrate that cultural power. Most historians assume that the instrumental purpose of legal fictions renders their verbal content either neutral or impotent.[4] Yet like the "fictional" term of a metaphor, the ideal rose to which the real mistress is compared, legal fictions act on and change the reader's perception of the terms they displace. The solid beauty of real women looks increasingly fragile, external, and poignantly ephemeral after reading Elizabethan "flower" sonnets. In a parallel, far more prosaic manner, the procedural empowerment of legal fictions that imaged adultery as property damage, though known to be "false," influenced how men and women understood their marriages—their options, their roles and responsibilities. Obviously, legal procedure did not originate the idea that marriage was essentially a property relation, or that a wife's subjectivity was insignificant and dismissible. These were commonplaces of the English culture that invented the writs and torts, so it is hardly surprising to find them embedded in the discourse of the law.[5] Instead of merely reflecting the cultural biases that generated them, however, these discursive formulations must be understood as actively producing the continuing power of those biases. In people's everyday lives, the question of what adultery was "about" could not be answered without taking the law's procedural answer into account.

To a large extent, that answer was shaped not only by cultural assumptions and biases but also by a series of institutional pressures, from the late medieval to the early modern periods, that combined to make adultery a difficult subject to "discuss" litigatively in the King's law courts. These pressures, which I will take up in more detail later, included the exclusive jurisdiction of the ecclesiastical courts over all marital matters, the difficulty of representing what was essentially an emotional injury in the financial terms that courts were prepared to deal with, and the persistent challenge of conceptualizing the wife's behavioral transgression as an injury to her husband. The law's response was a series of leaps into fiction, in which the wife, her illicit sexual assertiveness—indeed, the adultery itself—virtually disappeared from the explicit text of the husband's Complaint, and the litigation was carried on through a succession of obviously fictional "stories" about violence, property damage, or the loss of a servant's labor.

There is nothing unusual about legal fictions controlling litigative procedures; they are found in all kinds of cases, where they display a wide variety of narrative forms.[6] What makes *these* fictions worth special study is the way they combine to obliterate the litigation's actual subject matter—adultery—as an explicit textual subject. Through six centuries and a variety of legal forms, the legal fictions at issue here worked to preclude plaintiffs' direct discussion of their wives' sexual transgressions while insisting discursively that what had occurred was a series of nonsexual incidents of damage to property. By declaring, in effect, that only stories built on these fictions would *count*, the law went beyond reflecting a preexisting cultural bias; it used the transformative techniques of metonymy, personification, and metaphor to construct stories that inevitably and powerfully influenced relations between women and men.

"The Pestilential Breath of Fiction"

In contrast to later chapters, which will focus on the deployment of literary narratives at trial (the Beecher-Tilton case), and in appellate courts (the female-plaintiff criminal conversation cases), this chapter focuses on the textualizing moment that begins litigation: the drafting and filing of legal pleadings. In modern litigation, these written allegations of complaint and answer initiate the lawsuit, establish jurisdiction, describe the injury, and outline the party's entitlement to an award of damages. In late medieval litigation, the same function was performed by the plaintiff's filing of a writ, often followed by a complex process of pleading or "counting," which set out the claim in numbered "counts."[7] Because many of the legal fictions that structured adultery cases appeared as jurisdiction-enabling allegations in complaints rather than as matters of proof at trial, it is important to understand how complaints work, and how jurisdictional legal fictions work within them.

Almost always lawyer-written, and drafted to respond to procedural and substantive legal requirements, pleadings even today are often the most formulaic, least individual texts generated in a lawsuit. Plaintiffs frequently include only the minimum facts necessary to make out a viable claim. More detail is considered strategically unwise; it may reveal too much too early, or may make it difficult to vary or supplement the original assertions at a later stage of the litigation. Although they play an important role in setting the parameters of the case, pleadings do not themselves constitute evidence or proof. Their function is administrative rather than persuasive: they "turn on" the machinery of the judicial system and notify one's opponent of the fact and general substance of the suit, but they play only a minimal role in deciding the case. Unlike testimony and other evidence introduced at trial, complaints do not ordinarily "go to the jury." Even a close reading of the complaint may not make it possible to predict the actual evidence introduced at trial.

In 1731, English law mandated the use of plain English rather than Latin or law-French in court pleadings (Baker 300). More than two hundred years later, the mystification of law language was still a major problem. In the late nineteenth century, progressive law reform on both sides of the Atlantic technically abolished the complex, ritualized pleading requirements that had characterized legal process since the early Middle Ages, sweeping away distinctions between law and equity, trespass and case, and doing away with the myriad forms of action, Latin terminology, and requisite verbal incantations.[8] From the vantage point of modern directness, centuries-old complaints seem profoundly disconnected from their underlying factual realities; they bristle with quaint obstructions and phrases from a language no living person ever spoke, and contain identical allegations of "fact" from one complaint to the next. Sometimes a legal fiction is patently counterfactual, like the allegation that the island of Minorca can be found in London's Cheapside. At other times, however, and commonly in the cases with which I am concerned, a reader unfamiliar with the ritual use of legal fictions would be unable to distinguish truthful allegations from fictional ones. In constructing a coherent narrative of injury that a particular court would have the power to redress, a plaintiff's lawyer typically interlarded truthful assertions with required fictions, making them all part of the continuous story presented to the court.

Yet the critical fictional phrases triggered important consequences, real-life results obtainable only by someone willing to describe his situation in those particular words. In this sense, legal fictions are splendid examples of J. L. Austin's category of "legal performatives," utterances whose significance lies not in their truth or falsity but in their ability to get something done simply by being said. The text of the complaint becomes the door-opening incantation that acts as a bridge between the individual and the law. Drafting that complaint, the lawyer translates his client's experience into the approved verbal formula necessary to have the case heard in the court of choice. This process of verbal fashioning redefines the plaintiff and his hitherto idiosyncratic experience as belonging to a category of discursively similar plaintiffs and experiences, textualizing his individual past through ritualized, counterfactual allegations. If this transformation—both coercive and, perhaps, comforting—is the necessary precondition for having personal wrongs adjudicated, it also erases a portion of the "personal" in defining those wrongs for the court.

Thus, when Henry Hide alleged that his wife had been beaten and carried away, the text of his complaint substituted a ritualized narrative of assault and theft for his likely actual experience of her voluntary departure in all its messy, perhaps ambiguous detail. Like metaphors, to which they are often compared and about which I will say more later, such legal fictions create complex linkages between the actual and the fictional—what Lakoff and Turner, in talking about metaphors, call "mappings between two conceptual domains" (4). Where poetic metaphors construct a resonant interaction between domains that, ideally, expands and complicates the meaning of each term, legal fictions permit the "reader," typically the court, to ignore differences and more particularly, to erase the real in favor of the fictional. The fictions' incontrovertibility prevents the alternate and actual facts of the case from claiming authority.

This incontrovertability is key. Unlike the factual allegations of a modern complaint, and unlike every other assertion made during litigation, fictional allegations could not ordinarily be challenged or defeated by the defendant's proof of their falsity.[9] They thus stand as striking, almost aberrational deviations from litigation's adversarial norm. The most profoundly defining characteristic of the Anglo-American litigative process is its continual positing of alternate "truths." Every story, testimonial fact, and argument is always structurally open to an opponent's counterversion, and this dialectic of strophe and antistrophe enforces (at least theoretically) an accountability to the subjective experience of litigants. Trial process insists that both parties' versions of an event be heard before juridical verdicts are reached, a requirement that significantly (though not always successfully) circumscribes the ability of either to construct a narrative of events wholly unconnected with "what happened." Yet the jurisdictional allegation that a defendant is "in custody," or that a wife has been "ravaged" by "force and arms" cannot be defeated by a direct and persuasive denial, because (at least with respect to questions of jurisdiction) the court will not permit the denial to be made.

In an important sense, the allegations made through legal fictions straddle the line between law and fact. In terms of the functioning of the legal system, legal fictions really are law, though they masquerade as fact. That is, unlike "real" facts, the questions about "what happened" that are intensely disputed by parties and witnesses and ultimately decided by the judge or jury as "trier of fact," the allegations made through legal fictions are not proved or disproved but operate like averments of applicable law to establish the rules or guidelines for deciding the case. Yet while they do legal work and accomplish legal tasks, the allegations produced by legal fictions take the discursive *form* of factual assertions, and they therefore play an important "factual" role by contributing specific elements to the plaintiff's complaint-story. Indeed, this combination of characteristics—reified and authoritative like law, yet narratively constituted as fact—helps explain legal fictions' usefulness and their power.

Legal fictions' ability to accomplish things that established statutory rules would otherwise preclude has been the focus of most appraisals of their merit, both positive and negative. Calling them "invaluable expedients for overcoming the rigidity of law," Sir Henry Maine praised their ability to "close the gap" between progressive movements in social opinion and the lagging inflexibility of the law (25, 23).[10] A century earlier, Blackstone used a description of the development of jurisdictional fictions to illustrate the law's constitutive benignity. Over time, he explained, the jurisdiction of the Court of the King's Bench had come to include all cases of trespass and assault, but not civil actions for debt. There was one exception to that rule, however: if the defendant was already in the custody of the marshal or prisonkeeper of the Court, the Court could hear whatever claims a plaintiff might have against him, including debt actions. Gradually, a legal fiction was developed whereby the plaintiff simply alleged in his complaint that the defendant *was* in such custody; the court, taking the case, refused to permit the defendant to deny he was in custody, and the case proceed to trial. "And these fictions of law," declared Blackstone, "though at first they may startle the student, he will find upon farther consideration to be highly beneficial and useful: especially as this maxim is ever invariably observed, that no fiction shall extend to work an injury; its proper operation being to prevent a mischief, or remedy an inconvenience, that might result from the general rule of law" (*Commentaries* 3:42–43).

However convenient such procedural innovations might be, they enraged Blackstone's onetime student, Jeremy Bentham. If Blackstone and Maine represent the positive pole in the historical debate about the virtues of legal fictions, Bentham represents the negative. In tirades against "the pestilential breath of fiction," Bentham compared it to a "syphilis, which runs in every vein, and carries into every part of the system the principle of rottenness" (*Works*, Bowring ed. 1:235; 5:92). In particular, he excoriated the "lie" whereby a man "is told that he is in jail; sometimes that he is lurking up and down the country, in company with a vagabond of the name of Doe; though all the while he is sitting quietly by his own fireside" (cited in Ogden xviii). Rejecting wholesale Blackstone's claims that such fictions were universally remedial, Bentham pointed out that their primary benefits accrued to the legal profession, not to individual litigants. Bentham considered the use of fictions mere theft, "having for its object the stealing legislative power, by and for hands that durst not, or could not openly claim it, and but for the delusion thus produced, could not exercise it" (1:243). The fact that courts competed for the most lucrative judicial business supplied an economic motive Bentham found deeply immoral and corrupting: "Fiction of use to justice: Exactly as swindling is to trade. . . . Every criminal uses the weapon he is most practised in the use of; the bull uses his horns, the tiger his claws, the rattle-snake his fangs, the technical lawyer his lies. Unlicensed thieves use pick-lock keys; licensed thieves use fictions" (7:283). Bentham challenged both the utility and the benevolence Blackstone had claimed for legal fictions, asking who benefited and who was harmed by their pervasive use and denouncing what he saw as their destructive moral impact. In Bentham's view, lawyers invented legal fictions to increase their access to money and power and to mystify and confuse the general public. Lawyers' positions as masters of the law's potent "word magic" enhanced their own prestige and ensured that ordinary citizens would be unable to negotiate the law's intricacies without them. The use of fiction, he declared, "affords presumptive and conclusive evidence of moral turpitude in those by whom it was invented and first employed" (9:77).

Yet for all of his invective against Blackstone in the *Fragment on Government*, Bentham's basic understanding of the content and structure of legal fictions was quite similar to Blackstone's. Though they disagreed about whether the fictions achieved positive or negative results, both Bentham and Blackstone assumed that the particular shape and subject matter of legal fictions was "merely" instrumental or even accidental, a nearly contentless convenience determined by the use to which the fiction would be put or the technical ends it would serve. To both writers, the verbal formulas that constitute the fictions are worth scarcely a glance, except to note their "falsity" and to determine their application. This failure to conceive of the discursive content of legal fictions as itself potentially significant is especially surprising in Bentham, whose writings display a lifelong obsession with language and a characteristically modern awareness that *all* language is always to some extent "fictional" and metaphorical, that "to language then—to language alone—it is that fictional entities owe their existence; their impossible, yet indispensable existence" (8:198).[11] His angle of vision too, which measured value by assessing benefits and harms to those affected, might have led him to examine how the language of a particular fiction affected its "victims."

To Bentham all lies were alike evil and, at least in the legal context, should be eliminated. Legal fictions were a necessarily corrupting influence because they legitimated, indeed celebrated as useful, acknowledged falsehoods. To Bentham, it was not necessary to examine the particular verbal formulations through which they worked. If we shift Bentham's critique to a context of cultural analysis, however, the question becomes not whether all lies corrupt by virtue of their untruth, but whether particular legal lies, such as those about marriage and adultery, can warp people's understanding of the subjects they purport to describe. The verbal content of many legal fictions may indeed be accidentally determined by certain preexisting, ancillary rules that the fictions are used to invoke. But origin and effect are two different things. In many cases, the very casualness of the fictions' construction is the source of their power: lacking the self-consciously artful qualities that permeate both legal opinions and traditionally literary texts, these minimal story paradigms speak with an unusual directness. The particular fictions chosen and the work they perform can help us to understand how the narratives of a culture's legal order affect those who live within its reach.

Indeed, the content of legal fictions is often surprisingly powerful. By substituting a fictional fact (the defendant is in custody) for a real fact (the defendant is in his home) and attaching consequences only to the words of the former, the law empowers the fiction. The fictional fact affects the legal course of events in the real world (because the defendant "is" in custody, the plaintiff's case against him can be heard) while the real fact disappears from the textual record, becoming legally irrelevant and consequently, one might say, a form of fiction. This empowerment of fiction accomplishes something both paradoxical and extraordinary: it brings about in actuality the situation that was originally asserted only fictionally. The allegation that a defendant is "in custody" may not be accurate when it is made. Yet because the court will not permit the allegation to be contradicted, and because its consequence is the unconsented-to assertion of legal jurisdiction over the defendant, the fiction forces him to submit to the plaintiff's attacks and to the court's power. The original allegation of custody thus produces a custody in fact, for though he may not be physically imprisoned, the defendant is most certainly within the punitive reach of the court, a "prisoner" of its jurisdiction. The distinction here between actual truth and metaphorical truth—between the defendant's body being in prison and his involuntary submission to the court as a form or image of custody—becomes blurred. The metaphorical assertion seems less and less "fictional" as the interaction of fiction and fact brings about actual changes in the defendant's situation.

To take another example, the plaintiff's allegation that he resides on the island of Minorca, "to wit in the parish of St. Mary Le Bow in the Ward of Cheap," has seemed to commentators and readers alike merely an amusing geographic impossibility, clever but substantively irrelevant. "There was little probability," Lon Fuller assures us, "that this isolated pretense would lead to a change in the meaning of the word 'London' that would extend it to embrace a spot of land in the Mediterranean" (18). But if we reexamine that fiction in the context of British colonialism and ask not what it did to the word "London" but how it affected Minorcans' understanding of the word "Minorca" (a point of view notably absent from Fuller's discussion), the fiction emerges as a striking instance of how official state power can *discursively* rewrite geographical boundaries. The legal fiction authorizes the law, through the performative power of its language, to absorb Minorca into the dominant, "civilized," well-policed City of London so that London's system of English courts, laws, and judges can exert authority over it. The operation of legal fiction is thus much more than symbolic. The island's autonomy, its existence as a separate social, physical, and economic entity, are all erased *as a practical matter* by the law's incontrovertible declaration that Minorca "is" in London. To Minorcans living under British rule, the fact that law language moved their island into "the Ward of Cheap" is a perfect illustration of Bentham's hated "theft" of legislative power. Like newspeak, the continually reinvented language that Orwell's Big Brother uses to control the history people can learn and even the thoughts they can think, the legal fiction of Minorca's relocation changes the ideas people can have about its degree of independence. The colonizing process, particularly its goal of psychological domination, is immeasurably furthered by the capacity of fictional language (a capacity we would identify as literary) to reinvent "reality" and thereby exert disciplinary control over domestic disputes of colonials.

". . . seized the wife of John and led her away with John's chattels . . . and broke down his hedges."

If we turn back now to the legal fictions that permeated early civil actions for adultery, we can begin to understand the active role they played in constructing the cultural meaning of adultery and marriage. The thread that connects these fictions is the work they accomplish: conceptualizing adultery as a compensable injury to the husband's property and removing wives from the law's discursive arena. Each of the fictions I will discuss—marital coverture, adultery as damage to property, as theft, as rape, and as loss of services—contributed to what became the tort of criminal conversation. The fictions fit into three conceptual groups: the underlying legal fiction of marital unity or coverture, which structured the law's "discussions" of all maritally related cases; the interlocking fictions used in the writs of abduction and ravishment to create a tangible property injury; and the reconceptualization of adultery as an injury to the husband's intangible property interest in the exclusive use of his wife's body and services. These fictions, which began as devices to obtain jurisdiction in specific courts, became part of the tort's fundamental logic and continued to shape legal discourse about adultery long after the need for them was past.

That legal fictions of adultery came to exert such cultural power also demonstrates an essential link between law and language. As Robert Cover has persuasively argued in "Violence and the Word," law as an operating system is always based on government's disciplinary power, on the potential exertion of actual force and the capacity for official violence. This is as true in civil litigation as it is in criminal cases, for the assertion of jurisdiction over disputes, the use of compulsory process, public testimony, damage awards, injunctions, and other manifestations of public power all demonstrate the state's continuing ability to *do things* to people. At the same time, however, law works through language, through a particular discourse of rules, statutes, orders, and decisions. The discourse of law exists quite separately from the "real world," even when it purports to represent actual events. To do its work, the law *needs* to exploit the capacity of language to create alternate realities, the capacity of fiction to construct within a textual narrative a world made up of both familiar, recognizably "real" elements and "fictional," blatantly counterfactual ones. That narrative amalgam, real and unreal, factual and fictional, is predicated on what only language, indeed only poetic language, can do. But a legal complaint is not a poem. It may be dependent on metonymy and personification, on verbal alchemy and rhetorical persuasion, but all these glories of literary form are there because—and this is key—they are the source of the complaint's practical power, what enables law to affect people's lives. These effects are both direct, as when a jurisdictional legal fiction allows a court to hear a case it otherwise could not take, and indirect, as when the law's extinguishing of married women's *legal* existence operates over hundreds of years to reinforce in women a sense of incompetence, marginality, and worthlessness. In short, the techniques of fiction are necessary to the effective promulgation of a legal discourse of power.

Of the fictions I look at here, the most fundamental and pervasive was the doctrine of marital coverture. Coverture was not a jurisdictional fiction, and it was developed in the context of marriage, not adultery. Though never explicitly alleged in criminal conversation complaints, it provided the underlying structural assumption essential to the litigation, the fiction of marital unity that gave the husband proprietary rights to his wife's property, and to the use of her body. Through coverture, a wife's legal existence was merged into that of her husband at the moment of marriage; a symbolic "death" at the altar that extinguished her separate existence as a legal subject and created the fiction that husband and wife were one person. For the duration of the marriage, she was "covered" by her husband; all the property and legal capacities she formerly enjoyed as a *feme sole* passed automatically to him, and whatever rights, obligations, and entitlements might once have belonged to either now were his alone. A wife could not own property, make contracts or wills, sue or be sued, or keep any wages she earned or any inheritance she acquired (Blackstone 1:442; Stone, *Family*, 136–42; Baker 550–57). Married women were removed from the sphere of public, legal speech and action, and were permitted to "speak" within the legal order only through their husbands, if at all. Coverture thus ensured that in adultery litigation a wife could be neither plaintiff nor defendant. It also prevented her from being a witness, because testifying for or against her husband would be admitting their separate existence, an impossibility that would destroy marital unity and domestic harmony (Blackstone 1:443). As commentators from Blackstone to John Stuart Mill to Lawrence Stone have noted, wife and husband were one person, and that one was the husband.

To understand the function of coverture in adultery litigation, it is important to remember that the concept of marital oneness was a cultural ideal as well as a legal fiction. At its visionary best, marital unity typified the desire of either partner for complete union, both spiritual and sexual, with the other. This unity is a central trope of John Donne's early poetry, from the lovers' "dialogue of one" in "The Ecstasy" to the "two souls therefore, which are one" in the "Valediction: Forbidding Mourning" to "The Canonization": "the phoenix riddle hath more wit / by us, we two, being one are it. / So to one neutral thing both sexes fit."[12] The splendid complementarity of Donne's images, their merger of two wholes into a single unified being, is especially remarkable for its insistence that neither partner dominates in love's new dual soul. The merged lovers form a "neutral" thing, "interanimated" by the flow of each into other, or, alternatively, they erase the gulf caused by absence by experiencing "not yet / a breach, but an expansion, / like gold to aery thinness beat" ("Canonization" l. 25; "Ecstasy" l. 42; "Valediction" ll. 22–24). But if lovers could share a fantasy of merged yet undiminished identity, the law of coverture arranged things quite differently. Once married, spouses constituted not a "neutral thing" at all, but an empowered male and a nonexistent female.

Coverture's erasing of the wife's identity may be read as a significant, unspoken subtext to Donne's love poems, particularly since these poems are thought to be written to his wife.[13] The poems construct a private lovers' world that, as the man implicitly assures the woman, will not be governed by "outside" legal rules that would efface or subjugate her. While still operating to obliterate identity, as public laws of coverture do, Donne's laws of love wittily reformulate the notion of identity effacement into a new principle of spiritual union, a combined identity that both lovers can participate in equally.

While the law's fiction of marital unity may thus have acted as an important counterpoint to Donne's poetic fiction of merger and equality, it also played a major role in constructing a cultural ideal of marriage in which compliant wives lovingly obeyed masterful husbands. Cultural pressures on women to willingly submit and men to confidently command were actively reinforced by legal fictions that treated all marriages as if the husband were really in charge. The law's coercive authority brought about in actuality its "fiction" of female extinction. Husbands received both affirmative powers, such as total control over their wives' assets and earnings, and serious responsibilities, such as being held liable for their wives' debts, torts, and criminal behavior. By refusing to permit either spouse to demonstrate that in their particular relationship the wife was free to make her own decisions or to control her own money, the law inevitably influenced the behavior and expectations of millions of couples. The legal fiction that protected litigative discourse from reality became a powerful determinant of that reality, increasing the actual power of husbands over wives.

Where a couple's behavior does not conform to the law's expectation, ridicule may be the result. In Charles Dickens's *Oliver Twist,* for example, where a wife has illegally sold the locket and gold ring that were an orphan's only identification, the husband is informed that he is "the more guilty of the two, in the eye of the law; for the law supposes that your wife acts under your direction." "If the law supposes that," Dickens's Mr. Bumble famously replies, "the law is a ass—a idiot. If that's the eye of the law, the law is a bachelor; and the worst I wish the law is, that his eye may be opened by experience—by experience" (*Oliver Twist* [1839] ch. 51). Mr. Bumble reveals the legal fiction of spousal unity as an obvious lie. The law may choose to believe that men control women, but the reality of Mr. Bumble's life is quite the opposite: his wife is independent, loudly vocal, and generally in vigorous control of him. If the law erases the Bumbles' actual marital relationship and replaces it with a stereotypical fiction of male dominance, Mr. Bumble eagerly returns the favor by personifying the law as an equally stereotypical bachelor, ignorant of what to Mr. Bumble is universal about wives: their domineering nature. Mr. Bumble wishes that the law's eyes might be opened by "experience," but experience—in the sense of the actual, idiosyncratic behavior of particular people—is just what both the law's fictions and Mr. Bumble's generalizations leave out.

Interestingly, however, the gap between law and experience is, in Mr. Bumble's case, also the gap between the ideal and the real, for in Dickens's universe, good women *do* act under the direction of men, remaining loyal and passive even when mistreated or ignored: from the patient Agnes in *David Copperfield* to the wives and mistresses of such sadistic mates as the dwarf Quilp in *The Old Curiosity Shop* and the brutal thief Bill Sykes in *Oliver Twist.* Mrs. Bumble's aggressive autonomy—exerted, not at all coincidentally, largely through the power of a commanding voice—is the mark of her capacity for evil, the "falseness" of a character at odds with what a "true" woman should be. In the world of *Oliver Twist,* the cultural ideal of marital interaction is reinforced by implicit reference to the law's fiction of marital unity. By making the two congruent, Dickens masks the coerciveness of the law, re-imaging it as an affirmative standard against which to assess actual experience.

But there are important differences between a generalized cultural fiction of male dominance within marriage and the specific operation of a legal system that refuses to recognize married women as independent subjects. Cultural principles have a flexibility, a historical responsiveness that allows them to change over time. In contrast, a fundamental legal fiction like marital coverture, while it may be functionally eroded here and there, works its way into a myriad of specific legal sites and becomes entrenched. The law's insistence that married women *do not exist* not only permeated substantive legal discourse in areas that explicitly concerned married women, but came to play a constitutive role in the very structure of legal process by preventing women from becoming speaking subjects.

With the doctrine of coverture as background, we can turn to the group of jurisdictional fictions that were used to bring adultery litigation into the Royal Courts in the late Middle Ages and early modern period. These were developed successively over several centuries, beginning with writs of abduction and ravishment and only much later developing into actions for loss of services and then into the separate tort of criminal conversation in the late seventeenth century. While the use of these fictions overlapped to some extent, they represent sequential stages in the development of a civil remedy for adultery. Their joint result was the fundamental "unmentionability" of female subjectivity, transgression, and agency; I will take up each stage in turn.

In his influential analysis of the central role of adultery in nineteenth-century fiction, Tony Tanner argues that the adulterous woman, because she violates society's requirement that the categories of "wife and mother" and "mistress and lover" be kept apart, "becomes the 'gap' in society that gradually extends through it. In attempting to ostracize her, society moves toward ostracizing itself" (13). For Tanner, adultery is so threatening to the contractual bases of society that, though it is omnipresent, every effort must be made not to see or mention it: "the invisible, inaudible deed becomes a silence and an absence in the text that gradually spreads, effectively negating what *is* made audible and present." Ultimately, in Tanner's view, the unmentionability of adultery is so destabilizing that it destroys the bourgeois novel and requires the production of new literary forms. "We can see adultery," he suggests, "as the gap, or silence, in the bourgeois novel that finally leads to its dissolution and displacement by postsocial fictional forms involving extreme states of physicality and/or/linguicity (or Proustian solipsism)" (14). Tanner's analysis contrasts the "repressions" of Victorian fiction with the eighteenth-century novel, in which "sexual activities are much more visible" and "sexuality in no sense threatens the structure of society or the institution of marriage" (13). Noting that adultery was actively prosecuted as a crime in the eighteenth century in England but not in the nineteenth, Tanner suggests that it was only in the nineteenth century that "adultery moved to the unspoken realm of those silent secondary laws of society, where rules and punishments are applied and meted out privately" (14).

Tanner's historical analysis, I would argue, is seriously undercut by the fact that legal discourse had made adultery an "unspeakable" gap centuries before the bourgeois novel was invented. Like many other literary critics, Tanner treats legal and literary discourse as fundamentally discontinuous, the former unvarying and non-narrative, the latter creative and culture-constituting. While the functional differences between the two are central to my analysis as well, I begin with an assumption of discursive similarity, a *continuity* of literary forms and strategies that makes the law's fictions about marriage and adultery crucial to any understanding of the role those structures play within culture and literature. By limiting his legal citations to criminal adultery statutes, Tanner also ignores the complex interactions of sex, marriage, and property that characterized civil adultery litigation from the outset. If we turn our attention to the operation of legal fictions in early adultery litigation, we will see first a pervasive "gap and silence" as profound and influential as any in later novels; second, the essential fact that it was *women's* transgressive desire, subjectivity, and agency that the law's discursive fictions erased (something paralleled in Tanner's nineteenth-century novels, though he fails to discuss it); and third, as I will develop in my later chapters, the way that "unmentionability" worked to stabilize legal discourse for centuries, yielding only recently and partially to a long siege by women in search of a legal voice.

Before the invention of the tort of criminal conversation, cuckolded husbands sought damages through the royal writs of abduction and ravishment, forcible trespass actions first developed in the thirteenth century. The proper legal site for adultery litigation at that time was the ecclesiastical courts. These had exclusive jurisdiction over all matters relating to marital relationships, because as a sacrament, marriage was a matter solely of church law (Pollock and Maitland 543). A husband's grievance about his wife's adultery raised religious issues of sin and sacrilege. Ecclesiastical courts inflicted shaming punishments on adulterers, such as requiring them to stand in white sheets in the marketplace, holding a candle and publicly confessing their sins (Stone, *Divorce*, 232). The problem was that ecclesiastical courts would not award money damages to injured husbands. Those who wanted financial reimbursement were therefore eager to meet the jurisdictional requirements for bringing cases in the more remunerative royal courts.

The royal writ of trespass could be used when the King's peace had been breached by an act of violence that caused damage to the plaintiff's property. Plaintiff-husbands therefore brought cases not of adultery but of theft.

The writ for abduction, a specific form of trespass, was used primarily when a wife had actually run off with her lover, perhaps under circumstances we would now liken to a consensual elopement (Baker 518). As Jeremy Weinstein puts it in his useful study of the history of adultery law: "for the husband to obtain a royal writ, his allegations of adultery had to be spiced up with allegations of other trespassory wrongs by the interloper, such as the taking of the husband's chattels or damage to his property" (212–13). Complaints for "abduction" consequently ignored the adultery at the heart of the husband's case (though it would become central at the trial stage), instead "treating the abduction of a wife entirely in terms of the chattels taken with her, usually her clothing and jewelry. If a wife simply left her husband for another man, there was no question for the royal courts. If she and her chattels were taken with what could be alleged to be force and arms against the king's peace, however, the king's courts had jurisdiction" (214).

Thus, the King's courts could take civil notice of marital infidelity only when it was formulated as a story about violence and injury to property. Plaintiffs therefore avoided mentioning sex, alleging instead a violent show of force and the theft of physical property. A typical fourteenth-century writ alleges that the defendant "wrongfully came with force and arms and seized the wife of John and led her away with John's chattels, namely jewelry, and broke down his hedges, against the form of the statute provided by the King for such a case" (writ B248, in Weinstein 215*n*149). Similarly, in the early seventeenth-century case of *Hide v. Cyssell* with which this chapter began, the plaintiff's trespassory writ alleged that the defendant "assaulted Elizabeth the plaintiff's wife, and beat and ill-treated her and took and carried away the said Elizabeth together with a gown, a petticoat, a smock and head-dress, valued at 20 pounds, of the plaintiff's goods and chattels and detained and kept her for five years" (Baker and Milsom 308). Were it not for the assurance of legal historians that the underlying complaint in each of these cases is in fact adultery, we might reasonably doubt it, so "factual" are the allegations of physical assault and chattel theft.

If we look more closely at the jurisdictional fiction that imaged the wife's adultery entirely in terms of the chattels taken with her, we can see that it is a complex combination of synecdoche and metonymy. At first glance, it seems to be a synecdochal representation of the wife (the "whole" woman) through a selective description of a small part of her (her jewelry or petticoat). Synecdoche can be a heightening device in literature if the part selected is of extraordinary value. In "The Good-Morrow," Donne's lovers, looking into each other's eyes, see reflections of their own faces:

My face in thine eye, thine in mine appears,
And true plain hearts do in the faces rest,
Where can we find two better hemispheres,
Without sharp north, without declining west? (ll. 15–18)

The lover's rounded eye represents the infinite whole that each lover has become. The eye's reflective capacity absorbs the other's face and heart; its shape suggests a new world, an alternate universe compressed to the intimate scale of a single eye; and its roundness defies both death and love's inevitable waning. Each lover's fullest self (assisted by the ancillary synecdoches of heart and face) is thus poetically represented by the lover's eye, while the eye's unique qualities suggest ways in which the lovers are enhanced by their love.

More often, however, synecdoche is a device for diminishment, especially when applied to human beings, because its telescopic process eliminates virtually everything that constitutes "personhood," reducing the complexity and agency that characterize subjectivity to simple object-status. This devalues what is left out and transforms what is left in into a thing. Efforts to diminish women by transforming them into objects, sexual or otherwise, have a classic affinity for this kind of synecdoche, producing familiar epithets that range from a "skirt" to a "piece of ass" to the wholly demeaning "cunt." The legal fiction's synecdochal reduction of women to clothes or jewelry effectively eliminates anything that might suggest interiority or independence.[14] The only thing "worth" mentioning about the woman is her gown or her necklace, just as the only thing "worth" mentioning when whistling at a woman on the street is her anatomy. In the trespass cases, the reductive synecdoche works to suppress rather than to magnify female sexuality, although sexual behavior is very much at issue.

Yet a closer look at the "chattel" allegations shows that they are more truly metonymies than synecdoches. Their poetic strategy metonymically substitutes the jewelry, headdress, or smock for the woman, selecting things not part of the woman herself but part of her context. To borrow the terminology developed in Roman Jakobson's well-known analysis of metaphor and metonymy, these objects are something contiguous with which she is identified, and which explains her "use" or value. Indeed, the gown and the jewels can function as jurisdictionally supportive "facts" only because they are the property of the husband, and thus emphatically *not* the wife's at all. In Jakobson's study of aphasics with similarity disorder, impairments that make it impossible for a speaker to call a thing by its name or by a synonym "force" him, through a process of metonymic logic, to project something from the "line of habitual context" into the "line of substitution and selection" so that contiguity becomes the determinant of verbal behavior (77–84). Thus, a patient will say "fork" for "knife," "heaven" for "God," "smoke" for "pipe" (83–84). In the legal context, it is adultery that, as in Tanner's analysis of the Victorian novel, becomes the "gap," the activity that cannot be called by its name, that forces a series of transformative fictions to fill it with assertions about property. The jurisdictional pressure to formulate a story about an injury to the husband's property requires that in the syntactical slot where the woman and her adultery would be expected to appear, metonymic replacement locates a physical object from her environment that does not so much represent as supplant and efface her.

It is important to remember that the husband does not own the wife. The law of coverture may deprive her of legally recognized subjectivity and agency, but it stops short (some might say it trembles on the brink) of making the wife herself a chattel.[15] The displacing fiction that constructs a trespassory injury could not, therefore, be the theft of the wife herself. Her husband *does* own, and thus has an obvious property interest in, everything she wears and uses, so his complaint alleges damage to all of the things that she took with her. The wife herself is textually irrelevant. She therefore disappears, becoming "unutterable," while her place is taken, in the metonymic logic of the complaint, by objects intimately associated with her, referred to because they have money value as property. Paradoxically, the legal fiction thus represents the wife through objects of property precisely because she herself is not property. The suit is brought, moreover, just at the moment when the wife's actual subjectivity and agency have been forcefully demonstrated by her sexual independence. The metonymic discourse of law thus recaptures her as her husband's at the very time that her *not* being his has been brought to public attention. The law's banishment of the wife from the arena of litigative discourse seems, from this viewpoint, like an anxious but effective linguistic extermination—as if female transgression can be punitively ignored but not confronted.

The wife's textual eradication also successfully commercializes the husband's story of loss. The new legal story is about an economic relationship between two men, husband and lover, and it is about financially assessable damage to property. This is what the court is in the business of handling; it can take the case and resolve the dispute through an award of monetary damages. As the wife fades from view, the complaint minimizes or eliminates the relationship of wife to lover, and wife to husband. The litigative conversation that ensues is entirely male-voiced, a transformation I will discuss in some detail in chapter 4. If Shylock's overpowering concern for the ducats that disappeared with his daughter is meant to display his abhorrently "Jewish" materialism, we might ask what is to be inferred from a process of allegation that dispenses with the daughter altogether. At least the complaint of Shakespeare's merchant alternates the name of his grief from person to property and back again. In criminal conversation cases, the language of the law permits the plaintiff to speak of his loss only in words that signify things, banishing the transgressive wife to gap and silence.

Trespass actions must always allege that the defendant committed the injury *vi et armis*, by force and arms. In the chattel fiction such allegations produce a metaphorical narrative of rape, though one that makes its victim invisible. By constructing stories about stealing and destroying physical property, in which the only active agent is the lover and in which objects representing the wife are looted, these jurisdictional fictions recount the metaphorical violation of the absent wife's body. A plaintiff who alleges that the defendant has broken his hedges and stolen his valuables, or that he has "beaten and ill-treated" the wife and stolen her clothes, constructs an obvious metaphorical narrative of forcible sexual injury. Yet we must remember that the allegations of physical force and violence were almost universally fictional. That is, not only was there no rape, there was also no forcible theft or battery, because the wife cooperated voluntarily. But because the wife, under coverture, had no legal capacity to consent, the defendant's "taking" of the husband's property became a forcible abduction.[16] Evidence of the wife's participation was therefore irrelevant, and "even if the jury found expressly that the abduction was not forcible, the husband could recover" (Baker 518–19).[17]

To the extent that a violent attack has "really" occurred, it is an attack on the husband's nonmaterial feelings of love, trust, male pride, and honor. The legal fiction transposes the "forcible" violation of the husband's honor by the lover, a figurative rape of man by man, first into the suppressed image of heterosexual rape and then into the actual words of the writ, which describe a violent but asexual theft and battery. The fictional text can thus be read as a double displacement of actual events, a convoluted set of textual pathways whose patterns represent the shadow of what has been exorcized from the surface of allowable discourse. That suggestive shadow nevertheless lingers, to return in a variety of forms.

While the writs of abduction and ravishment were still being mentioned by Blackstone in the 1760s, as a practical matter they had become a dead end by the end of the fifteenth century, after which none were brought (Blackstone 3:138, Weinstein 216). In the course of the seventeenth century, civil adultery litigation entered a new phase as two new husband's remedies appeared: first the action for loss of the wife's help or companionship (*per quod consortium amisit*); and then, toward the end of the century, the related action for criminal conversation, which for the first time explicitly alleged adultery. In both actions, the injury was characterized as an interference with the husband's *relational* interest in his wife. That is, the property interest that justified the plaintiff's trespassory complaint was located not in his physical property but in the intangible property rights he enjoyed through the contractually beneficial relationship of marriage. The new action made the husband's interest in his wife analogous to the (relatively new) enforceable interest that an employer had in the labor of his employees, a right which, if interfered with, could be the basis of a trespassory suit for money damages. By considering the relation of husband and wife as parallel to that of master and servant, the law enabled husbands to bring damage actions similar to already established master-servant cases.

In the new tort of loss of consortium, adultery was fictionally represented as a tortious interference in a service relationship. The action's roots lay in the fourteenth century when, in response to the labor shortage caused by the Black Death, the Statute of Labourers gave a master a legal remedy against anyone who wrongfully deprived him of a servant's labor. This right of action was extended at common law to allow actions of trespass for enticing servants away or inflicting injuries so serious that laborers could not perform their jobs. As the legal historian J. H. Baker notes:

> Although force and arms were alleged, the force was not used against the plaintiff; the action lay for the loss occasioned to the plaintiff by the interference with an existing relationship of benefit to him. Since the action lay in respect of the loss of services rather than the forcible wrong, it was natural that it should have been extended by analogy to situations where the plaintiff was deprived of benefit by non-forcible conduct. The extensions led to

> the diverse torts of enticement, criminal conversation, and inducing a breach of contract. (517, and see Weinstein 218–20)

Imaging the wife's adultery as the deprivation of a husband's right to benefit from his marital relationship, loss of consortium complaints formulaically alleged a loss of services, though in most cases the loss was both fictional and irrelevant to the true injury. In the 1620 case of *Hide v. Cyssell*, which began this chapter, the descriptions of Elizabeth's twenty pounds' worth of clothes are followed by the claim that, as a direct result of the defendant's wrongdoing, the plaintiff "wholly lost the comfort and company and also the advice and help in domestic affairs, which the plaintiff could and should have had and enjoyed with his wife during that time." Lost services were a fictional, jurisdictional allegation included to guarantee a hearing in the desired court, not a description of the actual "loss" suffered by the plaintiff.

While the husband could sue for loss of consortium, the wife could not. The underlying fiction of coverture gave the husband a proprietary right to his wife's services but granted her no corresponding right. When the defendant in *Hide v. Cyssell* protested that the wife should have been joined as a plaintiff, the court disagreed, holding that, despite allegations that the defendant had "beaten and ill-treated" the wife, the action was based on an injury not to her but to the husband, "for the loss and damage of the husband for want of her company and aid."[18] The wife's mental and physical harm is thus legally irrelevant, unless it causes consequential damage to the husband. If the wife is too "injured" to provide services, *he* has a cause of action against whoever is responsible for depriving him of his marital rights. Blackstone famously explains why entitlements run in one direction only in a section dealing with the "relative" relationships of husband and wife, master and servant, guardian and ward, and parent and child:

> In these relative injuries, notice is only taken of the wrong done to the superior of the parties related . . . while the loss of the inferior by such injuries is totally unregarded. One reason for which may be this: that the inferior hath no kind of property in the company, care or assistance of the superior, as the superior is held to have in those of the inferior, and therefore the inferior can suffer no injury. The wife cannot recover damages for beating her husband, for she hath no separate interest in any thing during her coverture. (3:143)

The child likewise has no enforceable property interest in his father or guardian, Blackstone goes on to assert, nor the servant in the master, and thus children, wards, and servants, like wives, cannot sue for injuries incurred by their "superior" (143). In short, relational property rights are nonreciprocal. In the late nineteenth century, when newly empowered female plaintiffs attempted to use the tort of criminal conversation to win damage awards against their husbands' female lovers, Blackstone's articulation of the asymmetrical powers and duties of "superior" and "inferior" would be resurrected and used as a conceptual wedge to block women from bringing such actions (see chapter 5). But when Blackstone was writing in the 1760s, the fiction of coverture and the wife's consequent legal nonexistence were taken so firmly for granted that the possibility of equal rights between spouses simply did not occur as a serious issue. The asymmetry caused by the legal fiction was thus written into the tort, where it became constitutive.

The shift from fictions about theft and destruction to fictions about lost services accomplished an important change in the "plot" of the law's fictions of adultery: it produced a story about marriage as activity rather than as ownership. The damaged "property" was intangible; the new narrative paradigm located the wife's value in her benefit-producing conduct rather than in the objects with which she was associated or adorned. The wife's active ministrations were presumed to provide her husband with "comfort and society." These might include the heavy physical labor of lower-class wives, or a round of afternoon tea and evening sex for the upper classes.[19] By situating marital rights and obligations in a continuing round of interactive domesticity, the new tort was not demonstrating less interest in property ownership or in the material side of life; rather, it was translating that interest to a more sophisticated notion of "property" that included contractual entitlements to the labor of others.

The law's "choice" of loss of services as an appropriate paradigm for adultery's injury may also be one of the earliest testaments to the rise of companionate marriage, which Lawrence Stone attributes to the late seventeenth and early eighteenth centuries (*Family* 217–24). Companionate marriage shifts the basis of marriage from relations of property to those of affection, and separates the realms of men and women by allocating political authority to the husband and domestic authority (including control over emotions, morality, and taste) to the wife. The wife becomes an active, though by no means necessarily equal, partner. As Ian Watt, Nancy Armstrong, and others have argued, this reconceptualization of domesticity is linked to the eighteenth century's invention of the novel. Looking at eighteenth-century fiction, we can see that it takes up the question of appropriate domestic service as a female marital duty with almost obsessive seriousness. Pamela proves her worthiness to be Mr. B's wife by carving and eating a chicken wing with modest and loving grace; Amelia shocked Fielding's readers by dressing a leg of lamb for her husband with her own hands; Parson Primrose's wife stays by his side even in prison, where she tells him she could bear even the abduction of their daughter "if you were but easy."

Yet nearly a hundred years before the appearance of the first "domestic" novels, we see the law selecting as its newly preferred marital plot a narrative not of ownership but of domestic interaction. The loss of services story thus seems an improvement over earlier chattel fictions; it discursively promotes the wife from object to actor, and we should not lightly dismiss such an advance. Yet the legal function of the new fiction is to equate "affection, care, and attention"—the services that would demonstrate the value of Richardson's, Fielding's, and Goldsmith's fictional wives—with enforceable property interests. The wife's useful labors are merely a new form of the husband's property. It is important to remember too that the allegations of loss of service, though crucial *legally*, were fictions invented to bring adultery actions within the jurisdictional ambit of analogous master-servant cases. Neither courts nor husbands considered the "real" injury to be the deprivation of service or affection. Rather, the linguistic fiction substituted for what was understood to be the true harm: the unmentionable adultery and its effect on masculine honor: "Provided a loss of service was made out, however trivial, the courts allowed juries to assess aggravated damages for the dishonour and injured feelings" of the cuckolded husband (Baker 519).

At the end of the seventeenth century, the claim for tortious interference with the husband's right of consortium took a new leap into straightforwardness by producing the action for criminal conversation. For the first time, husbands complained directly of the defendant's sexual misbehavior; the new action, still a claim for a trespassory property injury, simply "treated the act of adultery as a trespass in itself" (Baker 519). The husband's intangible property rights, which had included the wife's labor, were now also found to include the exclusive use of her body. The defendant's penetration of the wife's body was a trespass on the plaintiff's property rights because it was a taking, without the husband's consent, of something he "owned," namely, the right to be the only one to have intercourse with her.

While the injuring act was now the sexual transgression itself, the new action could not do without legal fictions; coverture was still a critical underlying fiction, and the new criminal conversation allegations also almost universally, and fictionally, claimed that the wife had been forcibly "ravaged" and that her services had been "lost." Because the tort developed out of the earlier loss of services action, the service allegations persisted long after their jurisdictional relevance was gone. In the nineteenth-century criminal conversation cases I examine in later chapters, plaintiffs routinely alleged loss of services whether or not the wife had actually ceased to perform them. In suing Henry Ward Beecher, for instance, Theodore Tilton alleged that by reason of his wife's adultery, he had "lost the comfort, society, aid and assistance of his said wife," though she had continued throughout the affair to live with her husband and to make great efforts to please him (see chapter 3).

And while the adultery was generally conceded to have been agreed upon rather than forced, the "force and arms" requirement for trespass actions still had to be met, so new cases also almost universally included an allegation that the sexual "conversation" had been achieved by force. "The usual declaration was to the effect that the defendant with force and arms assaulted the wife, and ravished and debauched her, so that the plaintiff lost her comfort, fellowship and society" (Baker 519). Where earlier writs alleged forcible abduction, theft, and destruction of property, the new cases claimed equally fictional allegations of a forcible sexual "taking." Since the wife had no right to determine her body's sexual employment, her consent was legally irrelevant. This meant that within the world of legal discourse marital sex, however violent and unwelcome, could never constitute rape, while all extramarital sex, even sex the wife passionately solicited, was in legal terms a "ravishment." The seemingly factual allegations of rape were thus written by the law's "story" of adulterous sex rather than by anyone's mimetic description of what had actually happened.

In later chapters, I will examine the tort of criminal conversation at the end of the nineteenth century in America, first through analysis of a nationally scandalous trial, the Beecher-Tilton case of 1875, and then through a reading of a series of cases in which married women sought to become litigative speakers by bringing criminal conversation cases against their husbands' female lovers. The legal fictions identified here as springing from institutional constraints on jurisdiction and from cultural assumptions about the nature of marriage haunt the later history of the tort with a vengeance. Though long past their original usefulness, they still permeated plaintiffs' complaints, set the terms of legal analysis, and forced courts to think about marriage and sex by referring to precedents set in the seventeenth and eighteenth centuries.[20] Even courts that congratulated themselves on the "wisdom" that made it "absurd in this enlightened age to regard the wife as a mere machine, made to labor and to talk as the husband directs" had to carefully disassemble the elements of criminal conversation and then formulate a new set of underlying legal principles to permit the tort's continuation (see, e.g. *Turner v. Heavrin*, 182 Ky 65 [1918]).

Yet certain moments in the tort's early history, such as the shift from claims of tangible property damage to claims of intangible loss of services, later proved extraordinarily useful. Where everyone connected with a seventeenth-century case for loss of services knew that the wife's failure to provide domestic services (ritualized as "companionship, care and affection") was not what the husband was "really" complaining about, late nineteenth-century courts found a fiction already in the law that could be made consonant with later cultural assumptions. As I will show in chapter 5, such courts took up the preexisting, legally empowered verbal formula and transformed it from a hollow phrase into a "true" and enforceable signifier for marital agony, an agony, moreover, that either spouse could properly avenge. The entrenched fictions of adultery litigation thus came, over time, to constitute not procedural tricks but foundational legal assumptions. They continued to affect real lives, both of women like Elizabeth Tilton whose stories went effaced and unheard, and of the generation of women who became the law's first female "speaking subjects," who, even when successful, were often derided and stereotyped as inappropriately "aggressive." And because our legal system operates through a discourse whose rules and empowered verbal formulas are often centuries old, the *legal* effect of these fictions is still very much with us today.

PART II

Theodore Tilton vs. Henry Ward Beecher: Criminal Conversation, 1875

PROLOGUE

Crisis of Confidence in the Courtroom

Between July 1874 and July 1875, the most important subject of discussion in America was New York author and editor Theodore Tilton's charge that Henry Ward Beecher had committed adultery with Tilton's wife, Elizabeth. Beecher, the nation's foremost preacher, was a national symbol of morality, idealism, and self-realization. His Sunday sermons attracted thousands weekly, and were read across the country by many thousands more. His writings included not only weekly sermons and essays, but also popular volumes of advice to young men, a life of Jesus, and a best-selling novel, *Norwood.* Son of an important New England minister, brother of Harriet Beecher Stowe and Catherine Beecher, Henry Ward Beecher and his family were looked on as embodiments of the American spirit: democratic, religious, energetically moral.[1]

The scandal about the preacher and Mrs. Tilton had been simmering since November of 1872, when free-love advocate Victoria Woodhull published the accusation in her *Woodhull and Claflin's Weekly*, but when Beecher finally authorized his Brooklyn Church to investigate the charges in July and August 1874, more than thirty reporters a day attended the church hearings. Media preoccupation with the scandal was said to be "unparalleled in journalism."[2] The *New York Herald* declared in July that "no event since the murder of Lincoln has so moved the people as this question" (Carter 115, 114; Rugoff 1981:493). The public's obsession became so intense that E. L. Godkin, editor of *The Nation*, wrote to James Russell Lowell that he was escaping to Vermont because the "nastiness of it, and the newspaper rhetoric on it" had made New York "almost uninhabitable just now."[3] Interest throughout what came to be called "scandal summer" was much more than local, however; in a single day in August, the *Chicago Tribune* gleefully devoted 22 columns to the Tiltons' marital correspondence, while articles about the case began to appear regularly in newspapers as far away as Marseilles and Rome.[4] During the second half of 1874, the *New York Times* ran 105 stories and 37 editorials about the scandal.

After two years of scandal, Tilton filed suit against Beecher in August

1874. The subsequent civil trial on Tilton's tort charges of criminal conversation and alienation of affections lasted for more than six months, from January to July 1875.[5] Even after so many months of saturation-level publicity, the trial stimulated a heightened interest. During the trial, every major newspaper in the country devoted front-page coverage to the case on a daily basis, "pushing politics off the front pages for months at a time" (Wendt 248). In suing the man who had once been his best friend and who had performed his marriage ceremony twenty years earlier, Tilton demanded $100,000 damages as compensation for the injuries *to him* caused by his wife's adultery with Beecher.[6]

Though the central question in the case was whether she and Beecher had committed adultery, Elizabeth Tilton's legal "interests" were not technically at issue. Neither plaintiff nor defendant, she was unrepresented by counsel and prevented from testifying by a procedural rule.[7] Elizabeth Tilton nevertheless appeared daily in the courtroom, a silent, constant presence among the boisterous spectators. On the seventy-seventh trial day, she rose "like an apparition" from her seat and attempted to read a statement. She was peremptorily silenced by the judge (*Tilton versus Beecher* 3:313–14, 323–25, 355–56). Nevertheless, conversations with her were recounted from the witness stand, her intimate letters to her husband were read in the public courtroom, and she was continually described and assessed by counsel for both sides.[8]

Popular involvement in the trial was intense. Huge crowds surged around the courthouse, often waiting all night for a chance to get a ticket for one of the limited spectator seats inside the courtroom, while "as many as three thousand persons a day were turned away, affording nearby saloons a booming business" (Shaplen 216). Scalpers sold the free tickets for as much as five dollars each. Immense bouquets of flowers were delivered to Beecher and to Tilton where they sat with counsel, until the courtroom reeked of hothouse plants and the competition by each party's supporters to produce ever more magnificent and showy bouquets thoroughly upstaged the ongoing interrogation of witnesses on the stand.[9] Jurors and spectators fainted in the June heat wave and were carried out. Trial transcripts, printed daily in several New York newspapers, were also sold to the public in booklet form as the trial continued.[10]

Final arguments to the jury lasted sixteen full days. On July 2, the 112th day of trial, after eight days of deliberation and fifty-two ballots, the jury announced that it was deadlocked. "It is a question of fact, a question of the veracity of witnesses on which we do not agree, your Honor, and I would say I think there is not a possibility of an agreement in this jury," explained Chester Carpenter, the foreman. Judge Neilson reluctantly dismissed the jurors, and the case ended without a verdict (3:1041–1042). When Beecher entered Plymouth Church that evening for his weekly prayer meeting, a crowd on the sidewalk cheered, while inside devoted parishioners sobbed (Shaplen 255).

In the following days and weeks, the media delivered a variety of verdicts. *Harper's Weekly, Scribner's Monthly,* and many others stoutly insisted that the nonverdict was tantamount to an acquittal, assuring their readers that "the majority of the jury in the late trial, like the majority of the public, held Mr. Beecher guiltless of the crime charged against him, and the result of the trial is virtual acquittal" (C. Clark 224–25). Many others were not so forgiving. In the *Nation,* Godkin editorialized: "It can hardly be said that this is a victory for anybody, but it is something very like a defeat for Mr. Beecher." Whether Beecher was innocent or guilty of the charge, Godkin declared, "It is a pitiful story, which must remain a permanent blot on his reputation, and must considerably diminish if not destroy his influence as a moral teacher" (18 July 1875, 22–23). In a lengthy assessment of the evidence one day after the trial's conclusion, *The New York Times* concluded that the facts "tell heavily against Mr. Beecher," something that "will be universally regretted, for it is a mournful sight to see a great preacher of religion resting even under the suspicion of a dark crime" (*Review of the Evidence* 33). Newspapers from Kentucky to London were more blunt, calling Beecher "a dunghill covered with flowers," and asserting that he had "acted with an imbecility that would have disgraced an uneducated girl" (*Louisville Courier Journal, London Daily Telegraph,* quoted in Shaplen 258).

In the following year, Plymouth Church raised Beecher's salary by $100,000 so that he could pay his legal expenses, sent copies of the final arguments in his defense to "every library, college, and important church in the country," and convened a second Church Council, which again acquitted Beecher of all charges (Hibben 282). Beecher continued to be a popular preacher and lecturer. Some historians assert that he recovered his position and the faith of his followers (C. Clark 224–29), while others conclude that he was taken less seriously as a religious leader, that he became a butt of mockery even in the religious press, and that "his lectures were often frequented by curiosity seekers rather than admiring parishioners" (Waller 146; Rugoff 1981:499–501). The Tiltons separated but never divorced.

Theodore Tilton's professional career was ruined by the scandal; he eventually "fled to Paris where he lived in poverty, writing poetry and playing chess" (Waller 11; Rugoff 1989:210). Elizabeth Tilton was supported for a time by members of Beecher's congregation, who hired her as a tutor. When she issued an unambiguous admission of the affair in 1878, however, she was swiftly excommunicated.[11] As Altina Waller concludes, "she grew old in Brooklyn, a virtual outcast, sustained only by the devotion of her daughter and a small radical group known as the Christian Friends" (145, and see Shaplen 272). Gradually, the scandal that "cast a stain upon the fair name of the Great Republic of the West" and the trial that counsel had confidently declared would "loom larger in history than any which has taken place for eighteen centuries" were forgotten (Marshall 13; 1:92).

CHAPTER 3

The Maintenance of Mutual Confidence: Sentimental Strategies at the Beecher-Tilton Trial

The Trial as Subject: Literary Form and Litigative Strategy

Though the immediacy of the Beecher-Tilton scandal has long since faded, its year-long reign as a national obsession invites analysis: In a decade filled with scandals about the vices and corruption of public figures like Grant and Tweed, what about this one led newspaper-reading Americans to experience it as the most significant event since the death of Lincoln? This chapter argues that one important explanation for the case's spectacular notoriety is that both the months of adversarial interrogation and the concentration on the single issue of credibility played into a profound preexisting cultural anxiety about the difficulty of distinguishing sincerity from hypocrisy. What Paul Carter has called the "obsessive, even compulsive quality" of Americans' involvement in the case becomes more understandable if we think of the trial as a convergence of structure, substance, and national concern about the difficulty of making reliable judgments about other people. Transformed from a titillating, gossipy set of newspaper stories into a formal public trial that became an increasingly undecidable interrogation of hypocrisy, the trial touched one of the country's rawest nerves. Following each day's testimony in their newspapers, Americans saw not just a beloved figure and longstanding role model on trial, but also the reliability of their own methods of judgment.[1]

With this cultural context in mind, I will concentrate on the rhetorical strategies deployed by lawyers in the courtroom, focusing on the forensic use of sentimentality to "solve" the case's central credibility problems and on contemporary critiques of such tactics of jury persuasion. I will also suggest broader connections among legal process, literary form, and the historical concerns of culture. The first section of the chapter sets out basic assumptions about the literary narrativity of trial process that underlie my analysis. The second and third sections use a reading of William Maxwell Evarts's closing argument for Henry Ward Beecher to compare Evarts's rhetorical strategy to sentimental strategies employed by such authors of fiction as Beecher's sister, Harriet Beecher Stowe. I connect Evarts's forensic rhetoric not only to literary sentimentality but also to theories of credibility and "mutual confidence" advanced by nineteenth-century evidence theorists like William Mowdesley Best and by recent cultural critics such as Karen Halttunen. The fourth section examines the era's powerful antisentimentalist critique, discussing first Tilton's inconsistent challenge to Beecher's sentimental strategy, then Mark Twain and Charles Dudley Warner's 1873 novel, *A Gilded Age*, which features a climactic murder trial at which the emotionally seductive rhetoric of an Evarts-like lawyer destroys the jury's rational decision-making capacity. Finally, the chapter ends with a discussion of the contrast in literary form between individual trial narratives and the inclusive, novel-like transcript of an entire trial or lawsuit.

In speaking of the "narrativity" of courtroom testimony and argument, and in analyzing it in such literary terms as genre, plot, character, and rhetoric, I am making what has become a basic assumption about the way legal process works: that all litigation is essentially conducted by constructing, presenting, and interpreting narrative versions of past events.[2] To win a case, litigants and their lawyers must transform the complex data of subjective experience into persuasive, coherent, consistent, morally inflected narratives. Significantly, the instrumental importance of such litigative narratives puts their intended readers in a uniquely powerful position. The "finder of fact," whether judge or jury, delivers the story-ending verdict that metes out rewards and punishments consistent with the fact finder's determination of "the story thus far."[3] From the plaintiff's or defendant's point of view, the only measure of success for any trial narrative is whether or not it convinces the jury-audience. Because courtroom storytelling is thus profoundly contingent on the response it produces, courtroom storytellers inevitably try to minimize uncertainty by shaping stories to elicit predictable, sympathetic responses. Witnesses and counsel frame their stories for maximal appeal to the specific audience of judge or jury, using what they know or infer about jurors' and judges' values, education, and literary familiarity. The particular story told, and the way it is told, represent the teller's best guess about what will persuade its intended audience.

In this sense, the jury can be thought of as "writing" the stories it hears. Those stories are also, importantly, told to steer the jury toward a desired interpretation. The moment of juridical intervention analeptically refashions what has gone before it, producing the denouement and retroactively privileging certain storylines while devaluing others. In this, it functions as an audience-participation drama like the 1986 New York dramatization of Charles Dickens's unfinished novel *The Mystery of Edwin Drood.* There, the final scene was determined—and varied—each night by the audience's voted selection of The Murderer, The Sleuth, and The Lovers from among the likely suspects in the cast. As time went on, actors began to vie with each other to be chosen, doing all they could in their early scenes to give hints that their character was indeed the murderer (Bennetts 2:1). Not only did each actor's desire to win affect the performance, but although the "truth" changed from night to night, the dramatic denouement produced by the audience vote always "proved" that their decision had been correct, that the selected "truth" had "really" been there all along.[4] In the same way, the delivery of a jury verdict ends the trial's provisionality and its illusion of interparty parity. Labels of truth and falsehood attach to various narratives, and while other readers of the trial record (appellate judges, newspapers readers) may disagree, they cannot experience early phases of the trial uncolored by the jury's *post hoc* assessment.

Once we recognize that the litigative conversation is not over until the jury speaks, jurors cease to be a passive audience before whom a fixed show is performed and take their place instead as full-fledged cast members. They are part of an ensemble piece in which one set of participants simply refrains from supplying an immediate response to its interlocutor. Such silent participants (one thinks here of Bergman's *Persona* or Stringberg's one-act play *The Stronger*) become critical touchstones whose actual or supposed response exerts an increasing shaping power over what is said to them. Thus, jurors are not the only "readers" in the courtroom; litigants, lawyers, and witnesses busily study each juror's facial expressions and body positions even as the jurors assess the demeanor of testifying witnesses.

Response-centered criticism has long argued that meaning is largely a product of the reader's interpretive activity rather than of the text itself. Readers approach texts with preconceptions; as Jonathan Culler has argued, the text must "be thought of as an utterance that has meaning only with respect to a system of conventions which the reader has assimilated" (104). These rules and assumptions derive in large part from the reader's wealth of prior experience *as a reader*, that is, the reader's remembered responses to similar plots, characters, and language. Someone who has read widely will be able to identify a text from its opening chapter as an epic or a tragedy based on a range of familiar linguistic identifiers such as tone, voice, vocabulary, or plot. She will then have specific expectations about how the story will "turn out," about which characters are to be admired and identified with, which recoiled from in horror. Many of these textual clues are linked to genre; once a reader knows what kind of story she is reading, tragedy or farce, hard-boiled detective fiction or soft-core pornography, she has a set of interpretive rules that she can apply with confidence.[5] To predict how a particular person will interpret a story about murder, it would be helpful to know whether the story was told in a manner more similar to *Crime and Punishment* or to the film comedy *So I Married an Axe Murderer*. This connection between genre markers and interpretation is also a key to understanding courtroom narratives.

In framing their cases for the jury, lawyers inevitably draw on the story forms that are most powerful in their culture at the time. They do so, moreover, not just to make their clients' claims neatly coherent and thus "tellable," but also to evoke the specific and predictable responses that jurors will have already learned, as readers, to stock characters and situations in familiar romances, farces, or sentimental tragedies. By suggesting that the facts of a case constitute a story much like others jurors know—especially if the analogous stories offer unambiguous moral assessments of character and action—a lawyer can provide a clear moral framework for jurors to use as a guide in making credibility determinations and evidentiary assessments.

A literary mode such as sentimentality—which dominated the Beecher-Tilton trial—can make this task seem easier. Nineteenth-century American sentimental fiction tended to divide the world into the morally unambiguous categories of good and evil—victim and perpetrator—while its textual strategies aimed to make readers identify with the deserving but abused victim, prototypically a child, slave, or orphan. If the victim hero/ine suffered at the hands of oppressive masters, teachers, or relatives, the familiar "trials and tribulations" plot pattern ensured that in the final chapter virtue would be rewarded and vice punished.[6] By suggesting to the jury that the "story" of the Beecher-Tilton case could be read as a familiar sentimental narrative, lawyers could assign characters to clearly demarcated categories of virtue or vice, fit complex and ambiguous fact constellations to paradigmatic plots of unjust treatment and wrongful deprivation, and cast the jury's job of producing a verdict as an opportunity to mete out rewards and punishments, producing an appropriately happy ending. Such literary surrogacy becomes a shortcut through the painstaking and difficult process of evidentiary evaluation: having accepted a proffered story formulation, jurors know how to assess each piece of evidence and resolve each testimonial conflict. The story assumes primacy, determining rather than reflecting the answers to questions about what happened or which party has the better legal claim. Especially in a lengthy, confusing trial such as Beecher's, the interpretive certainty of sentimental story logic can do more than simply guide evidentiary assessment; it can supplant it. This means that the party who can supply the most persuasive story formulation of the case's facts has gone a long way toward winning the case. It is not surprising, therefore, that many of the bitterest courtroom conflicts are about which party will control the story framework through which the jury "reads" the case.[7] It is not necessary, of course, that opposing parties conveniently champion different literary modes. At the Beecher-Tilton trial, both sides exploited sentimentality's emotional powers when it suited them, and both sides mocked sentimentality when such mockery seemed expedient.[8]

A brief example will illustrate the process of sentimental narrativizing at the Beecher-Tilton trial. As plaintiff's counsel, Theodore Tilton's attorneys made their opening statement to the jury before the first witness was sworn, giving them a powerful opportunity to preempt the story-making field by controlling each juror's initial assignment of the roles of hero and villain to one or the other of the parties.[9] After a lengthy recitation of the wrongs to which Tilton had been subjected by Beecher, Samuel D. Morris ended the first day of his opening statement for Theodore Tilton by telling the jury: "We come here from a blighted and desperate home. The children of my client are scattered in different parts. He will return to-night to as cold, as cheerless, and as desolate a home as there is in the land. And from that voiceless home and cheerless fireside he will come in the morning, to meet you, fathers, and brothers, and husbands, you coming from your happy homes, he from his desolate one" (*Tilton versus Beecher* 1:33). Even this fragment of Morris's rhetoric, which is consistent with his tone and vocabulary throughout the three days of his opening, reveals a great deal. First, Morris effectively exploits the familiar sentimental tropes of splintered family, cheerless fireside, and suffering father/brother/husband to demonstrate that it is Tilton, not Beecher, who should occupy the place of sympathetic victim-hero in the jurors' minds. Morris wants to elicit the kind of pity and compassion for a deeply wronged (but deserving, and compensable) hero that juror-readers had learned to feel by reading sentimental fiction, and, as a practical matter, to plant that characterization firmly enough that the coming months of testimony will be filtered through it.

Second, he sets up a narrative opposition that is not, as one might expect, between plaintiff and defendant but between plaintiff and *juror.* By positioning the jurors as possessors of successful family-defined identities ("fathers, and brothers, and husbands") and superior domestic comforts ("your happy homes"), Morris encourages them to look down in pity on Tilton for having undeservedly lost what they are imagined as enjoying. At the same time, however, Morris also implies that no family happiness is proof against a home-wrecker like Beecher, whose "crimes" threaten everyone's security, including the jurors.' Morris drove the point home two days later by assuring the jury that when they had rendered the verdict that would "brand the seducer as his crime deserves to be branded" they would "receive the prayers and blessings of every virtuous mother and of every virtuous daughter in the land, and a peaceful conscience will follow you through life, will be with you in the last solemn scenes on earth, and console you when at last you stand with your life-record before the ever-living God" (1:58). As a reward for reestablishing justice and virtue in the world through their verdict, the jurors will earn, in their own lives, the gratitude of others, a guilt-free conscience, and an easy passage at the Last Judgment. Morris exploits the rhetoric of sentimentality to the fullest: not only does he use sentimental stereotypes to shape the jurors' reception of the upcoming evidence, he also makes each juror's personal life a part of what is at stake in the trial. His forensic sentimentality constructs the reader as it constructs its own text.

While sentimentality, along with romance, realism, melodrama, and other literary modes, is still very much with us, it is important to recognize that each arose at a specific historical period, when particular cultural conditions made certain kinds of stories seem most "true." The fact of sentimentality's prevalence at an important trial in 1875 tells us a great deal, not just about which literary forms were popular during the period but also about the particular anxieties and concerns animating American culture at the time. Yet the "truth" of sentimentality in 1875 was anything but unquestioned. While its use at the Beecher-Tilton trial suggests its continuing power, the trial record also reflects continual attacks on sentimentality as artificial and unpersuasive, precisely the kind of response that "modern" readers sometimes have to the sentimental fiction of such authors as Harriet Beecher Stowe and Susan Warner.[10] What makes the Beecher-Tilton trial's million-word transcript an extraordinary site for cultural analysis is the way that it freeze-frames, through seemingly endless textualized rhetoric, a moment of intense cultural dynamism. Through it we can glimpse the sentimental synthesis, so splendidly transparent before the Civil War, still exerting a surprising rhetorical dominance even as it jousts uneasily with an antisentimental backlash and an often-unstated acceptance of modernist discontinuities.

The Fear of False Fictions: Convergences of Trial Structure, Case Content, and Cultural Concern

If the attention accorded the Beecher-Tilton scandal by the media and the American public gave it national importance, its crystallization into adversarial litigation transformed it, in the minds of many, into a matter of world-historical significance. "This is no contest between litigants to determine the right of property," asserted Samuel D. Morris to resounding applause as he began his opening statement for Theodore Tilton. "It is a trial the consequences of which reach to the very foundations of society. The home, the marriage relation with all that is dear in that relation, is upon trial in this case. Upon the result of your verdict to a very large extent, also, will depend the integrity of the Christian religion" (1:19–20).[11] To understand how millions of newspaper-reading "jurors" came to believe that their deepest personal, cultural, and religious values were at stake in Judge Neilson's Brooklyn courtroom, we need to find the connection among the structure of trial process, the substantive issues raised by this particular trial, and a pervasive concern of Americans at the time. That connection is the problem of hypocrisy.

All litigation simultaneously generates and undermines every witness's testimonial narrative. The problem of testimonial hypocrisy is thus built into the structural dynamic of every trial. While the witness's job requires that he produce a coherent narrative version of relevant events as he knows them, it insists structurally that every fact-based assertion be viewed with suspicion, whether attacks are mounted in cross-examination or by the conflicting testimony of other witnesses, or whether jurors merely learn from the adversarial pressure of trial process that no witness account should be accepted unquestioningly. Trial process treats any factual assertion as a possible lie. The dialectical alternation that characterizes procedures such as cross-examination, rebuttal, and final arguments dramatically enacts the resistance of trial process to any party's claim to have a monopoly on truth.

Among recent trial analyses, those of James Boyd White have consistently celebrated adversarialness for establishing "a culture of argument" in which "the conversation that it creates is at once its method and its point, and its object is to give to the world it creates the kind of intelligibility that results from the simultaneous recognition of contrasting positions" (267). White's analysis reads the "performed equality" of trial process as an affirmation of the possibility of multiplicity. What it ignores is the absolute commitment of that process to continuous, profound attacks on each position. Each party is given a participatory venue in which to speak, but no speaking is achieved except under siege. Where attacks on assertions of fact are missing because there are no fundamental factual conflicts, the case will be decided on a motion for summary judgment, obviating the need for trial.[12] The survival of a case to trial means that jurors must negotiate a battlefield of testimony and argument in which, at the same time that all narrators claim to be truth-speakers, all are to a greater or lesser degree under attack as hypocritical "fictionalizers." In rendering a verdict for one party, the fact finder delegitimates at least part of the other party's version of events—and perhaps parts of all versions—as constructed falsehoods.

If every trial thus enacts a contest between conflicting but purportedly truthful narratives, the Beecher-Tilton trial was a performance of mind-numbing length that had a single subject: credibility. Importantly, the case turned not just on credibility in general but on the component of credibility that is testimonial honesty. Consider for a moment other kinds of legal claims and offers of proof. In bank fraud or antitrust cases, the facts may be only minimally in dispute. Such cases are established primarily through reams of corporate or financial documents and records, and the majority of witnesses may simply identify and interpret documents. The validity or implications of these interpretations may then be challenged by the opposing party without the question of the witnesses' testimonial credibility arising. Typically, the outcome in such cases most often depends on the establishment of such complex law/fact hybrids as the existence of an unfair restraint of trade, whose proof may depend substantially on statistical evidence and statutory interpretation. Even in criminal cases that turn on eyewitness identification, testimonial honesty may be virtually irrelevant. When a witness claims to have seen the defendant commit the crime, the witness's perceptual credibility—her ability to see, or hear, or remember the details of the event under the particular circumstances—may be very much at issue, while her sincerity, her honest belief in what she is saying, may remain unquestioned. Her identification of the defendant as the person who robbed her may be attacked on the ground that it was too dark to see clearly or that the incident occurred so long ago that her memory of it must have faded, but with rare exceptions, such challenges do not amount to a suggestion that the witness is intentionally constructing a false fiction.[13] Similarly, when a criminal defendant such as John Hinckley raises a defense of insanity, both sides may agree on or even stipulate to the "facts of the case." The verdict then turns on the jury's assessment of the opposing conclusions of expert psychiatric witnesses about the single issue of the defendant's mental capacity. Though the experts may bitterly disagree and though their criteria, methods, and deductions may be challenged, it is rare indeed for such a witness to be accused of lying or testifying insincerely.[14]

In the Beecher case, however, it was clear from the outset that if one party's witnesses were telling the truth, his opponent's witnesses must be lying, at least about the central disputed facts. "Does not our view exclude his view?" demanded William Maxwell Evarts in his closing for Beecher. "Does not our view convict him of wilful, purposed contrivance of evidence against the truth to beguile your judgment and mislead your verdict?" (3:691). It is important to remember that even the most flagrantly hypocritical witnesses tell the truth most of the time, because the bulk of their testimony is about secondary matters, background details and undisputed events. In the Beecher-Tilton case, both parties agreed that Elizabeth Tilton and Henry Ward Beecher had a longstanding, intimate relationship; they disagreed only about whether that relationship had included consummated sexual intimacy. Unsurprisingly, there were no eyewitnesses to the alleged adultery. Instead, 111 circumstantial witnesses, including Beecher and Tilton, recounted and disputed the existence and meaning of various conversations, documents, and tangential events.[15] The area of disagreement was thus small but crucial, and it turned as much on matters of interpretation, on what certain epistolary or conversational phrases meant, as on whether or not particular events had occurred. Beecher and Tilton each testified and each supplied meanings for contested documents; the jury's task was to decide whether such testimonial declarations were credible truth or self-serving hypocrisy.

Theodore Tilton testified that in July 1870, his wife tearfully confessed to him that she had had an affair with Beecher for over a year (1:396).[16] Beecher had gradually overcome her resistance, Tilton testified, by convincing her that when two people loved each other, sexual union was wholly pure and not a violation of her marriage vow (1:396–97). Tilton's friend Frank Moulton and Moulton's very respectable wife Emma both testified to numerous conversations with Beecher in which the adultery was explicitly discussed and regretted, and in which Beecher sought help in hiding it from his congregation, his family, and the public (1:62–65, 75–89, 104, 129–30 [Frank Moulton] and 1:719–54 [Emma Moulton]). Letters were introduced in which Beecher seemed to confess to having committed a great wrong against the Tiltons, asking Theodore Tilton's forgiveness and declaring that "I humble myself before him as I do before my God" (1:401, 2:778–80, 793–94). Yet because the letters never explicitly mentioned adultery and employed ambiguous and emotional vocabulary throughout, their meaning became a matter of intense dispute. Though Beecher's memory consistently failed him on the stand—he answered "I don't know" or "I don't remember" to hundreds of questions—he did testify clearly that no adultery had ever occurred, and that he had never made improper proposals to Elizabeth Tilton (2:758, 765; see generally 2:729 to 3:136). Beecher testified that Tilton told him of Elizabeth's "inordinate affection for [him], or her exceeding affection" (2:761). To the jury, Beecher's attorneys argued that she had conceived so intense a passion for him that she may have believed it returned (2:48–49, 3:661–62, 746, 808). The only wrong he admitted against the Tiltons was having unfortunately been the means of Theodore's losing the editorship of *The Independent*, and having counseled Elizabeth to separate from a spouse who was mistreating her (2:770–72). Beecher's narrative cast Tilton as an adulterous and abusive husband whose selfish egotism had led to an intense jealousy of the older and more prominent Beecher and a determination to destroy him. Beecher was followed on the stand by a long parade of witnesses to his public character, service, and reputation (2:137 to 3:556). This condensation of the case into a testimonial credibility contest ultimately paralyzed the jury. Their foreman attributed the deadlock to a "question of the veracity of witnesses"; in dismissing the jury, the judge described their sole problem as "the weight of testimony and the credibility of certain witnesses" (3:1041, 1042).

Significantly, the trial's central credibility questions were presented to the jury as a series of problems in textual interpretation, whether the texts at issue were the hundreds of letters and documents whose disputed meaning became central to the case or the conflicting narrative versions of past events offered by opposing witnesses. Indeed, the fundamental ambiguity of language became an explicit and central issue at trial. As Beecher's attorneys declared in their opening statement to the jury: "Everything here turns upon a single question. When these people were talking upon generalities, when Mr. Beecher was using language that might cover one thing or another . . . to what were the parties referring? What did they have in their minds?" (2:87). Confronted with this plethora of ambiguous and conflicting narratives, jurors had to decide what criteria to use in getting from text to inference, from oral or written declaration to the "mind's" truth. Mere textual persuasiveness, like mere character reputation, was increasingly shown to be insufficient. The iterated onslaught of cross-examination, collateral challenge, and lawyerly deconstruction in a case that turned on a charge not just of sexual misbehavior but also of hypocritical proclamations of virtue encouraged jurors and juror-readers to lose confidence in their ability to make reliable inferences from the circumstantial evidence of everyday life. The vexed question of Beecher's honesty triggered an unsettling uncertainty that seemed to infect assertion of truth or virtue in every context.

What the Beecher-Tilton trial did, to the obsessive discomfort of both jurors and American newspaper readers, was to demonstrate that the dynamic narrativizing moment at the heart of all text-producing activities, from letter writing to explanatory testifying to the construction of a public persona, is also the precise moment at which the possibility of falsification and deception arises. The authorial control that is necessary to the purposeful transformation of subjective experience into coherent, communicable testimony can (and in some senses, must) serve other gods than truth. Clarity, performance, and eloquence thus always create textual surfaces haunted by the shadow of misleading hypocrisy. Most distressingly, from the vantage point of the juror-reader, the more persuasive the textual performance, the more difficult it is to distinguish false notes from true, because a textual surface can remain consistent and believable even if its connection to the referential world outside the text has intentionally been severed.[17]

The Beecher-Tilton trial thus presented a series of related questions, all of which raised the problem of what we might call "false fictions," plausible but essentially and intentionally false narratives. How can we distinguish a sincere witness from one who "performs" sincerity but is actually lying? How can we ever *know* what actually happened between two people in private so that we can distinguish between truthful testimony and equally "realistic" invention? How can we tell in our own lives whether someone we look up to as a teacher, preacher, or intimate companion is "really" good and deserving of respect or is a privately corrupt hypocrite and therefore a "false prophet" or "sinful spouse"? False fictions may take the form of a dissembling witness's misleading appearance and behavior, a believable but deceptive testimony, or the aggressively virtuous public persona of a privately dissolute man. The problem of identifying them was indisputably at the heart of the Beecher-Tilton jury's task, but a deep anxiety about the general difficulty of doing so was already troubling many Americans long before the Beecher scandal acted it out on the forensic stage.

As Karen Halttunen has convincingly argued in *Confidence Men and Painted Women: A Study of Middle-Class Culture in America, 1830–1870*, "the heart of the sentimental value system was a deep fear of the hypocrisy that was believed to be poisoning American social relations" (xvii). The socially successful hypocrite—the con man—became America's supreme criminal because he could "sever the connection between inner character and outward appearances by consciously manipulating the impression he made on others" (42). New urbanites, used to a world in which they had shared a lifetime of experiences or at least a common social, geographic, and economic background with almost everyone they met, now had no reliable way to distinguish an offer of friendship from the opening move in an elaborate con game. This problem is represented vividly in Horatio Alger's novels, which were meant to serve as entertaining advice manuals for readers. In *Struggling Upward; or, Luke Larkin's Luck* (1890), the hero, Luke, is befriended on the train to Chicago by a pleasant and well-dressed young man who proposes that they stay together at a hotel. Luke is delighted to have a knowledgeable and generous companion, but Alger quickly makes clear that the other's "object was to gain Luke's entire confidence, and remove any suspicion he might possibly entertain" in order to swindle him of his money (232). Luke's luck holds and he is able to reveal the man as a liar. In *Ragged Dick* (1868), the poor bootblack Dick, newly dressed in fine clothes, shows an out-of-towner around New York. Within the space of a few pages, they encounter an "agent of the Excelsior Mining Company" who promises them a fortune in three years if they will invest in his stock (26–27); are targeted by a con man who claims to have found a wallet stuffed with money, which he offers to give them for twenty dollars (33–37); and meet a newly arrived "countryman" who has been swindled of fifty dollars by a plausible con artist (50). Readers must learn from Dick to "look sharp" and shrewdly assess those they meet, for as one character notes, "you can't tell by looks . . . villains are generally well dressed" (44).

The placelessness induced by a rapidly changing society made hypocrisy "not merely a personal sin; it was a social offense that threatened to dissolve the ties of mutual confidence binding men together" (Halttunen 34).[18] Over time, the urban newcomer's dilemma was answered by what Halttunen calls "the sentimental typology of conduct," preached by a wide-ranging series of "advisers" who encouraged a "cult of sincerity" that asserted first that "all aspects of manner and appearance were visible outward signs of inner moral qualities," and consequently that aspirants could move confidently through the new antebellum society by following a set of behavioral prescriptions (40–55). Properly attended to, these rules would enable them to establish their own social acceptability and gauge the sincerity of others. One of the most popular of these advice books was Henry Ward Beecher's *Seven Lectures to Young Men*, first published in 1843. In it he warned of the "moral deterioration of youth, especially in the western cities" and the dangers of drinking, gambling, and urban brothels while preaching a gospel of success in which hard work, attention to one's appearance and behavior, and inner virtue would bring worldly success (Clark 57, Waller 25).

Halttunen focuses on antebellum America, when the first generation of young people left the familiar rural world for the uncertain opportunities of the cities. Yet the anxiety she identifies was still very much alive in the 1870s.[19] Indeed, one of the lessons of the public hysteria surrounding the Beecher-Tilton trial is that anxiety about hypocrisy remained intense—or perhaps reemerged—as the effectiveness of such antebellum solutions as the cult of sincerity eroded. By 1875 outward appearance, which might once have been believed to hold the key to inner character, was no longer accepted as a universally reliable index. The possibility of Beecher's adultery was thus troubling as much for its inconsistency with his decades-long eminence as for its obvious immorality. If publicly available evidence of virtue was of no use whatever in assessing the likelihood of private misbehavior, then all that was left was a dizzying sense of the fallibility of *all* knowledge and relationships, especially those we hold most dear and upon which our sense of our own identities most strongly depends.

Halttunen argues that the threat posed by successful hypocrisy is that it will "dissolve the ties of mutual confidence binding men together," because people will be unable to rely on the apparent virtue and sincerity of others.

The same sense of a profound connection among sincerity, confidence, and the functioning of society as a whole was articulated in the legal context by William Mowdesley Best in his influential 1875 treatise *The Principles of the Law of Evidence.* Like the writers of advice books who premised successful social interaction on an underlying trust in each others' sincerity, Best argued that the testimonial machinery of trial process was predicated on an assumption of the importance to society of a well-grounded belief in the honesty of others. Best introduces the subjects of proof and testimony by observing, "Mutual confidence between man and man being indispensable to the acquisition of knowledge, the happiness of our race, and indeed to the very existence of society, the great Creator has planted the springs of truth very deep in the human breast" (sec. 18:17). The natural impulses to speak and to believe the truth are sanctioned by both morality and religion, Best declared, for "were we to lose either our feeling of obligation to tell the truth, or our disposition to receive as truth whatever is told to us, there would at once be an end to all science and all knowledge, beyond that which every man had obtained by his own personal observation and experience. . . . Language would be useless, and we should be but little removed from the brutes" (17–18).

Best's analysis forges crucial links among the honesty of speakers, the trust of hearers, and the ongoing enterprise of civilization. Like Halttunen, he sees "mutual confidence" as the precondition for all positive social interaction, and therefore for all the culture-building enterprises of a society—government, science, discourse—that require communication. In Best's scheme, trials reaffirm a culture's belief in its own system of morality and truth by publicly identifying and condemning those who violate the culture-constituting "natural instinct" toward truth. After two years of destabilizing scandal about Beecher, the nation looked to the trial, with its official rituals of examination and deliberation, for just such a ritual of reassurance.[20] What it got can only be deemed a spectacular failure. The jury's refusal to provide a verdict one way or another stalled the process at what was intended to be only the midpoint of the drama, the weary moment when all assertions of truth had been thoroughly undercut by months of adversarial challenge. Had the trial "worked" as it was ideally supposed to, it would have climaxed at the moment of verdict, when a choice was made between warring versions of events. Either Beecher or Tilton would have been triumphantly unmasked as a lying "fictionalizer," and the jury's verdict would have retroactively labeled one set of narratives "truth" and the others "fiction."[21] However problematic and unsettling a jury verdict may be, it nevertheless provides a formal moment of closure that carries great weight. In the absence of any such authoritative resolution, the very blurriness of the line between fact and fiction becomes the only *official* verdict. The assessments of all private individuals become equal, and equally indeterminate. If the nation went into the Beecher trial troubled by its inability to discriminate sincerity from hypocrisy, it came out with less certainty than ever.

The dialectic of suspicion that characterizes trial process makes the courtroom an ideal setting for anxiety about the problem of believable hypocrisy to be climactically enacted. Worried about being "tricked" by publicly virtuous men like Beecher and unable to find reassurance in the prescriptive sincerity of sentimentality, Americans may have seen the law's relentless adversariality as an official, authoritative version of their own questionings and concerns. Moreover, while armchair "jurors" might have found their anxieties mirrored in the process of any trial, this trial was uniquely *about* hypocrisy. The nation's "choice" of the Beecher-Tilton case as a national obsession becomes, in this light, quite comprehensible. This is not to say that the case was the only scandal or the only trial to focus Americans' misgivings about the reliability of their neighbors' seemingly moral outward behavior; it was an era of scandals, of which Beecher's was only the most nationally publicized.[22] Fascination with the sexual misbehavior of famously moral public personages was also hardly unique to the 1870s; our own recent history has seen a wave of similar scandal-trials, with Paula Jones's lawsuit against President Clinton and Anita Hill's charges against Clarence Thomas at his Supreme Court confirmation hearings providing perhaps the most obvious parallels.

In pointing to a shared concern with hypocrisy as the link among the structure, substance, and social context of the Beecher-Tilton trial, my goal is not just to explain its extraordinary notoriety, but also to set the stage for an analysis of the strategic use of sentimentality—and antisentimentality—in the courtroom. Because the "sentimental synthesis" was originally designed to assuage anxieties about pervasive hypocrisy, its rhetorical dominance at the Beecher-Tilton trial comes as no surprise. Yet such a solution could no longer, by the 1870s, be proffered unproblematically. At the same time that William Maxwell Evarts was attempting to "solve" the Beecher-Tilton trial's credibility problem through the strategies of sentimentality, Theodore Tilton's attorneys were trying, somewhat inconsistently, to challenge sentimentality's assumptions, and in the world of literary discourse,

Mark Twain and Charles Dudley Warner were attacking the forensic use of sentimentality with passionate virulence.

The Juror as Sentimental Reader: "Why do you look at the growing beauty of their face and form and feel safe?"

If the structure and substance of the Beecher-Tilton trial were thus uniquely constituted to play into a well-established cultural anxiety about the difficulty of distinguishing glib confidence men from authentic moral paragons, the litigative strategy of the parties reflects a clear attempt to intensify and exploit that anxiety to their own advantages. We have already seen Halttunen's and Best's remarkably similar assertions that what is at stake in a test of hypocrisy is the "mutual confidence" that underlies the continuing viability of the participants' community. I want now to look at a series of statements made by William Maxwell Evarts in his eight-day closing argument for Beecher. Evarts, America's leading trial lawyer, had been Andrew Johnson's defender at his impeachment. A former attorney general and future secretary of state and senator, his rhetorical brilliance was matched by his seemingly easygoing courtroom manner.[23] Like the sentimental rhetoric used by Samuel Morris in his opening for Tilton, Evarts's deployment of sentimental strategies aims to evoke a specific response from the jury:

> Ah, gentlemen, you will find as we go on in this cause, and as you take it up upon its facts and compare it with known principles of human nature and human conduct, you will find at every stage of this business that the attack is not personal but against our society, against our civility, against our morality, against our religion. The attack is not that there are wolves in sheep's clothing, that vicious men dissemble and that they hide themselves under the cloak of sanctity to prowl on the society that they thus impose upon . . . it is that the favored, approved, tried, best results of this social scheme of ours, which includes marriage, and of this religious faith of ours, which adopts Christianity, is false to the core; that the saintly man and the apostolic woman are delivered over to the lower indulgences; and that that being proved, the scheme itself is discredited and ready to be dissolved. (3:659)

> Now gentlemen, whenever you establish the proposition that these breaches of external morality that threaten the very fabric of society, the central point, the purity of the family, can occur without preliminary moral degradation

> and preparation—without being accompanied by an inflammation of the low desires and the triumph of the flesh over the spirit—can be practiced with the maintenance of all the active benevolences and the exhibition of all the beautiful virtues of life, you have struck a blow not at Mr. Beecher, not at Mr. Tilton, but at your own wives and your own daughters. . . . Why do you look at the growing beauty of their face and form, and feel safe? . . . Why, all the while it may be going on in all our families, and nobody knows anything about it. What, shall we then discard all this, shall we believe that these sins come only by power against which no morality can guard, that there is no necessary connection between character and conduct; that these sins do not come from within, but that with all this purity they may arise. (3:663–64)

> We shall have to have a Wife Deposit Company, where we can leave our wives during the day, and we shall have to have some patent contrivance of paramour-proof alarms by which we can be called to the rescue when the insidious undermining of this external virtue (for there is nothing left in the world but external virtue) begins. (3:664)

What is going on beneath the wit, hyperbole, and fear-mongering in these passages? Quite simply, Evarts has made each juror's refusal to countenance attacks on Henry Ward Beecher a necessary act of affirmation of the reliability of virtue and value in the juror's own life. If Beecher's alleged corruption can exist without any hint tainting his publicly available behavior, if "there is no necessary connection between character and conduct," then our own judgments, based on similarly external "evidence," are unreliable, and we may well be unknowingly surrounded by diabolical confidence men, adulterous spouses, and corrupt institutions. The only way to solve the problem, argues Evarts, is to take a stand for the reliability of outward appearance and to refuse even to investigate accusations that, if true, would undermine the assumptions that prop up our own lives. What this argument does is to make the "sentimental typology of conduct" into a principle of evidentiary evaluation, encouraging jurors to accept certain kinds of evidence as if they established a conclusive presumption with respect to character based on sentimental logic while rejecting other evidence outright, not because it is demonstrably false but because its existence dangerously threatens the continued viability of the sentimental world view.

Two aspects of this strategy bear closer examination. First, Evarts shifts the locus of action away from Henry Ward Beecher's alleged sexual misbehavior and into each juror's consciousness. By the time Evarts is done, it is the *juror's* values, loved ones, and principles of judgment that are being tested by this trial, the juror's security of mind—not Beecher's—that hangs precariously on the verdict. As recent critics have persuasively articulated, this shift is the essence of the sentimental process in action: the sentimental text is an "act of persuasion" that works by forging a deep emotional bond of compassion and identification between the reader and the victim-hero/ine, what Philip Fisher calls an "experimental extension of the self of the reader" (98).[24] Having stimulated the reader to identify the sufferings of the orphan, the slave, or the prisoner as her own, the sentimental text achieves its object by altering the reader's world view and thus necessarily triggering action in the reader's life.[25] During the long months of testimony, defense attorneys had constructed Beecher as a man of sorrows, a suffering hero wrongly accused whose honor, virtue, and domestic felicity were being miraculously upheld despite Tilton's diabolical charges. Jurors were continually exhorted to feel deeply for Beecher, to pity, respect, and admire him.[26] Simultaneously, the attorneys worked to link Beecher to the jurors through a target response of intense compassion that would make them identify Beecher's plight as their own.

The sentimental reader reads to respond, finding in the narrative a blueprint for understanding and improving her own life. In its own terms, the success or failure of a sentimental text can be gauged by the intensity of response it elicits; its significant battleground is always, therefore, the reader's emotions. Sentimental texts thus interpret the lives of their readers. This makes the sentimental strategy splendidly useful to lawyers, for an empathic bond that leads to consonant action is precisely what final arguments aim to construct, particularly where the attorney's goal is to win sympathy, approval, or forgiveness for his client. By suggesting that a vote for Beecher is a vote for their own wives and daughters, Evarts offers jurors a way to "read" their own lives as reassuringly consistent narratives. Even more to the point, he makes a verdict-vote for Beecher a hopeful endorsement of their loved ones' virtue. By siding with Beecher, jurors can find a solution to their anxieties that will stave off for a while longer the modernist anguish of isolation, the sense that what is unseen in others and even in ourselves is profoundly, even dangerously inaccessible.

The process by which this shift is achieved is worth a closer look. One of sentimental literature's most effective rhetorical maneuvers is to rupture the narrative flow of events so that the author can make a direct appeal to the reader's most deeply felt experience, making the reader's personal pain the source of literary response.[27] When successful, the authorial intervention accomplishes not just a closer connection but a reversal of the typical relationship between reader and character. Ordinarily, the process of reading temporarily extinguishes the reader's own world of experience and emotion, transforming her into a vicarious "experiencer" of the character's position and emotions. In this type of sentimental reading, however, the intervention makes the reader's *own* experience the "real" heart of the text-reader interaction, while the narrated event and characters function as pale, representational stand-ins for the reader.

The true master of this strategy was, of course, Henry Ward Beecher's sister Harriet Beecher Stowe, whose 1852 best-seller *Uncle Tom's Cabin* continually makes the reader's deepest emotional experiences an essential component of the narrative action. Like Evarts, Stowe interrupts the flow of events in her narrative to construct a new scene in which the reader and her loved ones become characters in a narrative parallel to but separate from the story. A typical intervention interrupts the story of the slave Eliza's escape with her young son:

> If it were *your* Harry, mother, or your Willie, that were going to be torn from you by a brutal trader, tomorrow morning,—if you had seen the man, and heard that the papers were signed and delivered and you had only from twelve o'clock till morning to make good your escape,—how fast could *you* walk? How many miles could you make in those few brief hours, with the darling at your bosom, the little sleepy head on you shoulder,—the small soft arms trustingly holding on to your neck? (105)

At such moments, what happens is not simply that the reader identifies with Eliza and enters her world, but that a new story is constructed that brings the defining conditions of Eliza's predicament into the *reader's* world, so that it is the reader's child who must be saved, the reader's home that must be left behind, the reader's physical endurance that must be tested. If the process of transforming ourselves into fictional characters increases our empathy for Eliza, it also recasts our own future lives as open-ended narratives whose shape is as yet undetermined. Having linked our life stories to Eliza's and thus triggered anxiety about the outcome of our own stories, Stowe exploits the narrative uncertainty she has created to elicit responsive action from her readers.

Like Stowe, Evarts makes the sufferings of his client crucial components of the hypothetical horror stories he tells the jurors about their own lives, in which their wives' continuous adulteries can only be prevented through a "Wife Deposit Company" or a "paramour-proof alarm." Like Stowe too, Evarts suggests that how the reader actively responds to the story will determine whether or not it will come true. A vote for Beecher extinguishes one narrative of each juror's future life and constructs another, so that the vote becomes an act of defense and self-protection. An "incorrect" vote makes the juror responsible for Beecher's sins, and for the immorality of modern life. Such a vote becomes an act not just of suspicion but of aggression.

In another moment in *Uncle Tom's Cabin*, a scene in which a grieving mother lovingly takes her dead son's clothes from a drawer to give to Eliza's ragged son, Stowe interrupts the narrative to ask, "oh! mother that reads this, has there never been in your life a drawer, or a closet the opening of which has been to you like the opening of a little grave?" (154). That Stowe connects her "client," the escaping slave Eliza, to her reader through their common experiences of suffering has often been noted. What has not been sufficiently explored, however, is how this process reverses the relative roles of reader and text. Instead of the reader vicariously experiencing Mrs. Bird's grief for her dead child, it is Mrs. Bird, weeping over the little shoes and toy horse, who enacts the *reader's* grief over a similar loss. The textual narrative, though still significant in itself, has become the occasion through which the reader comes to terms with her own sorrow and, if the process works, achieves emotional equilibrium by shifting the locus of action to a third site, where she engages in compassionate action in the world.[28] Similarly, for those who responded to Evarts's appeal, Beecher's ordeal became a performative enactment of each juror's anxieties, and an occasion for resolving them.

The second strand of Evarts's strategy is his reformulation of the "mutual confidence" paradigm formulated in W. M. Best's treatise on evidence, from a two-sided model in which truth-tellers and truth-believers cooperate to enable the production of society into a linear model of cause and effect, in which belief alone is both necessary and sufficient to do the job. Whether or not a person tells the truth, it is his interlocutor's obligation to believe him. Best's description of the "natural impulse" toward truth contains two reciprocal elements: the impulse to *tell* the truth, and the willingness to *believe* that what we are told is true. In Best's system, of course, both are necessary for any mutual confidence to arise. It is precisely because society is grounded on the near-universality of both truth-telling and truth-believing that the punishment of the few liars who appear is no threat to the rest of the populace. Rather, the litigative quest for falsehood is reassuring, because the ritual identification and expulsion of unnaturally false speakers guarantees that those who are left can be trusted. In Evarts's reformulation, however, the coordinate requirement of the prevalence of truth-telling by others has simply been erased. No suggestion is made that the juridical task includes a tough analysis of competing testimonies to determine which ones are true and which false. Indeed, with civilization-producing activity shifted away from the community as a whole, where interactive relationships always include the possibility of legitimate challenge and question, and into each juror's heart and mind, there seems no need to venture beyond that internal realm. We can create or destroy Christianity and the security of our home lives simply by *believing* them created or destroyed.

Evarts argues, in so many words, that we must believe in the honesty of others whether or not they are actually honest, because belief makes civilization possible. A faint threatening whiff of heresy lurks beneath the rhetorical surface here, I would suggest, insinuating that our wives, daughters, and priests are not in fact what we need them to be, but that the last thing any of us wants to do is confront that possibility. The question of Beecher's possible hypocrisy thus stands in for the question that cannot be asked about "our" wives and daughters, and our loud refusal to accept even the possibility that suspicions against him might be justified forecloses the threat of hidden corruption closer to home. As a litigative strategy, this is truly brilliant: it induces jurors to refuse on personal, moral grounds even to consider the evidence against Beecher. It is much more effective than simply arguing that such evidence is weak or unpersuasive (though of course Evarts also did just that, for days at a time) because, if successful, this strategy wins the case for Beecher on his reputation alone, obviating the necessity for any close juridical examination of the months of damaging, if ambiguous, testimony.

The defense employed this strategy from the outset. "What is the use of an honorable life," asked Benjamin Tracy in his opening statement for Beecher, "if it is no barrier against false accusation; if in the face of foul conspiracy, its prayers and labors, generosities and heroisms are to be counted as worse than nothing—merely the disguises of a rotten hypocrisy?" (2:90–91). Tracy's question is grounded in a paradoxical logic by which, having insisted on a transparent continuity between what is seen and what is hidden (Beecher's parishioners believed in him, he added, because they could look "through his clear eyes into his transparent soul" [2:91]), he justifies the erection of an impassable defensive "barrier" between the two spheres. Because public benevolence guarantees private virtue, the existence of such virtue in a particular case must be presumed without investigation, and all accusations rejected as necessarily false.

The Antisentimentalist Critique and the Narrative Inclusiveness of Trials

Evarts and Tracy used the strategies of sentimentality to solve the central problem of Beecher's credibility at a time and in a context that subjected such strategies to a widespread critique. This section looks at two aspects of the antisentimentalist challenge: Tilton's somewhat ambivalent challenge to Beecher's conduct-as-character defense; and Twain and Warner's all-out attack on the emotional power of forensic sentimentality in *The Gilded Age*. The section concludes by contrasting the inclusive realism of an entire trial's transcript with the unambiguous and exclusionary sentimentalism of each party's proffered narrative.

If we return for a moment to Halttunen's thesis about the middle-class preoccupation with the problem of hypocrisy, we note that it identifies an *anxiety* about the possibility of being taken in by hypocritical confidence men and traces the development and gradual disintegration of a *solution*, the sentimental typology of conduct, which held that all forms of dress and behavior were the outward signs of inner character. As the quest for apparent sincerity produced ever more formalized prescriptions, however, the artificiality of all such rule-induced behavior became increasingly obvious, and the system's "built-in tendency for self-destruction" led to its dissolution (189). Lionel Trilling's important book *Sincerity and Authenticity* traces this problem to the French Revolution's preoccupation with the hypocrisy of old French society, causing an "obsessive concern with the possible—the all too probable—hypocrisy of the individual, even of one's own self":

> The Revolution brought to its highest intensity the idea of the public, and established, Dr. Arendt suggests, an ultimate antagonism between the unshadowed manifestness of the public life and the troubled ambiguity of the personal life, the darkness of man's unknowable heart. What was private and unknown might be presumed to be subversive of the public good. From

> this presumption grew the preoccupation with sincerity, with the necessity of expressing and guaranteeing it to the public—sincerity required a rhetoric of avowal, the demonstration of single-minded innocence through attitude and posture, exactly the role-playing in which Rousseau had found the essence of personal, ultimately of social, corruption. 'One cannot,' Andre Gide has said, 'both be sincere and seem so.' (69–70)

As Americans gradually came to recognize the inherent contradictions in a system of prescriptive sincerity, they often opted to rely on formal social behavior, allocating the "darkness of man's unknowable heart" to a private sphere beyond the ambit of social investigation. But if many sophisticated Americans had come, by 1875, to admire theatricality and social performance and to accept the idea that public and private selves might be drastically discontinuous without being diabolical, they were markedly uneasy about saying so publicly, and even more uneasy about the possibility that well-known models of morality like Beecher might be as "modern" in such matters as their most forward-looking followers. The complex attitudes toward sentimental rhetoric displayed at the Beecher trial demonstrate that such culturally defining concepts do not follow straightforward rise-and-fall trajectories, but circulate among groups over time, fading and returning in response to changing circumstances. Thus, while sentimental typology was under broad cultural attack both outside and inside the courtroom, it nevertheless retained real power for large segments of the population. It dominated the trial rhetoric of both sides in their appeals to the jury, even while the same counsel eagerly mocked the sentimental language of certain letters and documents; on occasion, counsel adopted strikingly inconsistent approaches to the use of sentimental strategies.

This inconsistency was most obvious in the strategically unfortunate vacillation of Theodore Tilton's attorneys. While attempting at times to challenge the logic of Beecher's conduct-as-character defense, at other moments they accepted its assumptions wholesale and tried, by offering negative rather than positive examples of his public conduct, to elicit an inference of private immorality. Thus William Beach, in his closing for Tilton, read statements from Beecher's sermons reflecting religious unorthodoxy on issues such as the doctrines of atonement and the divinity of Christ (3:996–98), quoted Beecher as having accepted the evolutionist arguments of Darwin (3:1005), and suggested to the jury that, though evidence of other sexual misbehavior could not be legally introduced, "you shouldn't assume that he had been a man entirely relieved from any suspicions of a like or previous offense" (3:885). Carrying the presumed connection between external and internal to its logical conclusion, Beach even argued that Beecher's plump body and full lips betrayed his licentiousness. The preacher "has never been conspicuous for self-denial and asceticism" in matters of eating, drinking, and other "pleasures of the senses," he observed. Then, "reading" Beecher's body as the authentic, unfalsifiable register of an undisciplined sensuality, he announced that "every lineament of his features declares him to possess those appetites in a marked degree" (3:844).[29]

Attempting to use the logic of Beecher's own forensic strategy against him, Tilton's attorneys thus argued that vulnerabilities in the preacher's public persona could be read as manifestations of private corruption. At the same time, however, they tried to erode the underlying power of the trope of "character." Beach asked whether,

> considering . . . the rather erratic and extravagant career of Mr. Beecher as a teacher, looking at the tendencies of his thought and sentiments as delineated in his spoken words, considering the impulses of his nature, as we read them through his utterances, is he deserving of the high encomiums he has received . . . and is he by the simple authority of his character and his word to overturn the power of demonstrative proof? (3:1010)

Note how, stripped of its presumptive association with affirmative teachings, thoughts, and sentiments, the word "character" itself becomes emptied of clear, easily available meaning. By the time the word appears, near the end of the sentence, it has become problematic, which effectively precludes its talismanic saving power from working to Beecher's benefit. Instead of murky arguments about "character," Beach suggests, he will offer the real goods, unambiguous and persuasive "demonstrative proof."

Beach also attempted a direct attack on character theory itself, an attack based on the clash between the sentimental, unitary view of character and a modernist conception that assumed profound discontinuities. For Lionel Trilling, the awareness of the "ambiguity of the personal life, the darkness of man's unknowable heart" becomes the springboard into the modernist conception of the self. It divides modern man's often alienated self-consciousness from what now seems to have been a naive faith in appearances and in the easy availability of meanings. In an attempt to elicit skepticism about inferences from Beecher's public conduct, Beach offered the Trilling-like assertion that "we cannot see the heart" (3:843). At the same time, however, he did not want to erode the effectiveness of his own "character" arguments or to offend the sensibilities of more traditional jurors. He was forward-looking, but tentative. "We cannot search the secret recesses of human nature," he declared:

> We but see the superficial character in the public acts of men . . . but yet they give us no clear and satisfactory clue to the true inwardness of a man. . . . We cannot well say of a man, even one with whom we are personally acquainted, however estimable may be all his characteristics and associations, and apparent acts—we cannot after all say to him or of him, that he is a faultless human being. (3:843)

Beach's argument, while it stresses the discontinuity between "public acts" and "the secret recesses of human nature," nevertheless frames the problem as one of inaccurate perception rather than of man's terrifying potential for evil. It suggests that a morally unambiguous "character" exists, though we may have trouble discerning it, and retains the sentimental vocabulary—the term "true inwardness"—to refer to that inner self. Indeed, his conclusion that a publicly virtuous man may not, after all, be "faultless," suggests that he is attempting to reassure and even protect his listeners from the really disturbing implications of his argument. Though forensic rhetoric often adopts somewhat contradictory strategies, Beach's closing argument seems to be at war with itself in ways that blunt its effectiveness. Unwilling to propose a consistent conception of character, either sentimental or realist, Beach tried to offer both at once. This mixture of genres sent thoroughly mixed signals, a literary conflict that may well have undercut his narrative persuasiveness.

The distrust of professed sincerity displayed by Trilling and Beach is directed at the problem of evaluating individual character, the difficulty of making reliable inferences about the "inner" person from available data about his "outer" behavior. When the critical focus shifts from sentimentality's role in constructing individual character to its forensic function in linking lawyers to jurors, sentimental trial rhetoric looks dangerously manipulative, marked by the "role-playing" and "social corruption" Trilling reports Rousseau as deploring (69–70). At the same time that Evarts, Morris, and company were putting their faith in sentimentality's capacity to forge powerful emotional bonds, others in American society were becoming deeply suspicious of sentimentality's power to elicit action based on "feeling" rather than "reason," particularly when that power was exerted in juridical contexts. The antisentimentalist critique is perhaps best represented by Mark Twain and Charles Dudley Warner's 1873 novel, *The Gilded Age*, which climaxes in a devastating indictment of the dangers of sentimental strategy in the courtroom. The novel was written, as Justin Kaplan has noted, "at a time when every day brought news of some revelation in the Beecher affair" (xiv–xv).[30] Writing two years before the Beecher scandal's culminating trial, Twain and Warner seemed presciently to understand that the rhetoric of sentimentality was already on trial in America.[31] By situating their critique of sentimentality at the crux of lawyer-jury interaction in a capital case, they treat the sentimental mode not as one among many ways of narrating a story's events, but as a dangerous narrative instrument of manipulation, a powerful forensic tool. I want to discuss the novel briefly to illustrate the widespread fear among Americans that the juridical use of sentimentality posed a profound threat to justice, law, and society.

The Gilded Age did more than provide an American era with a name tag: it imaged American culture as a giddy series of interlocking get-rich-quick schemes, ruled by a pervasive corruption and hypocrisy. The novel satirically demolishes the sentimental synthesis, insisting again and again that the essence of appearance is its manipulability, not its transparency. When the warm glow of a stove is revealed to be the light of a single candle, for instance, the novel's hero, Colonel Sellars, assures his freezing guest that "what you want is the *appearance* of heat, not the heat itself" (53, emphasis in original). The plot dances through myriad hypocrisies; among them is the quasi-tragic story of Laura Hawkins, a beautiful orphan whose innocent childhood ends abruptly when she is seduced and abandoned by a Confederate officer. When her ex-lover appears years later, she follows him to New York and shoots him.

Twain presents the climactic murder trial as a storytelling contest between Evarts-like lawyers for control of the jurors' melting hearts. The prosecutor, calling Laura a "fiend in the form of a beautiful woman," reminds the jurors in his opening statement that they are "citizens, husbands, perhaps fathers" (377). Using Stowe's and Evarts's technique of narrative interruption, he constructs a hypothetical horror story about the jurors' own lives, which only their verdict can keep from coming true: "They knew how insecure life had become in the metropolis. To-morrow their own wives might be widows, their own children orphans, like the bereaved family in yonder hotel, deprived of husband and father by the hand of some murderous female" (377). The rhetoric of the Hawkins trial, like that of the Beecher-Tilton trial, is frequently more concerned with stimulating the jurors' self-interested emotions than with presenting the "facts" of the case.

The challenge for Laura's attorney is to wrest the role of sympathetic, juror-allied victim away from the dead man's family and give it to Laura herself. Lawyer Braham begins by flattering the jurors as "men with hearts to feel for the wrongs of which she was the victim" (381). He describes Laura's life:

> the sport of fate and circumstances, hurried along through shifting storms and sun, bright with trusting innocence and anon black with heartless villainy, a career which moves on in love and desertion and anguish, always hovered over by the dark spectre of INSANITY, —an insanity hereditary and induced by mental torture. (382)

He then unfolds a sentimental formulation of her life story, from her rescue as a "sweet little girl found among the panic-stricken survivors of a steamboat wreck" to the moment when "the villain Selby . . . plucked the sweetest bud . . . and having enjoyed its odor, trampled it in the mire beneath his feet" (382–83). Spectators collapse in tears, but Mr. Braham only "paused as if overcome by his emotions" (383). At the trial's end, he closes with a rousing peroration, demanding for "a deluded woman rendered irrational by the most cruel wrongs . . . that justice which you and I shall need in that last dreadful hour, when death will be robbed of half its terrors if we can reflect that we have never wronged a human being" (392). When the prosecutor makes the fatal mistake of delivering a rational closing argument, "convincing the reason without touching the feelings," the defense inevitably triumphs (392). Laura is acquitted by reason of temporary insanity.

The novel has frequently been interpreted as an attack on abusive insanity pleas, sentimental literature, and the general incompetence of juries, whose "melting hearts" and "perfectly macaronian bowels of compassion" Twain had frequently ridiculed.[32] What has not been adequately noticed is the degree to which Twain's critique turns on the intersection of law, narrative, and sentimentality. The attack claims not, or not only, that jurors are stupid but that they display the emotional receptivity—the melting heart and easy compassion—that, minus the sneer, constitute the ideal sentimental reader. In the narrative of events before the trial, Twain presents the murder as the act of an unequivocally sane but immoral woman.[33] Yet at the trial, Laura's lawyer successfully suppresses the jurors' capacity for rational deliberation and judgment by drawing them into a story of suffering, exploitation, and madness. Serious criminal trials are precisely the places where the need for detached, unimpassioned reasoning is greatest, the novel suggests, yet the sentimental tango danced between coldly manipulative lawyer and overemotional juror vitiates, in the author's eyes, the trial's status as a quest for truth or justice. In Twain's text, Laura Hawkins's acquittal poses an overwhelming danger to ordered society as constituted through law, precisely because sentimental storytelling works just as effectively in the jury box as in the novel-reader's living room.

Indeed, sentimentality is a great deal more dangerous in the courtroom than the home, the novel implies, because so much more is at stake: not only the fate of accused criminals, but the legitimacy of the law's judicial process for dealing with crime and disorder. Ultimately, sentimentality challenges the "mutual confidence" among men that Best's treatise identifies as so necessary to a functioning, "civilized" society. Twain and Warner's "modern" antisentimentalism insists that cold reason is a better tool than warm responsiveness for evaluating the "truth" of witnesses and their stories.[34] The emotional involvement, the personal stake in the story that Stowe and Evarts work so hard to construct in their readers and listeners, is exactly what Twain and Warner find so inimical to justice. To demonstrate the dangers of such manipulability, they play with the novel's denouement, first providing a "fictional" image of Laura shut away in a horrifying Hospital for the Criminally Insane; then intervening in the narrative and substituting a "true history" of her complete post-trial release from confinement; and finally concluding with an abrupt authorial "murder" when she dies quite suddenly of "heart disease" (402–3, 422–23). Readers who resent being emotionally manipulated by this narrative sleight of hand should, the novel implies, rethink the consequences of such vulnerability in legal contexts, where the fascinating storyteller may be defending a very real criminal rather than a fictional heroine.

The jury at Laura Hawkins's trial has to decide between conflicting narratives of her life, actions, and mental state. The events and characters in each party's story are virtually the same, but the unambiguous moral valence and interpretive characterization given to each are in direct opposition, as they were at the Beecher-Tilton trial. At all trials, of course, the need to make each party's story demonstrate an entitlement to prevail creates a pressure to eliminate gray areas, compromising details, and moral ambiguities. Constructed, therefore, on a principle of exclusion, litigation narratives tend to reproduce sentimental paradigms of victim and perpetrator, plots and characters whose dynamics depend on the absolute avoidance of any moral ambiguity.[35]

Trial process as a whole, however, can never enact the one-dimensional morality of sentimental fiction or melodrama, because it encompasses not only the necessarily opposing narratives of both parties but also the testimony of witnesses who often refuse to follow their lawyer-directed scripts and the nonpartisan commentary of the trial judge. Thus while each party's narrative is constructed on a principle of exclusion, the trial as a whole operates on a principle of inclusion, of multiple causation and ambiguity. Its adversarial structure foregrounds gaps, shadings, and inconsistencies, inviting constant attack, correction, and addition, and it provides at least two plausible versions of central, contested facts. In literary terms, complete trial transcripts therefore always pull toward realism and modernism, genres often defined by their insistence on all forms of complexity—moral, motivational, and formal. The trial's structural embrace of multiplicity makes it difficult for either party to remain untarnished; even a clear verdict in one party's favor at the trial's end cannot wholly erase the shadows thrown on his story by the insistently adversarial process.

The tension between the moral binarism of sentimentality and the chiarascuro produced by trial process can be strategically useful in devising a forensic game plan. An opponent who constructs himself, as Beecher did, as a moral paragon and purely sympathetic victim risks losing his affirmative image in one swoop if his claim to fit the heroic stereotype is persuasively undercut. Sentimental fiction disintegrates whenever extenuating circumstances muddy the moral field on which its pure victims and fiendish oppressors must perform. A sympathetic sentimental character, unlike a sympathetic realist character, cannot be victim and perpetrator simultaneously.[36] Without challenging the basic fact that his opponent has suffered wrongs, a litigant can move that opponent out of the hero's role by showing that he has inflicted sufferings on others, or that much of his pain is the (even indirect) result of his own misdeeds. Once jurors lose uncritical compassionate identification with the opponent, the way is opened for a recasting of events and the presentation of a new narrative.

In a recent article, Wai Chee Dimock distinguishes the defining characteristics of criminal law from those of the nineteenth-century novel by opposing the law's "frugality" with the novel's "luxury of signification." Her analysis contrasts the increasingly narrow legal definitions of crimes and the circumscription of allowable punishments with the "symbolic latitude" for distribution of appropriate rewards and punishments available in fiction (223–24). Applied to fiction, the thesis works well; indeed, *The Gilded Age* is a perfect example, as the sudden death of Laura Hawkins from "heart disease" metes out the harsh but appropriate retributive justice denied by Twain's jury of captive fools; the fictive universe can achieve what criminal process in the "real" world cannot.

Considered in relation to the Beecher trial, however, Dimock's categories become problematical. In her analysis, law as a system is inherently exclusive, or narrowing, while the narrative products of authorial imagination are expansive, continually locating new meanings and ethical possibilities. Yet at the Beecher trial, which can be taken as a paradigm of mid-Victorian American legal process, the narratives under individual authorial control were markedly "frugal" in their range of signification, however infinite they may have seemed in absolute word count. They were unambiguous, single strains carved from multiple possibilities. But the trial process as a whole, including myriad "frugal" narratives, generated a complete transcript that displays many of the characteristics Dimock identifies only with the expansive possibilities of fiction, and specifically with the realist novel. As an inclusive "modern" novel, the trial transcript undercuts factual and moral certainty, surrounds each party's narrative with alternative meanings, doubts, and possibilities, and frequently interrupts the textual flow of witness narrative to permit a variety of attacks. Indeed, to carry the analogy a step further, the transcript of this particular trial is arguably more post-modern than realist in its refusal to provide a verdict, close factual gaps, or suggest the existence of an unambiguous "reality" outside the multiple and conflicting verbal representations of witnesses and lawyers. By shifting from a consideration of individuals' narratives to a reading of the six-month trial as a single text, we are forced to rethink the literary genres through which the narratives work, and to construct a new and quite different textual subject.

This expanded vantage point was perhaps best represented by the national news media, whose response to the trial's inconclusive resolution provides a fitting conclusion to my argument. The day after the trial ended, *The New York Times* published a lengthy analysis of the evidence, later published separately as a pamphlet. The Beecher-Tilton jurors may have failed to provide the closure of a unanimous verdict, but the newspaper did not hesitate to fill the gap. It delivered an unequivocal judgment, finding the facts strongly against Beecher and expressing a clear belief in his guilt. Yet the *Times* refused to assert Tilton's innocence, rejecting almost wholesale the details of his self-serving narrative. Admitting that "it is a mournful sight to see a great preacher of religion resting even under the suspicion of a dark crime," the *Times* editors declared themselves unable to "feel pity or respect" for Theodore Tilton. "That Tilton should have known of his wife's guilt; that he should have gone on living with her; that he should even have consulted with her alleged seducer as to the paternity of one of her children, and that, finally, he should declare on this very trial that she is a 'pure, white-souled woman'—all this puts him a long way outside of the range of public sympathy" (33). The newspaper's conclusion demonstrates the ultimate inability of either party to circumscribe the narrative possibilities available to juror-readers. The very exclusivity of each side's narrative tends to suggest the possibility of a third (or of multiple thirds) made up of some of each, and even, on occasion, of conclusions propounded by neither party. For example, the *Times* saved its severest criticism for Elizabeth Tilton, whom both Beecher and Tilton, for different reasons, had insisted was pure, innocent, loving, and "whole-souled." Although not a word of direct criticism of Elizabeth had been uttered at the trial, the *Times* dismissed her as "degraded and worthless," declaring that "a city full of such women would not be worth the trouble and misery which this one has occasioned" (34).

CHAPTER 4

Silent Woman, Speaking Fiction: The "Ministry of Catherine Gaunt" at the Beecher-Tilton Trial

Introduction: "the true defendant in this cause"

As noted at the end of chapter 3, *The New York Times* showed no hesitation at the conclusion of the six-month Beecher-Tilton trial in condemning Elizabeth Tilton as utterly "degraded and worthless," declaring that she was in fact an adulteress.[1] The central allegation of Theodore Tilton's civil suit, on charges of criminal conversation and alienation of affections, was that Mrs. Tilton had committed adultery with Henry Ward Beecher, the nation's foremost preacher. The nature of her intimacy with Beecher, indeed, the specifics of her sexual behavior, were thus at the heart of the case. Yet in confidently branding Elizabeth Tilton with a label that would permanently destroy her reputation, and with it her claim to middle-class respectability, the *Times* announced a conclusion based on the testimony of everyone *except* Mrs. Tilton herself. At the trial, both Beecher and Tilton took the stand; each had the opportunity to tell his own story to the jury, and each was subjected to weeks of wearying cross-examination.[2] More than one hundred witnesses testified for one man or the other. Beecher and Tilton were each represented by a benchful of prominent lawyers, among them two former judges and a former U.S. attorney general (C. Clark 209); the lawyers spent sixteen full days summing up the case for the jury, presenting at exhaustive length every possible argument in their clients' favor and every possible attack on their opponents (*Tilton versus Beecher* 3:556–1019).

Since she was neither plaintiff nor defendant, Elizabeth Tilton's legal "interests" were not technically at issue in the case. She was not called to testify and could not have testified even if she had been, because a procedural rule intended to further "marital confidence" precluded spouses from testifying either for or against each other.[3] She was unrepresented by counsel. Yet her utter exclusion from the litigative conversation in the courtroom was not achieved wholly without protest: on the seventy-seventh day she rose "like an apparition" from her seat among the spectators and attempted to read a statement. She was peremptorily silenced by the judge (3:313–14, 323–25, 355–56).[4]

Elizabeth Tilton's absence from the evidence-giving adversarial arena was the product of criminal conversation's classically homosocial structure.[5] As discussed in detail in chapter 2, the tort of criminal conversation traditionally erases the wife's agency, reducing her to a species of "damaged goods." The husband's claim against his wife's lover seeks compensation for the injury *to him* caused by interference with his property interest in the exclusive use of his wife's body and services. The litigation is between the two men; the wife's function in the case is as its contested object, her sexuality something that links the men and to which a money value is to be attached. Though her behavior is thus central to the litigative story, her "consent" to the adultery—her willingness, aggression, emotional involvement, in short, her subjectivity—is legally irrelevant, and therefore outside the story's narrative boundaries.[6]

The Beecher-Tilton case thus simultaneously accused Elizabeth Tilton of rank sexual immorality and refused her any opportunity to defend herself, a contradiction so obvious that even Benjamin Tracy, one of Beecher's attorneys, called her "the true defendant in this cause—she whose lips are sealed and whose hands are tied, while the battle is waging over her body. She can make no outcry, and strike no blow in her own defense" (2:5).[7] If she was presented to the jury as the victim of an almost pornographic bondage, it is crucial to remember that Elizabeth Tilton was bound and gagged not by Beecher or Tilton but by "the law," the structure of legal process in general and criminal conversation in particular. Tracy's vivid description is an appropriate introduction to the role of Elizabeth Tilton at the Beecher-Tilton trial: not only does it identify her as the person most truly under attack, but it also points out that the suppression of her voice in the legal arena precludes her self-defense, recognizing the necessity of legally empowered speech to individual freedom. Significantly too, Tracy's provocative characterization eroticizes Elizabeth Tilton's enforced silence. The bound woman is a sexually available—indeed, a rapeable—object *because* she is prevented from defensive self-assertion. As we will see, Elizabeth Tilton's exclusion from the case's verbal interplay made her "available" for a broad range of intimate discursive violations, assertions about her sexual behavior and desires that she, thoroughly "sealed" and "tied," could not fend off.

But if the legal requirements of the criminal conversation "story" thus dramatically suppressed the live voice of its only potential heroine, the project of constructing her remained central at the trial. Beecher, Tilton, and others testified to conversations with or about Elizabeth.[8] Lawyers described and analyzed her appearance, personality, motives, and behavior.[9] Dozens of her letters and notes were admitted and read to the jury (see 1:448–52, 487–94, 499–500, 503–4, 601, 682, 688). While she sat silently in the courtroom, Beecher and Tilton each constructed, out of documents and interpretive argument, the "Elizabeth Tilton" needed to further his case. In narrative terms, she became the silent fulcrum of their oppositional litigative stories, the blank but pivotal space into which each man could write the character his self-justifying story required. In Tilton's narrative, she was the loving wife reluctantly seduced by a powerful and charismatic public figure; in Beecher's she was an abused and unhappy woman who had become so enamored of him that she imagined her passion to be returned.

The critical document in this process of litigative "fictionalization" was a letter Elizabeth Tilton had written to her husband, in which she described her intense personal response to reading Charles Reade's sensationalist bestseller *Griffith Gaunt* (1866). "Through the ministry of Catherine Gaunt, a character of fiction," she wrote, "my eyes have been opened, for the first time in my experience, so that I see clearly my sin." Because the letter apparently accorded Reade's novel the power to interpret the letter-writer's life, the novel itself became crucial to the trial's project of determining whether or not she had committed adultery with Beecher. Lawyers summarized and interpreted the novel at length. Forensic manipulation of Elizabeth Tilton's private record of a life-changing reading experience recast it as evidence from which the jury might legitimately infer, or refute, the fact of her adultery.

This chapter explores the extraordinary phenomenon of Elizabeth Tilton's "absent presence" at the Beecher-Tilton trial, connecting it to *Griffith Gaunt*, the novel through which she was constructed for the jury. First, by studying the lawsuit's simultaneous exclusion of and obsession with Elizabeth Tilton, I explore the ways that the nineteenth-century American legal system frequently erased the self-authoring female voice, substituting for it a male-authored fictional construction. Second, by contrasting Elizabeth Tilton with Catherine Gaunt, the heroine of *Griffith Gaunt*, I investigate the connection between silenced woman and empowered heroine, sentimental reader and sensationalistic text. Elizabeth Tilton's sentimental, spiritual response to Reade's wildly sensational novel suggests that the individual reading experience, rather than the genre-related attributes of the text, determines how the reader will understand and be affected by the work. Third, by interrogating the narrative fictionalizing that occurs at all trials and by exploring the use of explicit literary references at the Beecher-Tilton trial, I argue that trial process necessarily blurs the boundary between fact and fiction. Considered together, these points suggest that a legal order that suppresses women's voices and excludes them from the adversarial arena reduces women ultimately to textual "constructs" indistinguishable from explicitly fictional characters in novels.

"Bless God, with me, for Catherine Gaunt"

At the Beecher-Tilton trial, Theodore Tilton testified that in July 1870, his wife Elizabeth had tearfully confessed to him that, after long resistance, she had given in to the passionate importunities of Beecher and had carried on an affair with him for close to eighteen months—that

> this friendship, contrary to my expectation or belief, had been in later years more than friendship, it had been love; that it had been more than love, it had been sexual intimacy; that this sexual intimacy had begun shortly after the death of her son Paul; that she had been in a tender frame of mind consequent upon that bereavement; that she had received much consolation during that shadow on our house, from her pastor, that she had made a visit to his house while she was still suffering from that sorrow, and that there, on the 10th of October, 1868, she had surrendered her body to him in sexual embrace. (1:396)

Tilton's narrative, framed as the recounting of a conversation in which he had informed Beecher of what Elizabeth had confessed to him,[10] stressed both her reluctance and Beecher's assurances that their adultery was so pure and sinless that it did not violate her marriage vows:

> Finally she had been persuaded by him that as their love was proper and not wrong, therefore it followed that any expression of that love, whether by the shake of the hand, or the kiss of the lips, or even bodily intercourse, since it all was the expression of that which in itself was not wrong, therefore that bodily intercourse was not wrong . . . that he had made these arguments to her during the early years of their friendship, and she had steadfastly resisted;

> that he had many times fondled her to the degree that it required on her part almost bodily resistance to be rid of him . . . that the occasions of her yielding her body to him had not been numerous, but that his solicitations had been frequent and urgent, and sometimes almost violent; that she made this confession to me because the sense of deceitfulness in her mind was a pain to her conscience. (1:396)

In the weeks of testimony that made up Tilton's affirmative case, his recitation of his wife's mournful verbal confession was supplemented by the claim that Elizabeth had at one point written a confession, in a document that had later been accidentally destroyed. Tilton's friend, Frank Moulton, and Moulton's wife Emma testified that Beecher had confessed to them as well. Letters and statements of Beecher's were introduced that never used the word "adultery" or made an explicit confession, but that seemed to express the sense that he had committed a great wrong against Theodore Tilton. Not surprisingly, Beecher denied every word and claimed that the letters were being misinterpreted (2:755, 758–74). Beecher's attorneys continually suggested to the jury that Tilton's case was nothing but false and lying "words, words words," being based on "no acts" at all (3:567, and see 2:37). It was therefore crucial that part of Theodore's case was based on a document containing Elizabeth's own words, the so-called "Catherine Gaunt letter" written four years before the litigation began, and therefore not vulnerable to the accusations of sham construction leveled against various documents offered into evidence by Tilton and written after the scandal had been revealed.[11] The significance of the letter, Theodore claimed, was that it recorded the moment when, suddenly and for the first time, Elizabeth became convinced that her adultery with Beecher was not in fact "pure" at all, but was a terrible sin. Significantly, that moment of insight had been triggered by reading *Griffith Gaunt.* This key document merits full quotation:

> June 29, 1871
> My Dear Theodore: To-day, through the ministry of Catherine Gaunt, a character of fiction, my eyes have been opened, for the first time in my experience, so that I see clearly my sin. It was when I knew that I was loved, to suffer it to grow to a passion. A virtuous woman should check instantly an absorbing love. But it appeared to me in such false light. That the love I felt and received could harm no one, not even you, I have believed unfalteringly until 4 o'clock this afternoon, when the heavenly vision dawned on me. I see now, as never before, the wrong I have done you, and hasten immediately to ask your par-

> don, with a penitence so sincere that henceforth (if reason remains) you may trust me implicitly. Oh! my dear Theo., though your opinions are not restful or congenial to my soul, yet my own integrity and purity are a sacred and holy thing to me. Bless God, with me, for Catherine Gaunt, and for all the sure leadings of an all-wise and loving Providence. Yes; now I feel quite prepared to renew my marriage vow with you, to keep it as the Savior requireth, who looketh at the eye and the heart. Never before could I say this. I know not that you are yet able, or ever will be, to say this to *me.* Still, with what profound thankfulness that I am come to this sure foundation, and that my feet are planted on the rock of this great truth you cannot at all realize.
>
> When you yearn toward me with any true feeling, be assured of the tried, purified and restored love of ELIZABETH. (3:741)

Responding to Elizabeth's epistolary assertion that Reade's novel had triggered a profound moral reevaluation of her past life, lawyers for both sides made the novel itself a central piece of "evidence" in the case. Though not technically admitted into evidence, it was freely discussed and quoted from. In a three-link chain of interactive analysis, arguments about the novel's meaning were used to interpret the letter, and the letter as interpreted was then used to fill the crucially empty place where "Elizabeth Tilton" belonged in the parties' litigation narratives. The character, inner life, and actual behavior of Elizabeth Tilton were inferred from parallels to Catherine Gaunt, the heroine of Reade's novel. Ultimately, complex acts of recognizably *literary* interpretation were offered to the jury for use in the juridical process of evidentiary evaluation. The seemingly clear boundary lines between fact and fiction, letter and testimony, literary heroine and "true defendant" were inevitably eroded, in ways that had very real adverse consequences for the silenced woman who was the trial's most important narrative subject. At the heart of this tumultuous courtroom controversy was the fixed and silent text of the letter itself, the record of an enigmatically personal, explicitly visionary experience. Reading *Griffith Gaunt* clearly stimulated Elizabeth Tilton to reassess both her past behavior and her future possibilities in what she felt to be a new, spiritual way. But what was the "sin" she now saw so clearly, what the love she had "felt and received"? In the bundle of texts, responses, and interpretations aggregated around Elizabeth Tilton and *Griffith Gaunt,* what was the relation between literary interpretation and legal argument? To unravel these interpretive interactions—between reader and novel, lawyer and evidence—we need to begin by looking more closely at both novel and reader.

Serialized simultaneously in English and American periodicals and published in book form in 1866, *Griffith Gaunt* was a scandalous best-seller on both sides of the Atlantic. It tells the story of Catherine Peyton, beautiful, rich, and headstrong, whose marriage to the weak-willed but handsome Griffith Gaunt goes from happiness through disaster to an almost parodic domestic resolution. A devout Catholic, Catherine's deepest passions are aroused for the first time in her life by the fiery sermons of her newly arrived priest, Father Leonard, whose words leave her "thrilled, enraptured, melted," and send her home to her husband of seven years all "hot and undiluted" (71). Through long hours of intimate religious conversation and a willingness to deceive themselves about the nature of their mutual attraction, Catherine and her priest fall deeply in love. Griffith, a hard-drinking but good-natured Protestant country squire, is incited from annoyance at his wife's apparently spiritual preoccupation to fits of uncontrollable jealousy by Catherine's maid Ryder, who is playing a complex game of her own to win Griffith's love. Meanwhile, the priest requires "all the self-possession he had been years acquiring not to throw himself at her knees and declare his passion to her" as he spends hours of "strange intoxication" confessing "his idol, directing and advising his idol, and all in the soft murmurs of a lover" (101). When, "literally unable to contain his bursting heart any longer, he uttered a cry of jealous agony and then, in a torrent of burning, melting words, appealed to her pity," Kate is "in a whirl" (102). She asks him to leave, but when he procrastinates she meets him in the woods with money to help his journey. Griffith, who has seen but misunderstood the forest scene, bursts in, convinced that the worst has occurred. In a jealous rage, "he literally trample[s] the poor priest with both feet" and rides off (109).

After returning briefly, Griffith again disappears, just after his voice is heard shouting for help. When his unexplained absence is linked to the discovery of an unidentifiable body, Kate is tried for her husband's murder. Deprived of defense counsel by the setting of the novel in the mid-eighteenth century, she defends herself, brilliantly.[12] Eloquent and intelligent, she cross-examines the witnesses against her, destroys the credibility of the malevolent Ryder by revealing the purportedly single maid to be both married and a mother, and ultimately obtains her acquittal, clears her name, and achieves a reunion with her husband. Griffith, meanwhile, has bigamously married Mercy Vint, an innkeeper's daughter who nursed him through a long illness during his mysterious disappearance. While he cowers drunkenly during the trial, Mercy bravely seeks out Kate, becoming her closest ally and most able defender. "Comprehending at last that to have been both of them wronged by one man was a bond of sympathy, not hate, the two wives of Griffith Gaunt laid his child [by Mercy] across their two laps and wept over him together" (197). Mercy testifies that Griffith is alive, thus winning Kate's acquittal. After the trial, Kate arranges Mercy's marriage to a former suitor of her own and, minimally subdued by adversity (and by a childbed transfusion that sends "some of Griffith Gaunt's bright red blood smoking hot" into her veins [209]) lives in peace with her now permanently submissive husband.

At first glance, Elizabeth Tilton seems a good candidate for status as a sensational heroine herself. The case has all the attributes literary critics have identified with the genre. Sensational bestsellers were often based on scandalous trials; Reade in particular kept enormous notebooks of newspaper clippings of criminal trials and other scandals and "insisted on the documentary basis of even his most outlandish" plots (Reynolds 101; and see Hughes 74–75, Burns 182–89). Sensational fiction of the 1860s and 1870s reveled in exposing the secretly immoral passions that burned beneath the surface of familiar respectability, "the disparity between apparently stable families and marriages and the horrifying secrets and extremes of passion that disrupt them" (Cvetkovich 45; and see Hughes 8, Reynolds 98–99). The Beecher-Tilton scandal placed Elizabeth Tilton at the center of a sexual rivalry between two well-known men who had national reputations as moral, spiritual, and intellectual leaders. Significantly, they also had large middle-class families and active social lives in "good" sections of Brooklyn Heights. In a matter-of-fact fashion borrowed from realistic technique, and in mundane middle-class surroundings familiar to its readers, sensational fiction presented incidents of lurid melodrama, often involving outrageous crimes, nightmarish or subversive sexuality, and barely plausible eccentricity (Hughes 15–27, 29–34; Pykett 30–35). In addition to its central allegations of adultery between Mrs. Tilton and Henry Ward Beecher, the Beecher-Tilton case featured the alleged adulteries of Theodore Tilton with a string of women, including not only a dramatic midnight attempt on the virtue of the Tiltons' maid, Bessie Turner, and a one-night stand with a seventeen-year-old girl in a town where he lectured, but also a passionate fling with Victoria Woodhull, the wildly unconventional free-love advocate who had first brought the case to public attention (1:278–79, 308, 553–57; 3:850; Waller 113–14). Newspaper readers were also treated to such melodramatic incidents as Elizabeth's flight from home in the middle of a winter night to escape her husband's physically violent abuse and her finding refuge only by lying down and weeping on the graves of her dead children (Fox 116–17). Eccentricity was provided by Tilton's description of a conversation in which he demanded that Beecher remove the "shadow" of illegitimacy from the future life of Elizabeth's fifth child, Ralph, by confirming the date that their "intimacy" began, which Beecher, weeping, did while Elizabeth, weeping, looked on (2:411–12). The trial was, as Milton Rugoff has declared, "the uncensored performance of a sex drama" (207).

The startling gap between the "ordinary" middle-class behavior one would expect from such externally respectable people and the scandalous incidents that became the delight of the popular press led E. L. Godkin to declare in a *Nation* editorial that the case provided "nearly as much amusement as if an unknown tribe worshipping strange gods had been suddenly discovered on Brooklyn Heights." Godkin warned that the participants lived in "a kind of mental and moral chaos, in which many of the fundamental rules of living, which have been worked out painfully by thousands of years of bitter human experience, seem in imminent risk of disappearing totally" (24 Sept. 1874, 201–2). One way of understanding the "story" of the case, then, is to see it as the kind of sensationally plotted fiction that Elizabeth Tilton found in novels like Reade's. More than one recent critic has linked the rise of the sensation novel to contemporary media obsessions with gruesome or shocking "real-life" sexual cases (Boyle 76, Reynolds 103–4). The media treatment of the 1875 Beecher-Tilton case suggests that the interaction between literary and actual scandal was not so much a response as a circulation: if sensation novels recast newspaper scandals in a powerful literary form, the popularity of such novels, and the consequent development of a "trained" readership, produced a climate in which both reporters and participants understood and imaged a case like Beecher-Tilton as a sensational "story." While the histrionic self-descriptions by the parties and their attorneys at the trial reveal that they saw themselves as melodramatic "heroes," the line between literary and actual event was further blurred by the literary register in which the media persistently contextualized the case: "we are reading the most marvelous of human dramas" declared *Frank Leslie's Illustrated Newspaper*, "greater in plot development and effect than Hawthorne's 'The Scarlet Letter', Charles Reade's 'Griffith Gaunt,' George Eliot's "Romola," or Shakespeare's 'Othello.' It has its only counterpart in 'Faust.' "

But if the plot of the Beecher-Tilton scandal seems perfect fodder for best-selling sensational fiction, the accused adulteress at its center does not fit the confident, transgressive mold in which such heroines are typically cast. Lurid newspaper accounts did their best to paint her as a swirling mass of amoral passion, as did, more subtly, Beecher's attorneys, but the effort was not notably successful. Sensationalist heroines are often described in terms of their convention-defying assertiveness, "an outright and gleeful threat to both social proprieties and the conventions of heroine construction" (Reynolds 98, and see Pykett 9–10). Such heroines often display an active, even aggressive sexuality, which the genre depicts as neither unnatural nor unfeminine, and a "tendency to usurp the hero's role as the instigator of the action" (Reynolds 120). "Sensation novels expressed female anger, frustration, and sexual energy more directly than had been done previously," declares Elaine Showalter. "Readers were introduced to a new kind of heroine, one who could put her hostility toward men into violent action" (1977:160).

But whereas Kate Gaunt, like her "sensational" sisters, Lady Audley, Magdalen Vanstone, and Aurora Floyd,[13] is strong-willed and sexually aggressive, Elizabeth Tilton seems to have been the essence of passive pliability. In one twenty-four hour period, she wrote a "confession" of adultery that her husband showed to Beecher, a "revocation" of those accusations when Beecher visited her where she lay in bed recovering from a miscarriage, and a "retraction" of the revocation when her husband came home and found out about the letter she had given Beecher (Waller 125–26, Shaplen 86–98). Shy with strangers, she was timid with the famous feminists and journalists who visited her husband and hesitant to exert authority over her Irish servants (Waller 56). Her correspondence, read at length at the trial, records a constant struggle to assume the shapes required both by her husband and by the mid-Victorian cult of sentimental Christian domesticity: to be pure, spiritual, submissive. "*This* I think I have decided" she wrote in a typical letter to her husband in March 1868. "No more chidings, scoldings! An inexpressible tenderness has grown up in my soul toward you. I never saw my path as clear as now—that whatever you may do, say, or be, it becometh me to be the Christian wife and mother!" (1:490). The letters are filled with continual self exhortations toward spiritual and religious improvement, and declarations of love for her husband, framed in a sentimental vocabulary ("those parts of your letter which give me your soul, tho' extravagant, thrill me all over with ecstasy" 10 Jan. 1867, 1:449). As she was a great reader of fiction and a much-appreciated listener,

Elizabeth's intimacy with Beecher had flowered as he read to her from drafts of his own best-selling sentimental novel, *Norwood* (1:455, 2:742). In short, Elizabeth Tilton approached the burning passions and bigamous illegitimacies of *Griffith Gaunt* with a set of skills and expectations developed through her participation in American sentimental and religious culture.

Significantly, the most striking aspect of her "Catherine Gaunt" letter is its spirituality, a quality of response that suggests an overpoweringly moral stimulus. Had Reade's novel disappeared, we might reconstruct it on the basis of this letter as a work of sentimental Christianity in the genre of *The Lamplighter* or *The Wide, Wide World*, in which the struggles of a heroine of almost perfect virtue to perfect her own Christian soul provide a model for readers who must grapple with their own powerlessness and frustration. Catherine Gaunt appears to Elizabeth as one of the "sure leadings of an all-wise and loving Providence," while the novel fulfills a function we associate with explicitly religious works, and prototypically with the Bible: it provides a redemptive morality to be applied to her own behavior and a set of spiritual goals toward which to strive. The letter's descriptive vocabulary is wholly religious; she refers to the heroine's "ministry," to herself as experiencing a "heavenly vision," to "sin," "penitence" and the requirements of "the Savior." Religious inducement to submit to the secular authorities that controlled women's lives has persuasively been identified as the central goal of sentimental fiction by such recent critics as Jane Tompkins, who argues that "learning to renounce her own desire is the sentimental heroine's vocation," and is understood to be "the achievement of Christian salvation" (176). If sensationalist heroines frequently triumph over law, convention, and the weak men in their lives, sentimental heroines tend to remain in positions of worldly powerlessness, achieving mastery through self-conquest and hard-won submission to both God and their husbands. So Elizabeth Tilton declares that the influence of Catherine Gaunt has stimulated not insurrection, but strength to renew and keep her marriage vows.[14]

Reading Elizabeth Tilton's letter, one would never suspect that an influential review in the New York *Round Table* could have condemned *Griffith Gaunt* as "an indecent publication" so "immoral," "so compact with crime, so replete with insidious allusions" that it was what "no modest woman can read without a blush, and what no man should think of placing before his wife or sister or daughter, whose perusal modesty cannot survive untainted" (3). Asked by Wilkie Collins to testify in Reade's libel suit against *The London Review*, which had reprinted the *Round Table* article, Charles

Dickens admitted that while he admired the work greatly, he would not have published it in his own magazine because many incidents "might be impurely suggestive to inferior minds (of which there must necessarily be many among a large mass of readers)."[15] Wayne Burns, Reade's modern biographer, goes even further, declaring that "the passages in question are not 'impurely suggestive to inferior minds,' they are purely (or merely) 'suggestive' (or pornographic) to all perceptive minds" (262). Reade's righteous indignation against those who dared suggest that his novel made sin attractive was vented in an open letter to the American press, in which he railed against those "prurient prudes" who "take my text and read it, not by its own light, but by the light of their own foul imaginations; and having so defiled it by mixing their own filthy minds with it, they sit in judgment on the compound" (1883:316).[16] Burns, unconvinced, expresses an opinion typical of those few modern critics who have considered *Griffith Gaunt* when he confidently asserts that "despite his published denials" Reade "most certainly . . . intended Kate's experiences and feelings to be titillating" (240).[17] Without exception, modern and Victorian critics identify the novel's eroticism as its most salient characteristic.

While they may disagree heartily about the advisability of encouraging female readers toward a more assertive sexuality, both sets of critics thus agree that, like other sensational best-sellers, *Griffith Gaunt* did just that. But if many readers found the work more salacious than seemly, Elizabeth Tilton was not among them. Her letter suggests that, for her at least, the novel's signifying center was precisely its capacity not just to render but to judge sexuality. *Griffith Gaunt*'s moral framework—which Winifred Hughes dismisses as an example of "the cautious hedging and . . . inevitable disavowal of his meaning" that colored all of Reade's novels, one of the "variety of ingenious solutions to the problem of Victorian censorship" employed by sensation novelists—was, for Elizabeth Tilton, the novel's heart (103, 30). What moved her was apparently not the novel's implicit call to rebellion against traditionally "feminine roles" but its explicit insistence on the dangers of undisciplined sexuality. Recent feminist critics have seen novels like Reade's as the stimulus for women to see "new possibilities for themselves" that included, ultimately, "new fantasies, new expectations, and even female insurrection" (Sicherman 214, Showalter 1978:115). Yet Elizabeth's letter declares that reading *Griffith Gaunt* led her to an acute consciousness of sin and a highly respectable resolution to "renew my marriage vow with you and to keep it as the Savior requireth."

What we have in the "Catherine Gaunt letter" is the record of a striking—though probably not uncommon—intergeneric encounter in which Elizabeth Tilton achieved a successfully sentimental and religious reading of a scandalously sensationalist text. Her response to *Griffith Gaunt* suggests that reader-text interactions may be a great deal less predictable than genre critics would have us believe. How a reader reads, and what she reads for, are much more important in determining what she makes of a particular text than whether the text itself is "inherently" pure or pornographic. That textual interpretation is, in large measure, more reader- than text-determined has become a truism of modern criticism, and a cornerstone of reader-response theory. Surprisingly, however, genre critics often fail to take the diversity of individual responses into account. The burst of recent critical attention to sensationalist fiction of the 1860s and 1870s has delighted in constructing a unified female readership influenced toward "a demand for greater individual autonomy" and "a liberalization of controls over sexual and familial norms" by reading these gleefully subversive texts (Garrison 158).[18] Such views provide notably inadequate mappings of reading experiences like Elizabeth Tilton's; a more nuanced approach would recognize that a reader's conception of both self and appropriate textual response will be shaped by discourses and influences other than those of the text she is reading.

Shirley Samuels notes in a recent essay that "the sentimental complex . . . situates the reader or viewer: that is, the act of emotional response the work evokes also produces the sentimental subject who consumes the work" (6). Having become over time a thoroughly "sentimental subject," Elizabeth Tilton went on to consume other works that were anything but sentimental in the ways she had learned; all texts were grist for her sentimental mill. A second factor in her response is that, inevitably, her "mill" was built in the shape of her particular past, so that fictive situations that paralleled or indirectly related to her own experience had special meaning for her. Here we should note that if she was an atypical reader, Elizabeth Tilton's sexual sophistication may have been as much the cause of her reaction to *Griffith Gaunt* as her sentimental religiosity. Where most readers probably found Catherine Gaunt's erotic temptation outside their experience, Elizabeth knew the dizzying combination of spirituality and sexuality that characterized Catherine's not-quite-criminal conversations with her priest.[19] Henry Ward Beecher's famous "Gospel of Love," which stressed the spiritual affinity of like-minded souls, had prepared the way for him to express more earthly desires. Elizabeth's memory, not fantasy, would have been evoked by Reade's assertion that "the heart does not speak by words alone: there are looks, and there are tones of voice that belong to Love, and are his signs, his weapons; and it was in these very tones the priest murmured to his gentle listener about 'the angelic life' between spirits still lingering on earth, but purged from earthly dross" (100). For Elizabeth, *Griffith Gaunt's* power was not its vivid rendering of female sexuality, something she would have found more familiar than shocking, but its explicitly moral grappling with the consequences of sexual attraction, a problem that was for her both current and overwhelming.

Elizabeth Tilton's response to the novel, then, came from both her literary and cultural training and her particular personal situation. Much as he abhorred this inevitable incursion of the reader's subjectivity into the reading process, Reade himself seems, interestingly, to have understood it. Accusing his readers of "mixing" their minds and imaginations with his novel to produce a "compound," he implicitly recognizes reading as an interactive negotiation in which reader and text interpret each other.

This process of mutual interpretation is the key to Elizabeth Tilton's "heavenly vision." In the text of the letter, we can see that she describes two distinct but related responses to reading *Griffith Gaunt.* The first seems to be a conflation of herself with Catherine Gaunt, a collapse of distance between the real and the fictional characterized by an identification with Catherine and an appropriation of her perceived qualities. In the second, the story of the novel opens a space or vantage point from which Elizabeth's own experience becomes recognizable as a "story," a parallel, perhaps interchangeable narrative version of Catherine's life. Elizabeth simultaneously uses *Griffith Gaunt* to step outside her own life, to a distance from which her past becomes a morally assessable narrative ("a virtuous woman should check instantly an absorbing love. But it appeared to me in such false light"), and to admit the assertiveness and spiritual strength of the novel's heroine inside her own consciousness, where they can bolster her self-confidence ("my own integrity and purity are a sacred thing to me").

Taking what she needs from the novel, permitting its "ministry" to work on her self-perceptions, is for Elizabeth a way to become—at least while writing the letter—the triumphant heroine of the story of her own life. Strikingly, her expectation of such a self-transformation not only seems to recognize her own and Catherine Gaunt's lives as "stories," but to image them as equally open to a continual process of interpretation. Just as a moment of insight at four o'clock alters her understanding of what had happened earlier in the novel, so this sudden "heavenly vision" triggers a new reading of her own past experience. The "story" of Elizabeth Tilton's relationship to Henry Ward Beecher is recast in the transformative text of her letter from the spiritually pure romance of Beecher's "story" to a parable of sin and false understanding, and the sexual activity at its center comes to signify not the pure consummation of love but its sinful betrayal. This openness to reinterpretation also opens the rest of the story, her future course, freeing it from the shackles of a single narrative pathway determined by the action thus far. The visionary moment detaches past from future. Elizabeth herself becomes a newly purified and spiritually superior heroine who can enter the next chapter of her life untainted by its previous events. And, just as she read Reade's sensation fiction through the filter of her own needs and experience, so she now "reads" her role within the sensational "Beecher-Tilton scandal" from a spiritualized, sentimental subject position.[20]

The process of reading thus engendered interpretive narratives that provided moral clarification for ambiguous sets of experiences, one set fictional, the other her past history. The interpretive negotiation through which reader and novel seem to flow into each other makes it, finally, difficult to locate within the text of the letter the boundaries between fictional protagonist and fictionally influenced letter-writer. Significantly, the letter was part of an intimate correspondence with her husband, and as such, its universe of referentiality—whether of shared past experience, private vocabulary, or assumed understandings—was utterly lost when the letter became part of the public record of the scandal and trial. That it registered a moment of intense meaning for Elizabeth Tilton is clear; how that moment implied the particulars of her relationship with Henry Ward Beecher much less so. The next section of this essay takes up the lawyers' forensic manipulation of the letter, an oppositional round of interpretive narratives aimed at explicating the "text" of Elizabeth Tilton's life.

"You see now, as in a mirror, the heart of this woman . . ."

It may seem quite strange that explicitly fictional events and characters could merge so smoothly with the very real ones in the Beecher-Tilton case. A central contention of this book is that literary elements always play some role in the discursive construction of litigation narratives, but the use of *Griffith Gaunt* at the Beecher-Tilton trial appears to be of another order than the typically subtle, even unrecognized, infiltration of literary form. Where the "ordinary" literary reference works through explicit or implicit analogy, as a reference point meant to shape the jury's response to the evidence, the fictional text at issue here *became* evidence, substituting directly for testimonial narratives that could not be produced. The Beecher-Tilton trial was, by any measure, an intensely literary event. Not only did the media compare it to familiar literary works, but the lawyers delighted in giving dramatic readings of Tilton's poetry (1:466, 467–68, 551), examining Beecher about the drafting of his novel, *Norwood* (2:742–43), condemning and defending Beecher by reading from his sermons and published lectures (1:334, 3:560, 1003–1006), and referring almost continually to a truly astonishing variety of literary works.[21] Even Theodore Tilton seemed to understand his wife in literary terms; asked by lawyers during the Plymouth Church investigation of the case to describe the religious character of his wife, he replied that the investigating committee should consult the ninth chapter of his novel, *Tempest-Tossed*, because he had based the character Mary Vail on his wife, using the text of her letters.[22]

Sometimes these literary references took the form of rhetorical genre markers rather than invocations of specific texts, as when John Porter described Tilton using a cluster of sentimental tropes, trying to convince the Beecher-Tilton jury that his client should be situated as the stereotypical victim of a villain's machinations (see discussion of Tilton's opening, ch. 3). At other times, lawyers read extracts to the jury from familiar texts, as when Tilton's attorneys read at length from *The Scarlet Letter* and declared that "with the prophetic eye of genius, Hawthorne had described the actual experience of Henry Ward Beecher," whose corrupt soul, like Arthur Dimmesdale's, was "penitent and repentant toward God, but timid and defiant and lying toward men. That is not the penitence that saves" (3:934–35). In both of these examples, literary form is offered not as evidence but as a morally loaded, narratively coherent framework that can be used to organize and give meaning to the mass of evidence and testimony with which the jury is confronted.

A third form of literary reference at the trial, and one that brings us closer to *Griffith Gaunt*, was the paradoxical use of literary fiction as a guarantor, and source, of factual authenticity. In his final argument for Beecher, William Maxwell Evarts challenged as incredible Tilton's assertion that Beecher had seduced Elizabeth by convincing her that their adultery was pure and sinless, declaring that nobody could have used such language and arguments, and that the alleged conversations must therefore have been lying "fictions" made up by Tilton (3:661–62, 713–14). Tilton's attorney, William Beach, responded by reading a passage from Sir Walter Scott's *Woodstock*, in which a priest attempts to seduce a young woman with just such an approach:

> Walter Scott is supposed to have been a tolerably good scholar in human nature. No writer has ever pictured so graphically and beautifully all the manifestations of our nature in its highest and best developments . . . and he has been considered as the great master of human passion, as the great printer of human nature. [describes plot of novel and reads passage] Well, here is the very sentiment which is attributed to Henry Ward Beecher by the mouths of two or three witnesses. . . . Well Henry Ward Beecher has read that undoubtedly. A man who reads Dumas will not neglect Walter Scott. . . . And very many of the brightest and highest conceptions of our own minds are derived from these sources of information, because there is very little originality in the world. . . . It is not surprising that Mr. Beecher should have used arguments of this character and addressed to this woman this sort of sentiment. Another great man, great as Beecher . . . puts into the mouth of one of his characters and gives the authenticity of his name to sentiments and arguments of like kind. And when Mr. Evarts says that no man of intellect ever dreamed of arguments of this character addressed under such circumstances to the seduction of virtue, I present him the example as delineated by Walter Scott. (3:864–65)

To us, Scott may be the ultimate romantic novelist, his plots far-fetched and his language often stilted, but to the Victorians, as John Henry Raleigh has argued, he was the equally ultimate realist, his works a repository of human nature captured in persuasive detail, his characters plausible, familiar flesh-and-blood portraits.[23] This suggests that to the participants in this trial, literary fiction was accepted as "true" not just in a theoretical or philosophical way, but in the legal sense as proof that something actually happened. It must have happened in the real world of 1860s Brooklyn, Beach argues, because it happened in the fictional world of Scott's seventeenth-century England. The trial was punctuated by continual accusations on all sides that parties and witnesses were "fictionalizers," and that Tilton was a "cunning rhetorician" (3:593) whose "manufactured" case was pervaded by an "air of general untruthfulness" that showed the "dramatic and artistic skill with which it had been gotten up" (3:641, 557).[24] Yet an *explicitly* fictional text, the result of painstaking, artificial construction set in an earlier and different period than that of its writing, is treated as "proof" of an allegation of fact. While the cultural acceptance of fiction as a source of "truth" is hardly surprising, its deployment in a legal quest for certainty about past events is fascinating.

Had the Beecher-Tilton trial occurred today, Tilton's attorneys might have attempted to introduce expert testimony, perhaps from a sociologist or psychologist, about the verbal patterns of seduction men might typically use, leading to an expert opinion that such a "line" was within the range of common and credible patterns. The reign of the forensic scientific expert not yet having begun in 1875, Sir Walter Scott is positioned as the expert, the "master of human passion" whose "printing" of a particular conversation demonstrates not painstaking "fictional" construction, but the accurate representation of "natural" fact. This contrast between what is "artificial" and what is "natural" is at the heart of the asserted difference between the "lying" stories and false testimony purportedly "concocted" or "dictated" by Tilton, and the "natural," recognizably "true" conversations and descriptions of Scott. Yet realms of truth and fiction cannot be kept apart. In a further recognition of the pervasive influence of fiction on the world of fact, Beach suggests that Beecher's arguments about pure and sinless love may have been based on his reading of Scott. The rhetoric of real life is thus not merely corroborated but produced by the texts of fiction, which are then offered as proof of allegations of fact. Art is accepted as an accurate imitation of life, indeed its verifying reflector, while life is understood to imitate and find inspiration in the superior rhetorical persuasions of art. Stronger evidence of the circulation of literature into legal and private discourse, of the blurring of boundaries between them, can hardly be imagined.

If we return now to Elizabeth Tilton's letter, it is clear that the semiotic slippage between heroine and reader, fictional and factual life story, was what made it so useful for Beecher's and Tilton's attorneys at the trial. While all trials use constructed and therefore "fictional" narratives of character and event, Elizabeth's absence from the testimonial stage had produced a narrative gap that was much more than ordinarily open to the incursions of fiction. The oppositional storytelling drive that powers all litigation means that the interpretive narratives of plaintiff and defendant will necessarily conflict at key points, dichotomizing along the case's fault lines. Because the same characters are central to both parties' narratives, there will be two versions of each person and action, diverging just at the points of factual dispute. As a result, character delineation in the narratives of testimony and argument will tend to correspond more closely to the shape of each litigant's need than to the actual person's past behavior. At most trials, this tendency is counteracted, at least to some extent, by the narrative subject's ability to enter the testimonial arena herself. Neither party is completely free to manufacture person X's behavior and motives out of whole cloth if X can appear and tell her own story, particularly if she is a credible witness.[25] But in criminal conversation cases, the testimonial interplay among plaintiff, defendant, and relevant witness that, ideally, forces trial process toward "truth" does not function fully or effectively. Elizabeth Tilton could not testify, nor was she represented by counsel. If her absence created the real problem of her unavailability as an explicator of her own texts and actions, it also created an equally real and notably uncircumscribed opportunity for counsel to "write" her into the story in whatever terms they found most useful.

The confessional language of the Catherine Gaunt letter seemed at first glance to provide exactly the "hard" evidence needed to close the gap and "produce" Elizabeth Tilton. On closer inspection, however, the letter's text was itself clearly gaplike, its terms ambiguous, the referents needed to decode its intense affective claims missing. The letter admits only the "sin" of loving and being loved; it does not mention sex, adultery, or Henry Ward Beecher. Searching for a narrative of events about Elizabeth Tilton's life that would not dissolve into ambiguity and absence whenever pressure was applied, Beecher's attorneys turned quite naturally and unironically to fiction, to the novel that Elizabeth had identified as stimulating a "heavenly vision" of her own sin and redemption. As William Beach had used *Woodstock* to prove that certain conversations had occurred, so William Maxwell Evarts, Beecher's lead counsel, used *Griffith Gaunt* to prove that the alleged adultery had *not* taken place.

Evarts treated *Griffith Gaunt* as a black-letter narrative of the relations between Elizabeth, her husband, and Beecher. For him, the correspondence between fictional heroine and actual woman was absolute: Elizabeth was sexually faithful to her husband because Catherine Gaunt did not commit adultery with her priest.[26] Indeed, argued Evarts, the novel, the letter, and the reader's life all can have "but one meaning, and it is an absolute refutation of all pretenses of carnal intercourse or bodily impurity of any kind on the part of this woman" (3:741). In one sense, the forensic conflation of woman and reader is appallingly appropriate: "Elizabeth Tilton" was already a wholly fictional character, "present" at the Beecher-Tilton trial only through the testimony and arguments of others. To interpret one fictional character in terms of another seems almost reasonable, and while Elizabeth's letter stops short of claiming to have lived every event of Catherine's life, it does invite an equation of fictional heroine with responding reader.

But Evarts's argument drew a different kind of connection between the two narratives: where Elizabeth Tilton's letter records a fluid, interactive negotiation with certain events and emotions in the novel, Evarts constructs an unambiguous, essentially static correlation between Elizabeth's entire life and the novel's entire plot. "You see now," he assured the jury, "as in a mirror, the heart of this woman, the life of this woman" (3:743). Evarts's interpretive narrative of the novel became in effect a typological instrument deployed to interpret the ambiguous text of her letter, which was then used to produce what he had been after all along, an unambiguous narrative of the letter-writer's life. In his hands, all three "Elizabeths" became freely interchangeable objects, verbal signifiers unconnected to any speaking subject and therefore able to be substituted for each other at will. Elizabeth's admissible written statements were ambiguous and inconsistent, and her exclusion from the trial's litigative discourse reduced her to a manipulable verbal construct. In contrast, the novel's seemingly straightforward narrative outlined a relationship that, however intense, unambiguously evaded sexual consummation. On the rock of what *didn't* happen in the novel, Evarts pitched a tent of declarative certainty.

Evarts was an adversarial advocate for his client. He used Reade's novel to rid Elizabeth Tilton of all "bodily impurity" because his task of persuading the jury that Beecher had not committed adultery necessitated exculpating her from the charge as well. But though he acquitted her of adultery, Evarts based Beecher's defense on the wholesale sacrifice of Elizabeth Tilton's honor, and here his flexible interpretation of *Griffith Gaunt* was of particular assistance. Not only did Beecher's attorneys deny that he had seduced Elizabeth, they suggested that whatever improprieties did occur were caused by her overwhelming passion for him, a passion he had neither encouraged nor reciprocated. To prove Beecher's innocence from Reade's novel, Evarts did not hesitate to make unequivocal, though unsupportable, assertions about its content. His argument rewrote the novel's story to conform more closely to the exculpatory narrative of "real-life" events that constituted Beecher's defense, a narrative that was, in all historical likelihood, also a fiction. Evarts simply erased Reade's explicit revelation of Father Leonard's sexual passion for his "idol" Kate, describing the "entangled affections" at issue as having been solely hers, and he ignored what Burns has called Reade's "frantic efforts to maintain Kate's innocence and purity . . . by shifting the burden of moral responsibility wholly onto Leonard" (256). In Evarts's version of the relationship between Catherine Gaunt and her priest, the only sexuality that exists is Catherine's. This instrumental distortion of Reade's *fictional* text was thus proffered to the jury as substantive evidence from which an exculpatory inference about Beecher's *actual* behavior could legitimately be drawn.

In his effort to eliminate all traces of ambiguity and impropriety from the book, Evarts naturally omitted the transatlantic scandal that had surrounded its publication, assuring the jury that *Griffith Gaunt* "is and *is known to everyone to be*, an exposition of how there may come to be unsuitable disturbances of domestic peace, unsuitable exaggerations of grounds of religious discord between husband and wife, by the entirely innocent, the entirely pure, and religious relation between a clergyman and a penitent or a devotee" (3:741, emphasis added). Accusing Tilton's attorneys of not being able to "tell a story about a crime or an iniquity, without missing the whole point of its guilt or its wickedness," Evarts declared that Beecher's only sin was to have "heedlessly and blindly allowed an intimacy that began and proceeded on the footing of pastor and parishioner to come to a point where it led to the wrong that is portrayed in this 'Griffith Gaunt' " a wrong wholly attributable to "the wife's affections" and in which the minister can "thank God I have not fallen except by errors of a course of respectful attention and affection, and not under any pursuit of carnal sin or under the impulse of any carnal passion" (3:746–47).[27]

Evarts's reading of *Griffith Gaunt*, like Elizabeth Tilton's, exploits the essential openness of both fictional and factual life stories. Both readings were produced with redemptive aims, but where Evarts sought the legal exoneration of his client, Elizabeth recorded her private search for salvation. The circulation of identity between heroine and reader that we glimpse in the letter was, crucially, part of a completely private, self-referential experience. Evarts's forensic deployment of the novel is more disquieting, because it suggests that in the narrativizing process by which the events giving rise to a lawsuit are transformed into testimonial and argumentative narratives for the jury, fact and fiction can be easily and even appropriately interchanged. This is a disturbing thought indeed, even to those who, like most of us, assume that courtroom rhetoric generally includes a certain amount of exaggeration and "fictionalizing." Evarts's argument dissolves the boundaries between literary text and historical events, and rewrites both fictional and factual narratives. This suggests that for him, the verbal presentation of evidence and argument through which trials are conducted is itself always and only a fictional text, wholly severed from the "real world" and accountable only to its instrumental goal of winning the case.

One might expect that Evarts's forays into the realms of fiction would be effectively countered by counsel for his opponent. But Tilton's legal interests were at odds with his wife's. Winning his case required him to prove her an adulteress; he had, if anything, an even greater motive to misread the novel. In his final argument for Tilton, William Beach presented what we would identify as a "reader-response" interpretation of *Griffith Gaunt*, arguing that when Elizabeth Tilton read the "word painting of a great author" depicting "the danger and the sin of perverted affection improperly bestowed upon a priest of God," her "conscience was disturbed" (3:919). Beach attempted to avoid the problem of Catherine's sexual guiltlessness by rejecting Evarts's flat-footed parallelisms of reader and text. Rather, he claimed "it was not necessary, for the purpose of awakening any such reflection, arousing the conscience to the true conception of moral offense, that the particular crime or sin of which she had been guilty was portrayed in this work brought under her knowledge" (3:919). Reading to the jury Elizabeth's assertion that she suddenly saw "clearly my own sin," Beach commented that "no woman writes a sentence like this without a consciousness that in her own life there has been a grievous fault." Thus, it was not necessary that Catherine actually commit adultery for the novel to stimulate Elizabeth's agony over her sexual misbehavior. Instead, "the slight and inconsiderable circumstances," a "single sentence casually read," triggers an intense personal response. The parallel between reader and heroine lies not in a precise matching of experiences, but in a more impressionistic process of identification and response.

Beach's theory of the case made Elizabeth an adulteress. While acknowledging Catherine's marital fidelity, he described her feelings for Leonard as "perverted" and "improper," an obvious exaggeration that helped construct a bond of sinfulness between heroine and reader. Interestingly, Beach also accepted without question Evarts's attribution of the "entanglement of the affections" in the novel wholly to its heroine. By ignoring Reade's vivid rendering of Father Leonard's losing battle with his sexual desire for his parishioner's wife, Beach lost an opportunity to regale the jury with the author's descriptions of the priest's "murmurs of a lover," his "bursting heart" and "burning, melting words." Perhaps he failed to exploit the dramatic possibilities of Reade's text because he realized such readings might have appeared inconsistent with his earlier declaration that any specific parallels between the novel's plot and Elizabeth's life were unimportant. Equally likely, he may not have read the book. If so, he based his literary interpretation and argument not on the book but on Evarts's summation, removing not only the real Elizabeth Tilton but Reade's heroine as well from the arena of available "evidence," until forensic rhetoric became its own source.

"I shall stand here on the watch, to see that you treat her with due reverence."

Perhaps the ultimate irony in Elizabeth Tilton's relationship to Catherine Gaunt is that while both women's life stories climax in dramatic trials in which they are implicitly or explicitly accused of serious, reputation-destroying crimes, Catherine is empowered in precisely the ways that Elizabeth is silenced. Catherine is both party defendant (and therefore direct and explicit subject of the litigation) and lawyer (and therefore able to examine witnesses and argue to the jury); Elizabeth sits mute among the courtroom spectators. While Catherine's lack of in-court defense counsel initially intensifies her "feminine" helplessness, it soon becomes the direct means to her unmediated victory. Authorized by the legal system to speak for herself, she becomes author and interpreter as well as subject of the "story" of the events leading up to the trial and the trial itself. When witnesses testify that she received a peddler in her bedroom on the night of the supposed murder, she forces them to admit that the interview took place in an anteroom outside her boudoir, which in turn was outside her bedroom, eliminating any impropriety. When the dead body is identified as Griffith's by means of a mole on its forehead, she demonstrates that an identical mole was known to be on the forehead of the peddler, Griffith's illegitimate half-brother, who has also disappeared. In each instance, Catherine destroys the credibility of the narrative introduced against her. Unlike Elizabeth Tilton, she is legally authorized to contradict, to oppose false narratives with true ones or, more precisely, to counter condemnatory stories with exculpatory ones in which she casts herself as a virtuous, wise, and womanly heroine. Then, in a lengthy and eloquent summation, she presents a new, whole, credible story that exonerates her and reduces the opposition's narratives to fragmentary falsehoods.

Catherine's summation mentions neither Father Leonard nor any other explanation of Griffith's volcanic jealousy. But these gaps in what a reader might call "the whole truth" provide important evidence of her self-creation as an author: authors create truth by creating persuasive narratives. As William Maxwell Evarts did in discussing the text that created her, Kate Gaunt understands how to exploit the power of interpretive storytelling. For her, the relation of voice to personhood to power is absolute. In the shift from discursive object to authoring subject, constituted through the receipt of *legal* authority to speak in court, she gains control not only over the story of her past but, at least as important, over the unfolding story of the rest of her life.

Catherine's reversal of the traditional exclusion of women from power-creating legal discourse is enhanced by her bond with Griffith's second wife, Mercy Vint. Mercy too has her moment of adversarial triumph in court, coolly facing down the prosecutor, and it is her evidence that wins Catherine's acquittal. Kate and Mercy represent a striking inversion of Eve Sedgwick's paradigm of homosocial interaction: their heroic intimacy—created through their having shared a male sexual object both desired but neither much respects—enables them to prevail over the masculine legal and social order. Indeed, Catherine's finest moment comes in attacking the prosecutor who has been aspersing Mercy: "For shame! This is one of those rare women that adorn our whole sex, and embellish human nature; and, so long as you have the privilege of exchanging words with her, I shall stand here on the watch, to see that you treat her with due reverence: ay, sir, with reverence; for I have measured you both, and she is as much your superior as she is mine" (202).

In sharp contrast to the way that Kate Gaunt's authoritative voice marks her self-creating narrative control, the suppression of Elizabeth Tilton's legal voice indicates her complete exclusion. Powerless to contradict or to explain the accusations against her, she could only listen mutely while Beecher, having seduced her with the lure of a pure and spiritual love, unhesitatingly grounded his defense on insinuations that she was both oversexed and mentally unbalanced. It is really no surprise then that, as noted at the beginning of this chapter, *The New York Times* concluded that Elizabeth should be "dismissed to the general contempt of mankind" (34). If this seems a rather extreme example of blaming the victim, it should remind us that the project of suppressing Elizabeth Tilton's voice began long before the litigation was initiated and far from the Brooklyn courtroom in which it was played out. While the legal order excluded her testimony from the trial, a decision permitting her to speak would not have been likely to produce any truly authentic self-expression. Elizabeth Tilton's correspondence and her out-of-court statements are a stunning record of inconsistency, registering throughout an urgent desire to be and to say what the men in her life wanted to have and to hear. Indeed, her various confessions and retractions must ultimately be read as the ventriloquized statements of whichever men happened to be dictating at the time. Beecher and Tilton recognized this, and each eagerly accused the other of dictating Elizabeth's written words while defending as spontaneous and sincere any statements that supported his own position.

These two forms of silencing are of course connected. A legal cause of action that structurally refuses to recognize women as speaking subjects is but a particularly dramatic instance of a more generalized devaluation of women's voices within the surrounding culture. Criminal conversation litigation, like Victorian culture in general, anxiously attempted to control the circumstances under which women could speak and, directly or indirectly, the content of their speech.[28]

Elizabeth Tilton's attempt to intervene in the Beecher-Tilton trial can also be read as a gesture toward Kate Gaunt, in which she "became" Kate by trying to reenact Kate's victory-winning forensic self-assertion. The statement Elizabeth Tilton was prevented from reading in court was printed in the published transcript of the trial. In it she declared "solemnly before you, without fear of man and by faith in God, that I am innocent of the crimes charged against me. I would like to tell my *whole* sad story *truthfully*—to acknowledge the frequent falsehoods wrung from me by compulsion—though at the same time unwilling to reveal the secrets of my married life, which only the vital importance of my position makes necessary" (3:355, emphasis in original). Three years later, in 1878, Elizabeth Tilton reversed herself yet again, publishing an unequivocal admission of the affair (Shaplen 266; Waller 145). By then, however, few were interested. Separated from her husband and publicly vilified, Elizabeth Tilton was, in Victorian terms, "ruined"; she lived out the remainder of her life in lonely isolation.

But before we consign her to silence and submission or reduce her to a mere pitiable victim, let us return briefly to Elizabeth Tilton's letter. If it constructs her as a sentimental heroine, it also gives her access to the particular brand of spiritual power such heroines characteristically achieve, an assertive mastery of self within the constraints of predetermined roles.[29] The letter is not, entirely, a register of unremitting submission. Along with her admissions of sin and petitions for pardon, Elizabeth included the uncharacteristically independent comment that Theodore's "opinions are not restful or congenial to my soul." And, after asserting her own readiness to renew her marriage vows, she rather haughtily challenges her husband's promises of future chastity by observing: "I know not that you are yet able, or ever will be, to say this to *me*."[30] Finally, her assurance of unending devotion is apparently to become available only "when you yearn towards me with any true feeling." Surely some of Catherine Gaunt's proud sense of superiority to her weak-willed and adulterous husband has crept into Elizabeth Tilton's verbal self-representation. And while these glimmers of self-assertion may be examples only of her imitative receptivity to the nearest strong personality, the "ministry" of a character of fiction may be more salutary than the dictation of a self-interested husband or lover. Reading *Griffith Gaunt* she became, at least for a time, a headstrong, articulate, judgmental heroine. If Elizabeth Tilton could not receive a permanent infusion of Kate Gaunt's assertive personality by reading, as Kate receives a permanently effective transfusion of her husband's submissive blood, still she could keep reading even in the isolation of her post-trial life, and one hopes she did.

As a final point, I want to acknowledge that this analysis may be read as merely the latest in a long line of textualizations of Elizabeth Tilton. The real woman who lived through these events is, of course, as elusive and unknowable as ever. Once again, she has been subjected to analysis, her intimate relationships made the stuff of public discourse, the ambiguities of her life (or more accurately, of the texts that "evidence" her life) used to produce conclusions that she could neither influence nor control. Yet if Elizabeth Tilton's posthumous reputation can thus be actively reformulated, a twentieth-century revival of interest in the Beecher-Tilton case can no longer affect a living woman's life, feelings, or thoughts. This chapter has tried to affirm Elizabeth Tilton's devalued voice; while such investigations are clearly necessary to the work of feminist historians and cultural critics, it is also important to recognize that they cannot be carried out without, to some extent, "fictionalizing" their subjects.

PART III

Female-Plaintiff Criminal Conversation Cases: Rewriting the Law's Story of Marriage

PROLOGUE

Revision Through Four Cases

Wales v. Miner, 1883

In October 1881, plaintiff Miner sued defendant Wales for the seduction of Miner's former wife, Eglantine. Miner alleged that Wales "wrongfully and wickedly persuaded, seduced, debauched and carnally knew the said Eglantine Miner . . . that thereby her affections for the plaintiff were then and there alienated and destroyed," and that he had been "wholly deprived of the comfort, fellowship, society, aid and assistance" of his wife. Wales had been a lodger in the Miners' home. Evidence was presented at the trial that an intimacy developed between Wales and Eglantine Miner, "that she had been seduced by appellant, and that they were guilty of continuous adultery on various occasions, from the year 1873 until Christmas, in 1879." When her husband objected persistently to the relationship, she left him. After keeping house for Wales for some time, in 1881 Mrs. Miner divorced her husband and married Wales. The jury returned a verdict for the plaintiff of $1,000.

On appeal, the Supreme Court of Indiana upheld the verdict and the sufficiency of the evidence. To the defendant's claim that damages were excessive "because appellant may have been seduced by the wife, and not the wife by appellant," the court held that "as against the rights of the husband, the wife is incapable of consenting to her seduction." The court noted that the plaintiff had been married more than twenty years when his wife met Wales. "And when we take into consideration" the court continued, "that appellee, in his advanced years, has been deprived of the society, affections and assistance of his wife, his name dishonored and his family disgraced, his mental anguish, pain and vexation, his peaceful home broken up and all his marital relations overthrown by the destroyer of his wife's virtue, we think that a very low estimate or limit should not be placed upon the amount of damages that should be awarded by a jury in such a case" (*Wales v. Miner*, 89 Ind. 118 [1883]).

Kroessin v. Keller, 1895

In 1895, Mary Kroessin sued Wilhelmina Keller for criminal conversation, "the right to recover being based solely on alleged adulterous acts between plaintiff's husband and the defendant." Asked on appeal to determine whether a woman could bring a criminal conversation case against another woman, the Supreme Court of Minnesota disallowed the action. The court held that while at common law a cuckolded husband could prove that he was damaged simply by showing adulterous intercourse because of "the disgrace which attached to the plaintiff as the husband of the unfaithful wife . . . no such disgrace has ever rested upon the wife" of an unfaithful husband. Furthermore, while "a wife's infidelity might not only impose on her husband the support of children not his own, but still worse, cast discredit upon the legitimacy of those really begotten by him," no parallel dangers followed from a husband's adultery. Therefore, the husband's adultery caused no legally redressable damage to the wife.

At common law, the court noted, "the man was always conclusively presumed to be the guilty party. In the eye of the law, the female could not even give her consent to the adulterous acts, and, as a result, it was no defense in this form of action that the defendant had been enticed into criminal conversation through the acts and practices of the woman." With these principles in mind, it was clear to the court that the "grounds or elements constituting this action . . . cannot possibly exist or be involved in a similar action brought by a wife. And what has been said about the unavailability of the defense that the defendant was himself the victim and not the seducer, is suggestive of what the courts might have to hold to be the rule of pleading, and what they might have to inquire into, upon the trial of an action of this kind. Would it be held . . . that it was no defense for the female sued to allege and prove that she was the party seduced, and that the greater wrong and injury had been inflicted upon her, not upon the plaintiff wife?" Rejecting such actions as "better calculated to inflict pain upon innocent members of the families of the parties than to secure redress to the persons injured," the court refused to furnish wives "with the means of inflicting untold misery upon others, with little hope of redress for themselves." While it continued to permit husbands to bring criminal conversation actions against their wives' male lovers, the court refused to grant wives the same rights against their husbands' female lovers (*Kroessin v. Keller*, 60 Minn. 372, 62 N.W. 438 [1895]).

Foot v. Card, 1889

In 1888 Laura Foot sued Maria Card, alleging that in 1872 she was "living happily with, and in the enjoyment of the conjugal affection and society of, her husband Enos Foot" when Card, "by her arts, blandishments and persuasion, induced the said Enos Foot to begin, and from thence to continue an adulterous intercourse with her; and that she thereby alienated from the plaintiff his conjugal affection, induced him to deny to her his conjugal society, and persuaded him to abandon her." Defendant objected to the complaint on various grounds, but primarily that a wife could not bring a criminal conversation case against another woman because such a remedy was not available to wives at common law and was not founded in any authorizing statute. The case went up on appeal to test the sufficiency of the pleadings to state a cognizable case.

While it recognized the absence of applicable statute or precedent, the Supreme Court of Connecticut nevertheless permitted the case to go forward. Declaring that the right to conjugal affection was "a valuable property" that husbands had been able to vindicate in court "from time immemorial," the court held that "whatever inequalities may result from the marriage contract, husband and wife are equal in one respect, namely, each owes to the other the fullest possible measure of conjugal affection and society—the husband to the wife all that the wife owes to him. Upon principle, this right in the wife is equally valuable to her, as property, as is that of the husband to him. Her right being the same as his in kind, degree and value, there would seem to be no valid reason why the law should deny to her the redress which it affords to him." Since "by universal consent it is the essence of every marriage contract that the parties thereto shall, in regard to this particular matter of conjugal society and affection stand upon an equality, we are unable to find any support for the denial in this reason and the right, the injury and the consequent damage being admitted . . . the law will furnish a mode for obtaining adequate redress for every wrong," whether or not there is a statutory authority for doing so (*Foot v. Card*, 58 Conn. 1 [1889]).

Hunt v. Hunt, 1981

In 1981, Bonnie Hunt sued Kay Hunt for alienation of affections and criminal conversation, alleging damages from the defendant's interference in her marriage and carnal intercourse with plaintiff's now ex-husband. A jury awarded Bonnie damages totaling $50,000. Kay appealed, urging the appellate court to judicially abolish both torts. The Supreme Court of South Dakota did so. While it noted that "with the passage of time" wives had been permitted to bring such suits against other women in most states, the court found repugnant the idea that either spouse had a legally enforceable property interest in the other spouse's continued attention and affection. "We believe alienation of affections and criminal conversation, as viable legal remedies, are outmoded archaic holdovers from an era when wives were considered the chattel of their spouses rather than distinct legal entities. Wives are not property. Neither are husbands. The love and affection of a human being who is devoted to another human being is not susceptible to theft. There are simply too many intangibles which defy the concept that love is property." In outlawing the torts, the court also noted that the South Dakota state legislature had abolished adultery as a crime, "thus decriminalizing the very behavior upon which an action in criminal conversation rests" (*Hunt v. Hunt*, 309 N.W. 2d 818, 821 [1981]).

CHAPTER 5

Rethinking the Law's Story of Marriage: The Bonds of Sentiment

Appellate Parables and the Law's Skeletal Stories

As the cases summarized in the prologue suggest, late-nineteenth-century American appellate courts were presented for the first time with criminal conversation and alienation of affections suits brought by women against other women. Could a woman be a criminal conversation plaintiff? Was there a way to reconcile the gendered assumptions about marriage and sexuality that structured the law's paradigmatic criminal conversation story with the law's new requirement that married women be recognized as independent speaking subjects? I will argue in chapters 5 and 6 that instead of the law simply self-destructing (which, as we will see, was certainly possible), its exterior stability was maintained for quite a long period by refashioning the tort's implicit logic. The law's two fundamental factual requirements—that the plaintiff prove marriage to the adulterer and prove adultery between the plaintiff's spouse and the defendant—remained in place. In this way, "the law" of criminal conversation can be said to have survived unchanged from its late seventeenth-century formulation. What did change was the operative definition of marital rights and responsibilities, the marriage story that fleshed out and gave meaning to what I call the law's "skeletal story" of criminal conversation. I argue that appellate courts changed the substantive meaning of marital rights and obligations by giving each spouse an enforceable property right to the love and affection of the other, and that this right was defined by incorporating a sentimental discourse developed in the context of literary fiction. At bottom, my claim is that literary elements can play a key role in producing changes in the law.

Chapter 6 argues that the success of female-plaintiff cases contributed over time to the virtual demise of the tort. The nineteenth-century female-plaintiff cases at first cast the sexually active male spouse as the passive and voiceless victim of a female seducer's sexual aggression. Uncomfortable with this application of the classic criminal conversation script, courts changed or rewrote it. As a new marriage story emerged that rejected mutual affective entitlements, replacing them with a relationship that preserved each partner's independence and autonomy, the narrative logic of the tort was stretched past its breaking point. Most states have now outlawed it.[1] Yet while only about a dozen states now permit criminal conversation and alienation of affection suits, in 1997 there was a surprising resurgence in cases in those states, opening the possibility that the torts will have new life.

The key to the legal changes examined here is the inherent narrativity of appellate discourse. Through subtle shifts in the cache of literary fictions on which they draw, appeals courts can preserve "the law" as it stands while refashioning it to be compatible with the changed attitudes and assumptions of contemporary culture. Chapter 2 examined the way that legal fictions structured early criminal conversation pleadings. I noted there that, as Sir Henry Maine describes them, legal fictions function as concealment mechanisms, whereby "a rule of law has undergone alteration, its letter remaining unchanged, its operation being modified" (25). Legal fictions are obvious counterfactual assertions that the law treats as though they were true; everyone knows of their existence and purpose, though not all may approve. Though similarly aimed at preserving the appearance of legal continuity, the shifts in genre inflection I analyze here are much subtler, often, indeed, barely visible. I do not claim, for instance, that the appeals court judges who wrote the decisions considered here were self-conscious in their use of sentimental tropes and characters to define the legal parameters of spousal rights and obligations. As discursive enterprises, legal and literary writing necessarily share the resources of language, including plot, story, imagery, and genre. Packed with complex cultural freight, these elements can supply subtle inflections, enough to change the dress, manner, and meaning of the character fleshed out upon an unvarying skeleton, whether or not the author can name all of the tools he or she has used.

Since its invention in the late seventeenth century, criminal conversation litigation had been an exclusively male and male-voiced domain, the civil tort action a cuckolded husband brought against his wife's lover. As discussed in chapter 4, though the outcome of the case could effectively ruin her future life, the erring wife was neither plaintiff, defendant, nor witness; no legal channel existed through which she could voice her version of events.[2] And bringing any claims of her own against female partners of her husband's infidelity was both legally and morally unthinkable. The husband's right of action derived from his marital entitlement to the exclusive use of his wife's body and to her domestic services. These were nonreciprocal property rights accruing to him from the marriage contract. No parallel entitlement existed in the wife. A philandering husband might cause his wife untold humiliation, grief, and economic hardship, but his adulteries inflicted no injury that a court of law was obligated to recognize or compensate.[3] Even if the law had recognized an injury, wives would still have had no effective legal remedy because the doctrine of marital coverture, which merged the legal existence of the wife into that of her husband, precluded married women suing in their own names. If a wife was injured through the negligence or intent of another, a case for damages against that person had to be brought on her behalf by her husband; any damages awarded automatically became his property. This result would have surely undermined the viability of a claim based on the husband's sexual misbehavior, since it would have permitted him to profit financially from a serious injury to his wife that he participated in inflicting.[4] In addition, the wife's legal disability was seconded by a powerful cultural ethos that considered female adultery a crime akin to treason yet dismissed male sexual infidelity as trivial misbehavior that virtuous wives would do well to ignore. As many historians have documented, the ideal woman was modest, private, and domestic; she would never venture into a public arena like a courtroom as an aggressor, particularly when such an appearance was premised on her "failure" as a wife and her willingness to publicize—and profit from—the details of her husband's sexual activities.[5]

Yet when the Married Women's Property Acts gave nineteenth-century American women the power to sue and be sued, to conduct business in their own names, and to keep their own property (including damage awards), married women flocked to become the authors of a uniquely American legal story, the female-plaintiff criminal conversation case.[6] In state after state, unhappy wives brought suits against other women who, they alleged, had "debauched and criminally known" their husbands, causing them grief and humiliation and causing their husbands to neglect home and family. Lawyers for the female defendants (another new class of litigants) moved to dismiss the actions, arguing that women could not properly bring criminal conversation cases. Some trial courts agreed and dismissed the suits. Others, relying on both statutory changes and cultural progress in the status of women, permitted the cases to go to trial, often producing substantial damage awards. Either way, the losing party could raise the female-plaintiff issue on appeal, compelling state appellate courts to confront the full range of legal questions involved.

Surprisingly, this unique category of female-plaintiff adultery cases has received no modern critical attention.[7] Yet it provides an extraordinary window on the convergence of law, gender, and culture in late nineteenth-century America. The textual base for this chapter and the next is a group of over one hundred appellate court opinions, primarily from the years 1870–1910 (see table of adultery cases). With few exceptions, they are state rather than federal court decisions; like all torts, civil adultery cases are governed by state law. While state courts often rely on the persuasive logic of out-of-state precedents, they are not bound by them. Moreover, each state court must work within its own previous precedents and interpret the text of its own applicable statutes.[8] The decisions I discuss are therefore frequently inconsistent in results and exploratory in tone. To achieve a broad basis for comparison, I have examined cases with male and with female plaintiffs, and suits both for criminal conversation and for the related tort of alienation of affections. Alienation of affections, an American hybrid first recognized in New York in 1866, is a claim brought against anyone who deprives the plaintiff of the "love, society, companionship and comfort" of his spouse. While a count for alienation of affections is often joined to one for criminal conversation, as in *Tilton v. Beecher*, the wrong alleged need not be sexual. The "gist of the tort is an interference with the wife's mental attitude toward her husband, and the conjugal kindness of the marital relation"; actions may thus be brought against relatives and others and, as Prosser notes, "the meddling mother-in-law is more frequently a defendant than the wicked lover" (920–21). Because both torts represent forms of interference with the marital relation and with marital rights, they are often lumped together, and appellate courts rely on precedents from either, virtually indistinguishably, to delineate the exact parameters of legally enforceable spousal rights and duties. Prosser asserts that "there is no good reason for distinguishing them," and with clarification where necessary, the discussion below draws on both kinds of cases.

Earlier chapters discussed the production of narratives at the trial level. The present chapters shift away from the adversarial, fact-centered, many-voiced trial narrative to the single-voiced law-making text of the appellate court opinion. When lawyers speak of "the law" of criminal conversation—or for that matter, of libel, robbery, or real estate—they are usually referring to legal principles set out discursively in the text of appellate court opinions rather than to legislatively enacted statutes.[9] This is especially true in areas such as tort law, which derive from common law and which even today are not primarily statute-dependent.

Trial judges and juries make decisions about disputed facts; appeals court judges write decisions that set out, explain, and apply relevant law.[10] They decide, for example, not whether the defendant raped the victim but what the general legal rule governing the admission of a rape victim's sexual history into evidence should be, and whether in light of that rule the trial judge erred in permitting the jury to hear about the victim's past. As recent critics have shown, the boundary between law and fact is a great deal more blurred than distinct, and the influence of the case's particular facts on the appellate outcome is often significant.[11] Yet, notwithstanding what Kim Lane Scheppele has called the "mutually constitutive" relationship between law and fact, trial and appellate discourses differ significantly in the directional axes of their relevant narratives. Reversing the drive of trial narratives, appellate court decisions treat the specifics of a case as a mere framework for announcing the general principles of law that cases stand for.

While an appellate opinion obviously has consequences for the individuals who brought and defended the case, its significance lies in the paradigmatic story it articulates: wives as well as husbands are entitled to the comforts of marital affection, so wives whose situation is similar to that of the wife in this case can bring actions against women who cause the loss of their husbands' affection.[12] What is important in the appellate narrative is not the situation's uniqueness but its replicability. The point is to delineate clearly a prototypical situation and the rules that govern it, so that real people—lawyers in the first instance, but ultimately any person within the jurisdiction—can assess themselves in relation to that situation and conform their own behavior to the legal rules the narrative presents. If trial-level narratives are instrumental because they exist to elicit a specific verdict response from the trier of fact, appellate court narratives are equally instrumental because they are the means by which the law establishes its governance (often without our awareness that it has done so) over virtually every area of our private and commercial lives. This does not mean that the rules set out in an appellate opinion are self-evident or unambiguous once explained; indeed, the fact that the ruling is expressed through language and narrative means that ambiguity and interpretability can never be eliminated.[13] Despite the court's best efforts to frame its holding as narrowly and precisely as possible, subsequent cases will necessarily present different constellations of facts, requiring a continuing process of interpretation to determine the law's meaning and applicability. And over time, as the membership of a particular court or the political climate changes, new cases will write new rules. While they stand, however, the power of appellate court narratives lies in their ability to "make law" by articulating legal principles directly and through broadly applicable examples.

As a consequence, appellate court narratives tend to have the feel of allegory or, more precisely, of parable. Generic plots and representative stock characters appear in stories that range from brief abstract exempla to lengthy and moving dramas. The characters who appear in such stories are not unique individuals; rather, they stand for a class of people similarly defined. Like the prodigal son or the faithless steward, their names identify categorical roles and attributes rather than unique familial connections.[14] In the criminal conversation cases read here such characters include "the adulterous husband," or simply "the wife"; in another kind of case the characters might include "the police officer," "the rape victim," "the testator," and so forth. The court erases individuals' names and refers to them by function or situation because, as with the man who fell among thieves, that situation is useful to the story only for its nonuniqueness, for the likelihood that it will happen again and again.[15] In *Bennett v. Bennett*, for instance, a New York appellate court in 1889 affirmed a jury verdict for Elvira J. Bennett by saying:

> The actual injury to the wife from the loss of *consortium*, which is the basis of the action, is the same as the actual injury to the husband from that cause. His right to the conjugal society of his wife is no greater than her right to the conjugal society of her husband. Marriage gives to each the same rights in that regard. Each is entitled to the comfort, companionship and affection of the other. The rights of the one and the obligations of the other spring from the marriage contract, are mutual in character and attach to the husband as husband and to the wife as wife. Any interference with these rights, whether of the husband or of the wife, is a violation not only of a natural right, but also of a legal right arising out of the marriage relation. It is a wrongful interference with that which the law both confers and protects. 116 N.Y. 584, 590 (1889)

In this spare narrative, barely more than a statement of abstract principles, the court follows typical appellate practice by instantiating its definition of marital rights and obligations through a brief narrative about "the wife" and "the husband." Neither is an individual. Their identities are created at the moment of marital contract; marital law constructs them simultaneously by giving them precisely the same functional attributes, here defined in terms of entitlements and responsibilities. The third character is the law itself, which has created husband and wife from the dust and ribs of its power. While the "interference" with the marriage remains so abstract that no personified subject is grammatically represented to accomplish it, the law that has actively "conferred" life on marital spouses also powerfully "protects" its creation. M. H. Abrams defines a parable as "a short narrative presented so as to stress the implicit but detailed analogy between its component parts and a thesis or lesson that the narrator is trying to bring home to us" (6). Here, the narrative's minimal plot of an "interference" that destroys the mutual "comfort, companionship, and affection" of the marriage partners and the law's responsive willingness to "protect" what has been meddled with presents a clear lesson for readers about both the nature of each partner's rights and obligations and the role of the law in making and preserving them.

While *Bennett*, like many appellate decisions, began with a very brief précis of the facts of the case, it is often impossible to determine from a decision the parties' first names or the exact events giving rise to the lawsuit. Yet if a court can do without facts, it cannot do without narrative. Even when a court wants, as the *Bennett* court apparently did, to present a purely analytical statement of legal principles, it cannot avoid writing a text with recognizably literary elements. However restrained and abstract its narrative voice, minimal gestures toward character and plot appear. At the other end of the spectrum are decisions that go out of their way to exploit the dramatic impact of familiar, emotionally inflected story forms. When a court wants to use a vivid, affecting illustration to render its conclusions emotionally persuasive it may turn not to the facts of the case but to a sentimental melodrama of its own construction. One prime example is *Duffies v. Duffies*, 76 Wis. 374 (1890), an alienation of affections case in which the Supreme Court of Wisconsin, while upholding a husband's well-established right to sue anyone for the loss of his wife's society, refused to find a parallel right in the wife. After a dry if detailed examination of several centuries of English common law, the opinion suddenly springs to narrative life as it delineates the "unchangeable conditions" of husband and wife:

> The wife is more domestic, and is supposed to have the personal care of the household, and her duties in the domestic economy require her to be more

> constantly at home, where the husband may nearly always expect to find her and enjoy her society. She is purer and better by nature than her husband, and more governed by a sense of duty and right, and she seldom violates her marriage obligations, or abandons her home or denies her husband the comforts and advantages of her society by any inducement or influence of others, without just cause. Actions against others for enticing her away from home and her husband's society are not frequent. She is protected from such wrong, not only by her integrity of character, but by greater love for her family and the comforts and genial influences of home life. (383)

Having established the domestic universe of "the wife," the court constructs a contrasting commercial universe in which "the husband" operates:

> With the husband the case is different. . . . The husband is charged with the duty of providing for, maintaining, and protecting his wife and family. . . . The exigencies of even his legitimate business may keep him away from her and his home for months or years. He is exposed to the temptations, enticements and allurements of the world, which easily withdraw him from her society, or cause him to desert or abandon her. Others may entice him to do many things, for business or pleasure, which may deprive his wife of his society. The wife had reason to expect all these things when she entered the marriage relation, and her right to his society had all these conditions, and is not the same in "degree and value" as his right to hers. (383)

Perhaps the most striking aspect of the court's elaborate storytelling here is how far it has ranged from the facts of the case. Mrs. Duffies actually sued her mother-in-law, not someone who "enticed" her husband away while he was on a business trip.[16] Yet in the course of an eleven-page opinion, her claim is mentioned only in the opening paragraph's recital of the allegation that the elder Mrs. Duffies had caused her son to "refuse further to live and cohabit with the plaintiff and to support and maintain her and to support and maintain their child." On appeal, of course, the question was not what happened but whether the law permits a wife to bring a suit for loss of consortium against anyone who causes her husband to abandon his home. To ground its holding, the court erases the intrafamily struggle between the two Mrs. Duffies and replaces it with a powerfully imagined parable about conflict between home and workplace, wife and husband, shared "society" and commercial freedom, a conflict that the husband must win if modern industrial society is to flourish.[17]

By telling a different story than the one Mrs. Duffies told in her legal complaint, the court shifts the frame of reference through which relevant legal rights are defined. The capacity of appellate court opinions to create new stories and then to use them as the basis for the opinion's legal holding is fully exploited here. The new story turns one kind of conflict into another kind. The new story's characters are not individuals but categories: "the husband" and "the wife." The cluster of generic attributes used to define this wife—purity, domesticity, sense of duty—efface the obvious diversity of actual wives. The nature of a husband's legal rights and obligations are then defined in relation to this stereotype, a stereotype drawn from familiar texts illustrating the ideology of separate spheres. In the new story, each spouse has her or his own sphere of operation—the wife confined in the home and the husband out in the commercial world—yet both spheres are defined as part of the marriage. The husband's activities outside the home fulfill his spousal responsibilities just as much as the wife's work in the kitchen fulfills hers.

By making the husband's duties as a financial provider his sole marital obligation and then linking their fulfillment to unlimited travel and alluring distractions "for business or pleasure," the court defines freedoms usually associated with bachelorhood as generated by the marriage contract itself. This permits the court to conclude not only that a husband may be entitled to remain away from home "for months or years," but that by doing so he will be meeting, not violating, his spousal obligations. Without precisely saying so, the court even suggests that sexual infidelity is such a foreseeable "temptation, enticement or allurement" to men who are away from home earning their incomes that it becomes a husbandly privilege. The law must not define the husband's marital obligations so as to require him to come home; to do so, the court concludes, would dangerously restrict commerce and would also produce "numberless" lawsuits foolishly tying up the courts (383). The wife's financial security depends on the husband's continued freedom to travel (including inevitable "temptation"), which depends on the wife's homebound silence. In this story overwork and adultery do not threaten marriage; aggressively litigating wives do. It comes as something of a jolt to remember that were these numberless suits brought, the defendants would not be the erring husbands but those who enticed them away and who appear in the story only as vague pronouns ("others") or impersonal abstractions ("exigency," "temptation," "allurement").

By deploying stereotypical characters and a story line that glorifies the necessity of commercial pursuits, the *Duffies* court is using literary elements to legitimate its legal conclusion that marital consortium imposes different obligations on men and women. The emotional impact of its story—both the praise of morally "superior" wives and the plight of hard-working traveling husbands—keeps the focus away from the actual female-plaintiff alienation of affections litigation against likely defendants. In writing its own story and using it to justify and define gendered legal rights, *Duffies* is merely an extreme version of the narrativity that, to a lesser or greater extent, characterizes all appellate opinions.

While the appeals court decision's instructive function tends to push it toward parable and the use of affecting narrative, the substantive legal requirements for whatever kind of case is being decided also contribute in important ways to the appellate opinion's narrative structure. For every cause of action, the law establishes specific factual elements the plaintiff must prove to win his case. Taken together, these facts produce an inner core—a skeletal narrative—that underlies every discursive framing of the case, whether in the initial complaint, an argument to the jury, or an appellate court's discussion of applicable law. In a common law robbery case, for instance, the prosecution had to prove not just an illegal taking of property by the defendant, but a show of force (that is, a threat of violence) and a taking "from the person." No motive was required (though if shown, it would of course increase the persuasiveness of the prosecution's case), but the victim's physical presence was a necessity. Robbery cannot be committed in an empty house. The story of a robbery is thus always fundamentally different from the story of a burglary, which, at common law, was breaking and entering the dwelling house of another at night with the intent to commit a felony therein.[18] The factual requirements of the law construct in one case a plot centered on a confrontation between two people: a fearful victim and an exploitive, perhaps assaultive robber; and in the other case a plot about the violation of domestic, private space. There will be as many story variations as there are cases, of course, and at least two opposing ones at each trial, but beneath the surface of each the same generic skeleton will be visible.

In a traditional case of criminal conversation, only two facts must be proven: the plaintiff's marriage to the woman he accuses of adultery, and the fact of sexual intercourse between that woman and the defendant.[19] Through all the tort's historical transformations, this minimal requirement has never changed, and it is in this sense that I argue the law has maintained an aura of continuity. Yet even these two facts inevitably produce a story. The criminal conversation story has, at a minimum, three pivotal characters, a temporal sequence of events, and a moral as well as legal calculus with which to assess them.

In one sense then, the law's two factual requirements produce the criminal conversation story in case after case, century after century, without significant change. But—and this is a very important but—the requirements themselves came into being within a complex system of cultural, historical, and ideological assumptions that are, like the turtles in the story, absolutely interconnected "all the way down."[20] When a new cause of action is invented, as criminal conversation was in the last decades of the seventeenth century, its legal/factual requirements inevitably depend on the web of assumptions about the legal and social world in force at the time. For the tort to continue as a viable legal cause of action, those assumptions must either remain in force or be replaced by others compatible with the law's skeletal requirements.

As it was originally developed, the bones of the criminal conversation skeleton were structured by a cluster of assumptions we can analyze in literary terms as contributing principles of causation, characterization, and plot resolution to each fully fleshed litigative story. First, the narrative is held together by two causal links that generate criminal conversation as a compensable tort: the assumption that a wife's adultery necessarily causes injury to her husband, and that the person responsible for that injury is the wife's lover, not the wife herself. For the causal chain between lover's seduction and husband's injury to be unbroken, the possibility that the wife either originates her own behavior or is the person primarily affected by it must be denied. Instead, the lover causes injury to the husband "through" the wife, her body functioning merely as his instrument.[21]

These causal assumptions depend in turn on gender-based assumptions about character. Prominent among these is the assumption (at once legal, cultural, and perhaps religious) that a wife is not fully responsible for her actions because she is by nature emotional, manipulable, and not a fully "rational" being. As a *feme couvert,* moreover, she is not properly the person who controls the sexual use of her body. In terms of characterization then, for the causal linkage necessary to the tort to function, the wife *must* be narratively situated as an object of property while the two men, in contrast, *must* be responsible for themselves and their actions. Moreover, they must be owners of property and wielders of the legal system, public speakers who can assert their rights and present their defenses.

Third, the tort of criminal conversation requires litigation for its denouement. Adultery may begin in the privacy of the bedroom, but "criminal conversation" ends in the glare of the courtroom. If we think in terms of Aristotle's requirement that all whole stories have a beginning, middle, and end,[22] a situation, conflict, and resolution, criminal conversation suggests a sequence in which the litigative verdict provides an ending or resolution to a story that began with marriage, continued through complicated problems of sexual infidelity, climaxed at the trial, and was resolved through the payment of damages to the injured husband. Criminal conversation stories transform intimate experiences of conflict and suffering into public, commercial discourse. The cultural meaning of the story must therefore take the role of legal process into account. The popularity of the litigative solution, especially in the eighteenth century, suggests a society willing to assess intimate and emotional injuries in financial terms, to image illicit sexuality and insults to male honor as reimbursable "costs." As Lawrence Stone declares in discussing the early history of the tort, "it is difficult to imagine clearer evidence of the beginning of a shift from an honour and shame society to a commercial society than this evolution of litigation as an acceptable alternative to previous standard modes of revenge for cuckoldry by physical assault or duel. After all, trading injured honour for monetary damages is a commercial transaction taking place in a legal market" (1990:238).[23]

In the nineteenth century in America, three aspects of American law affected the kinds of narratives produced in particular cases. The first is what I have been calling the law's "skeletal story" for each tort, the fundamental requirement that the facts of marriage and adultery be proved in each case. In the torts of criminal conversation and alienation of affections, these required elements were not established by local statute but through the decisional law made by appellate courts and the generally understood but not text-based set of legal principles known as the common law. Firmly set in place during the tort's early history in England, these rules were carried across the Atlantic unchanged, and can be found in all American cases.

The second influential aspect of law is the law of marital rights and obligations, what a husband or wife, by virtue of the marriage contract, is entitled to receive from or required to provide to a spouse. These rights are at issue in civil adultery litigation, of course, but they also arise in other kinds of cases that concern marriage, such as a suit for separate support.

Marital rights and obligations can be defined in general terms, that is, without necessary reference to a specific kind of lawsuit. On their own, such rights are not necessarily enforceable in a court. Even if a husband has a legal right to exclusive sexual intercourse with his wife or to her affection and attention, he cannot ask a court to order her to provide these things; rather, he must turn to an existing cause of action such as a suit for divorce (against his wife) or criminal conversation (against her lover), and he must ask for the kind of legal remedy appropriate to that cause of action. Because marital rights and obligations can be understood as having a legal existence separate from the substantive facts that must be proved in a particular cause of action, the nature of those rights can be reformulated without necessarily affecting the ongoing viability of the tort. This is a key point. In the cases I consider below, the site of greatest rhetorical flexibility was in the definition of marital rights and responsibilities. Courts were able to leave in place the tort's basic legal requirements so that the tort itself did not appear to be undergoing a radical redefinition, while rewriting the underlying story of marriage by reformulating the nature of each spouse's rights and responsibilities.

The third relevant aspect of the law is the Married Women's Property Acts, state statutes that in varying formulations released married women from the disabilities of coverture. Beginning in Mississippi in 1839 and continuing on a state-by-state basis through the end of the century, the acts gradually gave married women increased legal rights, framed to meet particular perceived problems.[24] Their motivations were largely economic. Up to this point, as Lawrence Friedman and others have stressed, "most litigation over married women's property was not litigation between spouses or within the family at all . . . Typical cases . . . were about the family's external relations, not its internal life" (211). By the middle of the nineteenth century, statutory clarification was needed so that, for instance, a wife who ran a rooming house while her husband panned for gold in California could make a binding contract to buy coal or bring an action against a wagon driver who ran into her and injured her.[25] The statutes "concerned that most basic of institutions, the family, and seemed to work radical change; yet the debates were only modest and fitful. Newspapers made almost no mention of the laws. Little agitation preceded them; great silence followed them" (Friedman 211). Though feminists had certainly worked for their passage, the acts won legislative approval by garnering the support of conservative businessmen who wanted to remove obstacles to continued commercial growth. Some scholars have suggested that in significant ways the gains from the acts were illusory; indeed, by seeming to guarantee equality and change while acting primarily to retain patriarchal economic and social power structures, the acts may have delayed more fundamental substantive progress for women (see Basch 1982 and Warbasse).

Yet as Martha Minow has argued, "legal rules and practices daily influence how people act by affecting the expectations they hold and the risks they take" (822).[26] However limited their intent, the statutes were framed rhetorically in terms of equality—if not between men and women, at least between married and unmarried women. While legislators surely did not have adultery litigation in mind when they passed the acts, women and their lawyers recognized in the statutes the potential to expand women's legal remedies. Because the statutes typically spoke only in the most general terms about rights and powers, their applicability to a particular kind of lawsuit could only be determined by bringing a test case. The Ohio statute at issue in *Westlake v. Westlake*, 34 Ohio St. 621 (1878), for instance, provided that "All personal property, including rights in action, belonging to any woman at her marriage or which may have come to her during coverture . . . or have grown out of a violation of any of her personal rights, shall . . . remain her separate property, and under her sole control" (632). It was left to the appellate court to decide, as the *Westlake* court did, that a wife's right to marital consortium is a "personal right," and that a right of action growing out of a violation of that right is a wife's "separate property," on which she has a statutory right to sue "against one who wrongfully induces her husband to abandon or send her away" (632, and see *Parker v. Newman*, *Eliason v. Draper* [relevant statute interpreted to permit cases]).

If women were to be permitted to bring civil adultery cases against other women, a new set of story-making assumptions would have to be found that would recognize wives as speaking subjects with enforceable marital rights, yet that would be somehow compatible with the law's unchanging skeletal requirements for the tort of criminal conversation.

The Anguish of a Sensitive Wife

When the Married Women's Property Acts made it possible for nineteenth-century American wives to bring legal actions previously restricted to men, appellate courts found themselves for the first time considering whether women could bring criminal conversation and alienation of affections suits against other women. As the criminal conversation case was traditionally constructed, the complaint charged that the lover had injured the husband's property interest in his wife. If the traditional paradigm remained in effect, a successful gender-reversed case would have to be premised on some legally enforceable property interest that a wife had in her husband, some right that was violated by his sexual infidelity. Without such a right, there could be no injury; without an injury, no lawsuit. But were the wife's rights the same as the husband's? Once freed from the disabilities of coverture, could she simply pick up the male-voiced criminal conversation script and apply its language of dishonor and defilement to the experience of male infidelity?

To permit the cases without changing the torts' skeletal legal requirements, courts changed the parameters of the law of marital rights and obligations—the law's story of marriage. From its origin as an aristocratic narrative about property damage and the injury to male honor, criminal conversation became in the nineteenth century a middle-class, sentimental story about the destruction of marital intimacy. This was achieved in some courts through explicit breaks with past precedent, in others through a more subtle redefinition of the "traditional" discourse of marital rights, and in still others by expanding women's available legal remedies toward the more recent tort of alienation of affections, which did not require proof of sexual infidelity. Whichever route the court chose, its description of marital rights and obligations—in particular its instantiation of the all-purpose term "marital consortium"—referred less and less to male sexual property rights and more and more to a mutual spousal obligation to provide domestic attention and affection.

A closer look at the "traditional" formulation helps explain the problem faced by the courts. In *Tinker v. Colwell*, 193 U.S. 473 (1904), the one major case in which the U.S. Supreme Court dealt with criminal conversation, the long-established principles of the male-plaintiff criminal conversation case are eloquently delineated.[27] "The cause of action by the husband," declared the court, "is based upon the idea that the act of the defendant is a violation of the marital rights of the husband in the person of his wife, to the exclusion of all others, and so the act of the defendant is an injury to the person and also to the property rights of the husband" (485). The court agreed with cases holding that "the essential injury to the husband consists in the defilement of the marriage bed, in the invasion of his exclusive right to marital intercourse with his wife and to beget his own children. This is a right of the highest kind, upon the thorough maintenance of which the whole social order rests" (484). The husband is entitled to damages "for his wounded feelings and honor, the defilement of the marriage bed, and for the doubt thrown upon the legitimacy of his children" (481). Criminal conversation is regarded as an "actual trespass upon the marital rights of the husband, although the consequent injury is really to the husband on account of the corruption of the body and mind of the wife, and it is in this view . . . that the consent of the wife makes no difference; that she is incapable of giving a consent to an injury to the husband" (483).

Tinker provides a powerful articulation of the connections among male sexual "honor," property rights, and the construction of a social order that requires the erasure of women's subjective capacity for consent. The inequality of husband and wife, his entitlement to control the sexual use of her body, is "a right of the highest kind" so important to the continued stability of "the whole social order" that the punitive resources of the legal system are to be marshaled for its "thorough maintenance." Because the husband's superior position is socially necessary, granting wives the same property-based powers over the sexual use of their husbands' bodies would upset not only the established hierarchy within marriage, but the web of hierarchical relations that ensures social stability. Here it is worth noting that Blackstone's discussion of criminal conversation in the *Commentaries* occurs in the section that deals with a group of asymmetrical "familial" relations: husband and wife, parent and child, master and servant, and guardian and ward (3:8:139–43). Adultery, defined as "criminal conversation with a man's wife," can be remedied, Blackstone notes, by an action of trespass "wherein the damages recovered are usually very large and exemplary." In an oft-quoted comment at the section's end, Blackstone declares:

> We may observe that in these relative injuries, notice is only taken of the wrong done to the superior of the parties related . . . while the loss of the inferior by such injuries is totally unregarded. One reason for which may be this: that the inferior hath no kind of property in the company, care and assistance of the superior, as the superior is held to have in those of the inferior; and therefore the inferior can suffer no injury. . . . The wife cannot recover damages for beating her husband, for she hath no separate interest in anything during her coverture. (3:143)

Without a "kind of property" in her husband's sexual behavior, a wife "can suffer no injury" from his infidelity; but so long as the law of coverture and the cultural concept of marriage make her "the inferior," no such property right can possibly exist. The critical, position-defining role played by the wife's reproductive function, moreover, underscores the nonreversibility of the spouses' relative positions. "Thorough maintenance" of the husband's control (or, as we might call it, thorough policing of the wife's sexuality) is needed to ensure that "true" paternity will govern the inheritance of property.

So long as adultery was imaged solely in terms of property, inheritance, and reproduction, women's demands for reciprocal rights were easily rejected. This was the strategy adopted by the Supreme Judicial Court of Maine in *Doe v. Roe*, 82 Me. 503 (1890) and related cases. Limiting the scope of adultery's injury to possible stains on the legitimacy of children, the court was able to declare that a husband's adultery simply inflicted no injury. A wife's infidelity could force a man to support illegitimate children and cast suspicion on those who were really his, the court asserted, but "a husband's infidelity can inflict no consequences upon his wife. If she remain virtuous, no suspicion can attach to the legitimacy of her children" (504).[28] Keeping its rhetorical eyes firmly fixed on issues of inheritance and "legitimacy," the court's sleight of hand shifts the locus of inquiry from the husband's behavior to the wife's, until the key question raised by a charge of *male* adultery is whether or not the *wife* "remain virtuous." By making the avoidance of adverse "consequences" contingent on the wife's virtue alone, the court writes a marriage story in which the wife's sexual behavior is central, while the husband's occurs outside its narrative boundaries. As in *Tinker*, the wife's body is inextricably linked to other forms of property in which the husband has an interest, including his lineage, inheritance, and financial resources. Indeed, this web of interlocking threads situates the wife's body at the nexus of tangible and intangible property axes, so that the illicit "conversation" of her body with another man's inflicts a complex of connected injuries to her husband's property.

In sharp contrast, no web of legally consequential links is forged between his sexual misbehavior and its effects on her. So far as the story of their marriage is concerned, his adultery is irrelevant. Moreover, because it produces no "consequences" that affect the wife's legally enforceable interests, it cannot generate a criminal conversation story, cannot form the basis for a lawsuit. This is true not only because a husband's adultery could not produce illegitimate offspring (at least not within *his* marriage), but because, under coverture, the wife had few property rights that could be injured.

Paradoxically, this made the wife's sexuality enormously valuable to the marriage, while the husband's was essentially valueless. He could do what he wanted with his body because it neither represented nor guaranteed marital assets. Not part of the provision of what the wife was entitled to (mainly financial support) from the marriage, it could "play around" at will. The husband's sexual license was not impeded by such earlier doctrines as the medieval "marriage debt" (so dear to the Wife of Bath), which gave the wife a right to spousal intercourse and to the engendering of children, because the value of his body to the wife was presumably unaffected by his sexual fidelity.[29]

The situating of male sexual behavior "outside the story" is marked in the *Doe v. Roe* opinion by the court's rhetorical avoidance of it. The court's easy substitution of the wife for the husband as the target of moral evaluation suggests that while the sexual "virtue" of *every* woman—even those not accused—is always worth examining, a husband's sexual behavior is simply not to be discussed in moral terms. It is as if words like "virtue" and "suspicion" can cling only to female objects, while male misbehavior, invisible and "without consequences," evades even the rhetorical surface of the opinion. The general resistance to judging male infidelity shared by many courts was intensified by a parallel unwillingness to attribute to wives the sexual drive and pride of possession that underlie the concept of masculine proprietary sexuality. If courts were uncomfortable labeling male misbehavior a "defilement of the marriage bed," they found downright repugnant the prospect that wives might be accorded a right of sexual "ownership" in men's bodies, or that they might begin publicly to display the force of their sexual interest in their husbands.

What was needed was a way to tell a story of marriage that was "about" a new kind of property, that grounded the wife's right of action in something other than sexual possessiveness. The new story had to construct a link between the husband's sexual behavior and the wife's rights, situating his fidelity firmly within the story's narrative parameters and giving it value. At the risk of oversimplifying what actually occurred, we can say that the crucial characteristic of the new cases was their conceptualization of marriage in emotional terms.

The concept of companionate marriage is the first step toward an answer. By characterizing the ideal bond between spouses as founded primarily on love rather than property, the partnership notion of companionate marriage, which permeated discussions of marriage from the eighteenth century onward, exerted cultural pressures that gradually redefined the terms establishing the legal relations of spouses within marriage. In particular, this reinstantiation affected the legal concept of "marital consortium," the "bundle of rights" that a husband had in his wife.[30] From the founding of criminal conversation in the late seventeenth century, the injury inflicted by the wife's adultery had been verbally formulated in plaintiffs' complaints as a "loss of consortium." As originally construed, consortium tended on analysis to distill into an entitlement to sexual and domestic services. The emphasis on services was, at least in part, a jurisdiction-enabling allegation designed to categorize criminal conversation with other tort claims for interference with commercially beneficial relationships like those between master and servant.[31] The right to receive attention and affection had always been among those listed in the bundle, but it was typically a near-meaningless item in a long list of marital "services" that might include Blackstone's "company care and assistance" or, as in the 1620 case analyzed in chapter 2, "advice and help in domestic affairs."

One important reason that the marital "services" owed to a husband were described in terms of property and financially assessable services was that late seventeenth-century notions of individual autonomy and contractual rights were predominantly understood in terms of ownership rather than affect. In the work of social contract theorists like Locke and Hobbes, heart, soul, and emotional satisfaction were much less central to the construction of a successful individual legal subject than life, liberty, and property. In the *Second Treatise of Government*, for instance, Locke describes marriage as a "voluntary compact" that consists chiefly in "such a communion and right in one another's bodies as is necessary to its chief end, procreation; yet it draws with it mutual support and assistance, and a communion of interests too, as necessary not only to unite their care and affection, but also to their common off-spring, who have a right to be nourished, and maintained by them, till they are able to provide for themselves" (ch. 7 sec. 78). After discussing the union of various animals as designed to enable procreation and the rearing of offspring, he comments that human unions are made more lasting "that so their industry might be encouraged, and their interest better united, to make provision and lay up goods for their common issue, which uncertain mixture, or easy and frequent solutions of conjugal society would mightily disturb" (ch. 7 sec. 80). "Care and affection" are thus means to achieving the true goals of marriage: procreation, provision for and care of issue, and joint accumulation of property. While the spouses' rights "in one another's bodies" are apparently mutual, their extent is defined by the needs of procreation and so may well be ultimately asymmetrical, like the rights enumerated in *Doe* and *Tinker*. Individual emotional sustenance and affective completion through romantic love were not yet central to a theoretical scheme of marriage and citizenship.

Nineteenth-century courts searching for an acceptable way to find that a wife's rights were the same as her husband's soon discovered that they could accomplish much by emphasizing "consortium" and transforming it from an empty list component into a pivotal, legal entitlement to actually *receive* affection and attention. Instead of rattling off the elements of consortium as if they were parts of a single term, a New York Court in 1885 simply took the emotional term seriously, declaring that "the wife is entitled, as a matter of right, not only to the support and maintenance of the husband, but also to his love and affection" (*Warner v. Miller*, 17 Abb. 221, 223 [N.Y. 1885]). Whoever was responsible for destroying that love violated the wife's rights and was liable to suit for damages. To avoid the appearance of "making new law," the wife's right could even be declared to have been there all along, though perhaps invisible or unenforceable because of the disabilities of coverture. Thus, in the key case of *Foot v. Card*, 58 Ct. 1, 18 Atl. 1027 (1889), the Supreme Court of Connecticut declared:

> So far forth as the husband is concerned, from time immemorial the law has regarded his right to the conjugal affection and society of his wife as a valuable property, and has compelled the man who has injured it to make compensation. Whatever inequalities of right as to property may result from the marriage contract, husband and wife are equal in rights in one respect, namely, each owes to the other the fullest possible measure of conjugal affection and society,—the husband to the wife all that the wife owes to him. . . . Her right being the same as his in kind, degree and value, there would seem to be no valid reason why the law should deny to her the redress which it affords to him. Inasmuch as, by universal consent, it is of the essence of every marriage contract that the parties thereto shall, in regard to this particular matter of conjugal society and affection, stand upon an equality, we are unable to find any support for the denial in this reason. (1028)

Others echoed the Connecticut court's conclusions, though few had the temerity to declare them in force "by universal consent." Bigelow's treatise on torts, frequently quoted in these appellate opinions, declared: "the gist of the action, however, is not the loss of assistance, but the loss of the *con-*

sortium of the wife or husband, under which term is usually included the person's affection, society or aid" (153). The notion of an enforceable right to "conjugal society and affection" clearly reflects a shift of emphasis toward an ideal domesticity defined not by material relations but by mutual affective ties (see Stone 1979:217–53). Spousal rights were now grounded in process rather than property, as marriage became an ongoing, intimate interaction rather than a static relation of ownership. One consequence of this shift was that safeguarding assets and ensuring the legitimacy of issue necessarily became less crucial than maintaining a shared domestic atmosphere of trust and joint involvement, a "conjugal" realm of home, love, and family.

Yet the invocation of the term "companionate marriage" begins rather than ends our discussion. Though surely necessary to the conceptualization of the female-plaintiff criminal conversation suits, it falls far short of providing a sufficient answer. As Lawrence Stone has persuasively argued, companionate marriage has been a rising, even dominant ideal since the mid-eighteenth century, though we should note that some historians place its rise in the United States somewhat later, at least into the early nineteenth century.[32] Moreover, the concept of companionate marriage coexisted fairly comfortably with the doctrines of coverture that erased women's legal existence; it is, for instance, only peripherally associated with the passage of the Married Women's Property Acts. In short, the notion of marital unity based on love has not, from Milton's Eden onward, necessitated a conception of equal wifely rights.

I want to suggest that what was needed was not just companionate but sentimentalized marriage—a marriage story, developed through literary fiction, that privileged emotional ties over all others. My argument begins with Nancy Armstrong's persuasive claim in *Desire and Domestic Fiction* that fiction can be both the "document and agency of cultural history." Eighteenth- and nineteenth-century domestic fiction, she argues, while it "seemed to be concerned solely with matters of courtship and marriage in fact seized the authority to say what was female" through fictions that "contested a dominant political order which depended, among other things, on representing women as economic and political objects" (5, 15). Armstrong's thesis is that "the domestic novel antedated—was indeed necessarily antecedent to—the way of life it represented" (9). Novels created an enormously influential new ideal of womanhood, and consequently of individuality and marriage, based on ideally emotional subjectivity. For Armstrong, the literary plot of sexual exchange became the "safe" model through which "dangerous" political conflicts of class and ideology were discursively engaged.

Armstrong connects the rise of English domestic fiction to political and cultural change. I suggest that sentimental American domestic fiction, with its obvious and continuing links to English antecedents and contemporaries, supplied American appellate courts with an affectively based discourse about women, sexuality, and marriage. This new "marriage story," unavailable when the original criminal conversation narratives were written, was used to fill out the civil law of adultery so that, without changing the skeletal requirements for the tort, a new narrative body could be constructed. My argument identifies the relevant fiction as sentimental rather than "domestic" or "romantic," to emphasize the power of the sentimental synthesis in mid-nineteenth-century American culture—a power recently analyzed as pervasive in a variety of discourses.[33] My discussion of sentimentality in chapter 3 focused on its capacity to create a deep emotional bond between text and reader, and analyzed the ways that lawyers at the Beecher-Tilton trial used sentimental rhetoric as a forensic strategy to engage jurors' emotions. Here, my concern is not with sentimentality as a strategy for forging emotional relationships between narrative and audience, but with the cluster of values and personal characteristics consistently presented as positive or worthy in sentimental fiction. While both aspects of sentimentality concern emotion and ultimately implicate readers, my focus here is primarily on their typical perceived content rather than their interactive effect.

As a literary mode of organizing stories of marital experience, sentimentality contributes at least three shaping values not present in earlier marriage stories, even those based on companionate marriage. First, it locates the highest and most precious human attribute in each person's capacity to *feel* deeply and truly. From Stowe's admonition to her readers that they must begin their response to slavery by seeing that they "feel right" to the masculine and feminine models of "right feeling" typified by Southworth's heroic Ishmael or Cummins's gentle Gertie, sentimentality correlates personal value with the individual's ability to respond emotionally to the plights, needs, and experiences of others. Susan K. Harris has called the "privileging of sentiment, or feeling" one of the "two most prevalent culturally based codes in women's midcentury novels" (the other being a Christian value scheme), a firmly established set of assumptions that novelists and readers expected to share (1990:78–79). From the early work of Nina Baym, Ann Douglas, Jane Tompkins, and Philip Fisher to the more recent explorations of Shirley Samuels, Susan K. Harris, Joyce Warren, and Mary Lou Kete, critical disputes about the politics, degree of empowerment, conscious artistry, and relative feminism of nineteenth-century American sentimental fiction have all occurred within a framework of general agreement that sympathetic responsiveness is presented as a central affirmative value.[34] To distinguish it from derogatory uses of "sentimental," Baym and Fisher in particular have stressed that sentimentality is not "excessive, undisciplined, self-centered emotionality" but a "capacity of all human beings to respond to others' distress" (Baym xxxviii; and see Fisher 92, Tompkins 132). By focusing on emotional responsiveness, I am not refuting the persuasive claims of these critics that the heroines of sentimental fiction are tough, strong, smart, and powerful, or that the novels are often subtly subversive. What I am arguing, and will return to later, is that when male judges at the end of the nineteenth century wanted to depict women and marriage as defined by emotion, they reached back to what was by then an old-fashioned literary mode whose perceived characteristics seemed to fit the bill. They borrowed not the mode's political or religious agenda, but its centering of domestic life in a validated emotional domain.

When this concentration on sensitivity was applied to the law's marriage story, it centered the narrative on each partner's stimulating and experiencing a depth of emotional *response*. Thus understood, the marriage contract created in each spouse the legal *right* to be emotionally protected and sustained, and a corresponding *obligation* to provide (and not destroy) such affective sustenance for the other spouse. What was important about a husband's or wife's behavior was not what was done but what effect it had on the partner. Significantly too, the new paradigm redefined the right that had been violated by adultery from actively "masculine"—the right to be the exclusive "user" of a woman's body—to more passive, comfortably "female"—the right to receive love and attention from one's spouse.

Second, sentimentality allocates to women a "natural" superiority in the realm of feeling, a valorized affinity for emotional response, whether to the sufferings of others, to affection received, to religion, or to the maternal joys of child-rearing.[35] In *Anna Lee: The Maiden, the Wife, the Mother—A Tale*, an 1871 didactic novel of a model woman's progress through life, T. S. Arthur, one of the few male writers to use the sentimental mode, describes the emotional state of newlyweds Anna and James Hartley:

> James Hartley had been married three weeks—three of the happiest weeks he had ever spent; but happier far was his lovely young bride. A form of affection, as every woman is, she could love more deeply, and feel a more intense delight in loving. The more closely she looked into her husband's mind, and the clearer she saw and understood the moral qualities by which it was adorned, the purer and more elevated was her love. (74)

Arthur's Anna is intelligent, practical, competent, and articulate, qualities that set her apart from many of the other female characters in the novel. In the realm of emotion, however, her ability to "love more deeply" than her husband is simply a function of her sex: she is "a form of affection, as every woman is." This is not to say that Anna's love is like that of the selfish, frivolous women whose wifely inadequacies supply continuing contrasts to her excellence. Yet, even if "every woman's" affections are not as splendid and pure as Anna's, women as a group live more completely in their emotions and enjoy a greater potential than men for experiencing the joys (and consequently the sorrows) of love.

Applied to the story of marriage and infidelity that underlies criminal conversation, the emotional capacity and vulnerability of wives created precisely the link between husband's adultery and wife's injury that had been missing. The husband's philandering violated the wife's marital rights because it caused her to suffer emotionally. And where tradition assumed that the wife of an adulterer suffered less than the husband of one because no "shame or disgrace" attached to her position, the wife now could claim to suffer as much as or more than a man similarly situated because, as a "form of affection," love and its losses were more central to her existence.

Third, as Philip Fisher and others have shown, sentimental plots tend to focus readers' emotional attention on the sufferings of their victims, often disempowered children or slaves. Fisher argues in "Making a Thing Into a Man: The Sentimental Novel and Slavery," that "prisoners, children, animals and slaves—the weak and the helpless within society gain by means of sentimental experience full representation through the central moral category of compassion" (94–95).[36] Cummins begins *The Lamplighter* by describing poor Gertie's isolation and emotional impoverishment: "no one loved her, and she loved no one; no one tried to make her happy, or cared whether she was so. She was but eight years old, and alone in the world" (ch. 1). Like Fanny Fern's Rose Clark, Augusta Evans's Edna Earl, and myriad other sentimental heroines, Gertie begins narrative life not simply as a "weak and helpless" orphan who must make her own way but as a magnet for readers' pity and compassion.[37] While sentimental fiction's complex female characters often struggle with anger and other undisciplined emotions or possess such unstereotypical traits as obsessive scholarly interest, these "good" female heroines tend to display little sexuality.[38] Sex is still one area in which sentimentality works to divide the world into unbridgeable categories. A heroine may marry and thus implicitly gain sexual experience, but a "fallen" woman and a sexually flirtatious "belle" can never appear as protagonists, only as foils or objects of charity (Baym xxxviii). Readers who identify with the struggles of the virtuous young girl and wife are encouraged to see such sexually implicated female characters as permanently branded, disqualified from being heroines. While not quite as morally absolute as the line that divides a slave victim like Stowe's Tom from a sadistic slave owner like Legree, the gap between the sweet and loving Beatrice and the selfish, fashionable, dissipated Claudia Merlin, both of whom love Southworth's Ishmael, can never be crossed. We may pity passionate Claudia's self-destructive agony as she condemns herself to a life of misery by marrying a Viscount only for his rank, but we are invited to see her as a monitory figure, representative of a category of dangerous and even contaminating women that "we" must neither accept nor become.

In litigative terms, sentimentality's morally unambiguous categorizing obviously assisted cuckolded wives both to claim the position of sympathetic victim and to characterize female defendants as dangerous "Others" whose illicit sexual activity restricted them to the role of negative counterexample. Less obviously, the sentimental logic that shifted the focus of attention from the site of wrongful behavior to the site of emotional response made adultery a wrong inflicted on, *and occurring in*, the heart and feelings of the "innocent" victim rather than the unfaithful bodies of the erring spouse and his female partner. As Fisher explains in his brilliant analysis of a scene from Rousseau, in which an imprisoned man watches in helpless agony as a child is torn from its mother and killed by a wild animal, the sentimental focus is not on the active violence or the pain of the child but on the internal sufferings of the helpless witnesses. "Suffering," Fisher argues, is "the primary subject matter, perhaps the exclusive subject matter, of sentimental narrative" (105). This shift in focus made considerations of physical property rights and even of sexuality unnecessary in criminal conversation cases; damages were to compensate not the "corruption of body and mind" of the adulterous spouse but the emotional sufferings of the complainant spouse. If it was difficult to think of a wife as having a violable sexual "honor," there was nothing easier or more consistent with Victorian images of wives than to see them as virtuous and suffering victims.

Working together, these three elements of sentimentality brought the wife's emotional state, her response, into the criminal conversation story.[39] Once this occurred, the stimulus, the husband's sexual infidelity, could no longer be kept out of it. In the case of *Rott v. Goehring*, 33 N.D. 413, 157 N.W. 294 (1916), for instance, the Supreme Court of North Dakota upheld a wife's right to sue another woman for alienation of affections even though she could not prove adultery, and even though her husband had continued to live with her. In rewriting the meaning of the legal right to consortium, the court displayed an explicit pride in departing from precedent:

> Consortium means . . . something more than mere physical presence in the home. To entitle plaintiff to recover, it was not absolutely necessary to show actual abandonment—actual abduction—or adultery. To understand this, we do not need to go to any musty tomes, nor resort to ancient court decisions; we need consult only our own common sense,—our sense of right and wrong, and what we, ourselves, know of human nature. We all know that nothing else—not even death itself—will cause a sensitive wife so much anguish, shame, misery, and heartache, as to learn that her husband has been untrue to his marriage vows or transferred his affections to another. In such circumstances is the wife's agony any less—is the wrong done her any less—by the husband's remaining in the family home with her? We know that in such circumstances, the husband's presence only intensifies the wife's agony. (421)

The wife is entitled not merely to her husband's presence, but to his wholehearted affection and loyalty. More than that, the husband has an obligation not to behave in ways that induce "agony" in a "sensitive wife." Marriage thus imposes obligations of sexual fidelity based on the emotional consequences of infidelity, not on its effects on tangible property and lineage. It is important to note that the wife's right here depends on her being "sensitive," that is, frail, pure, and given to intensities of feeling. But just being a woman could be enough. Echoing T. S. Arthur's insistence that women love more deeply than men, the Maryland Supreme Court in 1900 noted that "whatever their legal rights have been in the past, [wives] have, as a rule surpassed their husbands in their capacity to appreciate and enjoy domestic happiness. When, then, the marital rights of a woman are unlawfully invaded so as to cause this 'loss of consortium,' why should she not be entitled to have the wrong done her redressed by the law as her husband would be under such circumstances?" (*Wolf v. Frank*, 92 Md. 138, 140 [1900]).[40] In a slightly different formulation, an Iowa court declared in *Price v. Price*, 91 Iowa 693, 697–98 (1894): "The marriage state is not one entered into for the purpose of labor and support alone. Considerations of the highest character, as the comfort and happiness of the parties to the marriage contract, and the welfare of their children, give to each the right to the affection, companionship, and society of the other, and whoever wrongfully deprives either of that right may be held responsible." Courts in these cases often spoke rather smugly of their departure from the "barbarity" of the past, which made a wife "the mere servant of the husband" (*Deitzman v. Mullin*, 108 Ky. 610, 614 [1900]), and of their magnanimity in replacing "the effete and inhuman doctrine of the common law" with "the more enlightened and humane principles so universally approved in our country" (*Humphrey v. Pope*, 122 Cal. 253, 258–59 [1898]). Yet their validations of the wife's right of action tend to stress her greater emotional and practical neediness, and to reinforce her legitimate sphere of interest as that of home and family (the "welfare" rather than the "legitimacy" of her children).

In this reading, her frailty and dependence gave her a right to her husband's sexual loyalty; his obligations to her were *greater*, not lesser, than hers to him. In *Clark v. Harlan*, 1 Cin. Super. Ct. R. 418 (Ohio Sup. 1871), the court asserted that if a husband's right to sue for loss of "solatium" arose from the marriage contract,

> the same result, *for stronger reasons*, should follow the loss of the husband's consortium by the wife. His care of her whole social life; his protection from injury of her person, of her property and of her good name, are alike demanded by the marital tie and the first principles of justice. He cannot lightly disregard the obligations he has solemnly assumed, or ignore the relation he bears to her to whom he has pledged his affections until the bond is severed by death or the judgment of the law. (423, emphasis added)

The husband's happiness and security are within his own power to produce, while hers depend on his care and protection. Her lack of intellectual self-possession, the "incompleteness" of her life without his active assistance, make her emotional well-being his responsibility.

In the old criminal conversation story, the wife's essential "incompleteness," her status as disempowered, even legally nonexistent relative to her husband, her emotional vulnerability and inability to control the circumstances of her life, were all central to the construction of a story about female infidelity that made the wife an unvoiced object. Here, those same "feminine" qualities do not rob her of status as a fully human actor but intensify it, becoming the rationale for an increase in husbandly obligation that ultimately enables her successful assumption of litigative power. In permitting the female-plaintiff cases, courts could have simply given to wives what husbands had enjoyed, an enforceable property right to the exclusive sexual use of their husbands' bodies (and a few did).[41] But even *Nolin v. Pearson*, 191 Mass 283 (1906), which held that "the absolute privilege of each to the conjugal society of the other must be considered as embracing the persons of both, with no distinction in favor of one as against the other" grounded the right to the partner's "person" or body in an image of marriage as domesticity rather than as sex: "this equal companionship and aid in the founding and maintenance of the home and in the rearing of offspring is the foundation upon which this most important of all the domestic relations rests" (287).

Instead of creating a proprietary entitlement to something in the husband, courts created a "right not to be hurt," a right to a state of emotional well-being in the wife, which he had the marital obligation to preserve. He had to be faithful not because his body belonged to her or because her sexual "honor" needed to glory in its exclusive possession, but because his infidelity removed the shield of protection that his love for her provided. In short, the law's story of marriage borrowed from sentimental fiction a new notion of what marital relationships were ideally *about*, producing in the case law an enforceable right to intimacy. By constructing the wife as sentimental victim, both the right and the injury are broadened in scope, losing their exclusive focus on sexual activity. The essential injury is no longer the "defilement of the marriage bed" but includes such domestically defined wrongs as the abandonment of the wife and children, the desecration of the sanctity of the home, the misery of the family left without financial and emotional support. Where it seemed logical to the Maine court in *Doe v. Roe* to conclude that a cuckolded wife simply suffered no damages, a 1900 Illinois Appeals Court, focusing on the emotional basis of marriage, concluded its opinion by declaring: "Upon what reasoning it could be held that a loss of the affections of a husband is less real and substantial than the loss of the affections of a wife we cannot perceive. We entertain no doubt that by the clear weight of both reason and authority a wife has, under our statute, precisely the same right of recovery for such a loss as the husband" (*Betser v. Betser*, 186 Ill. 537, 540 [1900]).

One consequence of the reimaging of marriage in terms of the reciprocal duties and obligations of marriage *partners* was that the wife's having a "story" of her own became undeniable. The female plaintiff was a conceptual impossibility in the eighteenth-century criminal conversation case because the original tort depended on a story of gender relations that reduced women to intermediary objects. When eighteenth- and nineteenth-century novels began to describe marital partners who owed each other a full measure of affection, support, and faithfulness, the emergence of female plaintiffs, protagonists in their own litigative stories of emotional injury, became inevitable. It should be no surprise that in some states, where Married Women's Property Acts had not yet been enacted or were hopelessly narrow, courts nevertheless legitimated suits brought by female plaintiffs based on their "discovery" of the mutuality of marital obligation. In *Bennett v. Bennett*, 23 N.E. 17 (1889), for instance, the New York Court of Appeals found that a husband's right "to the conjugal society" of his wife is no greater than hers to his, for each has an entitlement "to the comfort, companionship and affection of the other" deriving from the marriage contract, a right "which the law both confers and protects." The court continued:

> A remedy, not provided by statute, but springing from the flexibility of the common law, and its adaptability to the changing nature of human affairs, has long existed for the redress of the wrongs of the husband. As the wrongs of the wife are the same in principle, and are caused by acts of the same nature as those of the husband, the remedy should be the same. What reason is there for any distinction? . . . Since her society has a value in him capable of admeasurement in damages, why is his society of no legal value to her? Does she not need the protection of the law in this respect at least as much as he does? Will the law give its aid to him and withhold it from her? (18–19)

Bennett represents a typical mixture of declarative equality and paternalistic concern. Wives' rights are the same as husbands', yet wives need the aid and protection of the law "at least" as much as men, and implicitly more.[42]

If the appellate decisions I have been examining constructed gendered narratives of relations between husbands and wives; they also, and perhaps equally importantly, wrote gendered narratives of the relations between female plaintiffs and the all-male judiciary engaged in "protecting" and "preserving" their rights. Casting themselves as the strong masculine protectors of necessarily weak feminine virtue, the authors of these opinions suggested that litigating wives were engaging in prototypically "feminine" behavior by bringing their claims to court. Yet we should not forget that initiating a civil lawsuit is always an assumption of power and an act of aggression. A civil complaint turns on the machinery of legal process: it initiates a case that must be accorded time on the docket; the careful attention of judges, juries, bailiffs, and clerks; and ultimately, often, the exertion of government authority over the defendant's time, money, and business or private activities. In a criminal conversation or alienation of affections case, moreover, a wife presented a legal narrative that attacked her own husband for his sexual misbehavior and publicized the intimate details of their marriage and its breakdown. During this same period too, women who attempted to enter the courtroom as officially empowered speakers—not as parties but as lawyers—were often met with what one legal historian has called a "horror and disgust" now almost impossible to comprehend (Friedman 639).[43] How are we to understand the courts' rhetorical strategies for dealing with these new female plaintiffs?

It seems that once they had determined to permit the cases, courts neutralized the problematic aggressiveness of female plaintiffs by imaging them as seekers of protection. Instead of being characterized as power-mad invaders of male space or threats to husbandly peace of mind, such women were represented as leaning on the strong arm of the law, which indeed takes over the "husband's" role of vindicating and protecting his wife's interests. As the Cincinnati court declared in *Clark v. Harlan*:

> we can not but feel a deep conviction that the wife is in the highest sense a ward of the court, not because she is now, under the generous policy of our law, relieved from the old idea of conjugal servitude which placed her as a chattel under the control of her husband, but because it is only consistent with the relation into which the parties have entered that each must have their separate interest controlled only by mutual affection and regard, while subject, nevertheless to the protection of the law. (423)

The *Clark* court explicitly preserves its own patriarchal power, signified by its protective, authoritarian stance toward its vulnerable "ward." The guardian-ward relationship was one of the four (along with that of husband and wife) that Blackstone identified as constituted by asymmetrical rights and responsibilities. Like a wife under coverture, a ward during his or her minority lacks the capacity to act legally on his own behalf. While the decision speaks of the spouses' parallel "separate interests" and their "mutual affection," it is hard to imagine a court describing its relationship to a husband-plaintiff in a criminal conversation or alienation of affections suit as a matter of guardianship (and indeed, I have found none that did so). Thus, while congratulating itself on having released the wife from subservient status as a chattel, the court nevertheless perpetuates a gendered imbalance of power by characterizing its own relation with female plaintiffs as a protective guardianship. Paradoxically, however, this rhetoric of disempowerment, which defined women as weak, needy, and relatively helpless, was being deployed to render acceptable holdings that actually increased wives' power to enter the legal system as speaking subjects who could wield its litigative processes for their own benefit.

This seemingly contradictory strategy may also help explain why many appeals courts in the 1880s and 1890s reached back to a literary mode already several decades past its prime instead of grounding their decisions in contemporary story lines about the New Woman or in the literary realism then circulating in the novels of Howells and James. Certainly, the "sentimental synthesis" and the sentimental novel reached their peaks in the 1850s and 1860s. Most of the literary works referred to earlier, including *The Lamplighter*, *The Wide, Wide World*, *Uncle Tom's Cabin*, *Ishmael*, and *St. Elmo*, were written before 1870. By the last decades of the nineteenth century, new literary techniques were presenting women and marriage in new ways. In novels like Henry James's *Portrait of a Lady* (1881), William Dean Howells's *A Modern Instance* (1883), Margaret Deland's *Philip and His Wife* (1898), and Robert Grant's *Unleavened Bread* (1900), complex portraits of marital breakdown refused to depict spouses in the roles of victims and perpetrators and, while retaining an emphasis on the emotional subtleties of marital interaction, no longer privileged emotional responsiveness over all other personal or intellectual qualities.

By describing turn-of-the-century literary modes in this way, I do not mean to oversimplify either sentimental fiction or literary history. As recent scholars have shown, the heroines of the best-selling sentimental novels were often engaged in struggles for power over themselves and their world, and were defined by an ability to think as well as to feel.[44] Moreover, even during the 1850s writers such as Fanny Fern ridiculed sentimental stereotypes. Fern, whose enormously popular weekly columns made her the highest-paid author, male or female, of her day, frequently advised wives to cultivate emotional toughness, competence, and independence. In an 1852

Valentine's Day column, "Hints to Young Wives," Fern's fictional persona finds a love letter from her husband to her dressmaker. Advising her readers to follow her own resolutions, she declares: "If you have made the interesting discovery that you were married for a sort of upper servant or housekeeper, just *fill that place and no other*, keep your temper, keep all his strings and buttons and straps on, and then keep him at a distance as a housekeeper should—'them's my sentiments!' " (*Olive Branch* 14 Feb. 1852, reprinted in *Ruth Hall and Other Writings* 224–25, emphasis in original).

If countersentimentality was popular at mid-century, the coming of realism and naturalism a few decades later did not cause earlier fictional modes to disappear from the literary scene. Not only did popular magazines and novels continue to publish new stories in the sentimental mold, but such earlier writers as E.D.E.N. Southworth continued to achieve monumental sales figures well into the twentieth century through the continual reissue of her previous best-sellers in edition after edition.[45] So while other literary modes were certainly jostling successfully for prominence, sentimental fiction was still very much available in the last decades of the nineteenth century.

But the cultural valence of sentimental fiction appears to have changed from the earlier decades of its dominance. To the late nineteenth-century reading public and to the judges who drew on its vocabulary for their descriptions of "sensitive wives' anguish" and need for affection, sentimentality apparently provided a conservative, unthreatening view of female nature. Its vocabulary of agony and sensitivity offered a safe way to acknowledge the intense emotional lives of women without figuring them as powerful or aggressive. The popular association of sentimentality with a series of old-fashioned gender assumptions that were on the wane served in the cases at issue here to mask the actual changes in the law that these decisions accomplished. The similarity between the rhetoric used in the cases cited here and in the works of T. S. Arthur is especially revealing. While Arthur is one of the few male writers whose works are often labeled sentimental, his many novels, short stories, and didactic pieces do not tell the story of a young girl's struggle for independence and self-mastery identified and analyzed by Baym, Tompkins, and others as "women's fiction." Instead, in novels like *Tired of Housekeeping* (1843), *The Hand But Not the Heart* (1859), and *Anna Lee* (1871), Arthur offers stories of marital crisis and adjustment designed to instruct young women in the risks and duties of marriage. His heroines, though intelligent, refined, and strong, need to learn such practical middle-class lessons as how to manage servants, stay within a budget, and support their husbands' career advancement. Like the later judges who reshaped the law of marital rights and obligations around a discourse founded in emotion, Arthur exploits sentimentality from the point of view of a male outsider, perhaps a potential husband seeking to mold an ideal mate. He deploys its elements selectively, in the service of his own agenda.

It is important too to note that there were courts that welcomed the new woman and created appellate narratives featuring her as a prominent character. In permitting female-plaintiff criminal conversation cases, for instance, the Kentucky Court of Appeals quoted an Illinois case that had refused to be bound by the legal fiction that a husband could control his wife's tongue: "The legal supremacy of the husband is gone and the scepter departed from him. The wife has the legal right and aspires to battle with him in the contests of the forum, to outvie him in the healing art, to climb with him the steps of fame, and share with him in every occupation. Her brain and hands and tongue are her own" (*Turner v. Heavrin*, 4 ALR at 568, citing *Martin v. Robson*, 65 Ill. 129). Because the wife is now on an "equal footing with the husband as to her right to sue," she should be permitted to bring the same kind of actions for damages from adultery as a husband. Here, through a string of miniparables formed from metaphorical clichés, the court constructs a wife characterized not by emotion but by action, not engaged in a separate sphere of domestic tasks but able and willing to assert herself successfully in precisely the same public professional activities that have hitherto been her husband's exclusive bailiwick. She is described as vocal and aggressive, ready to compete with him as a lawyer and even "outvie" him as a doctor. No attempt is made to mask or undercut the challenging independence of modern women. Indeed, it is the breadth of their professional achievement that provides the analytical ground for increasing the litigative powers of sexually wronged wives, even though their occupational identities are not at issue.

While, as might be expected, cases from around the country offer a variety of stories, the sentimentalized marriage story is the one that emerged most fully and frequently. Yet even as these cases wrote a new marriage story that emphasized the emotional needs of married women, enabling them to appear in the assertive role of criminal conversation plaintiffs, the underlying skeletal legal story of the tort remained in place. Though subject to severe stresses, it remained vigorous and even revitalized by the advent of female plaintiffs until at least the 1930s. The tort showed—at least for a while—a surprising adaptability in reformulating its outdated assumptions so that new stories about women, sex, and emotions fleshed out the same framework. This flexibility can be traced not just to the law's narrativity, the fact that it necessarily operates through discursive texts that share important features with other forms of narrative discourse, but also and more importantly to the law's ability to profit from that discursive continuity by appropriating literary rhetoric, plots, and stories that carry changing cultural assumptions. In chapter 3, I argued that one strand of William Maxwell Evarts's defense strategy for Henry Ward Beecher invited jurors to use sentimental logic as a principle of evidentiary evaluation, so that literary principles that guide a reader's assessment of fictional characters came to perform an essentially legal function. Here I have argued that on the appellate level, literary formulations of marital relationships were employed to define the law of spousal rights and obligations; literary and rhetorical elements were put to work in a realm that we ordinarily think of as excluding the literary and the sentimental. But if the law was ready to ground its legal narratives in wives' full subjectivity, was it equally ready to ratify narratives that effectively eliminated the subjectivity of husbands? The next chapter takes up this question.

CHAPTER 6

Consequences of Change: The Sexually Passive Husband and the Erotically Autonomous Wife

Attack of the Barbie Commandos

In December 1993, a group of activists calling themselves the Barbie Liberation Organization surreptitiously switched the voice boxes on more than 300 "Talking Duke" G.I. Joe and "Teen Talk" Barbie dolls, and then replaced the dolls on toy store shelves. The result, as *The New York Times* described it, was "a mutant colony of Barbies-on-steroids who roar things like 'Attack!' 'Vengeance is mine!' and 'Eat lead, Cobra!' The emasculated G.I. Joes, meanwhile, twitter 'Will we ever have enough clothes?' and 'Let's plan our dream wedding!' " (Firestone A12). While some complained that the "terrorist" attacks were unfair to children, others found the sudden disjunction between expectation and performance hilarious. The activists, whose goal was to "make a statement about the way toys can encourage negative behavior in children, particularly given rising acts of violence and sexism," were delighted with the nationwide publicity, much of which, like the *Times* article, was both amused and sympathetic.

The Barbie doll raids worked, of course, not by explicitly critiquing gender stereotypes but by deploying them. It was only because the dolls' bodies and voices, both "actors" and "scripts," were so intensely gendered that their unexpected inversion could be so shocking. So long as the signifying characteristics of G.I. Joe's body and voice point to the same conception of macho maleness, the underlying gender stereotype that determines them remains relatively unobtrusive. It is simply "who he is." This is not to say that G.I. Joe's violent "personality" is unimportant, or that it does not affect every child's interaction with the toy. But because the doll's physical, vocal, and script-content characteristics are wholly consistent with preexisting expectations about G.I. Joe, they attract no particular attention. The doll's stereotypical maleness, though constitutive, becomes transparent enough to be played "through" by children who use it unself-consciously.

When stereotypical extremes of "male" and "female" are conflated within one body, however, they are instantly, insistently foregrounded. It becomes impossible to ignore not only how gender-determined every phrase and tone of voice is, but how completely irreconcilable these male and female "traits" are with each other. A tough-talking Barbie can be amusing, but she can't really be a *Barbie*; militant aggression is too incompatible with the well-established feminine essence Barbie has been carefully constructed to exude for so many years.[1] For the activists, the incompatibility of opposing stereotypes is precisely the point; it induces discomfort (making us aware how much we depend on gender-appropriate behavior to maintain social comfort levels), and it makes both male and female stereotypes look silly and artificial (leading, the activists hope, to their abandonment in favor of new, nonsexist behaviors by both doll manufacturers and children). The surgical switch places so much stress on the stereotypes that they self-destruct. If the commando raid succeeds, it will be by having so undermined the credibility of the dolls' stereotypical attributes that restoring the "appropriate" voice box won't restore prior comfort levels. Instead, new character conceptions and alternative scripts will have to be invented.[2]

The female-plaintiff criminal conversation cases I discussed in chapter 5 enacted a similar, real-life gender switch. Like the sweet-looking Barbies who were made to shout "Attack!," wives who brought civil adultery actions against their husbands' mistresses found themselves speaking the aggressive lines allocated to the part of "plaintiff" in the law's preestablished criminal conversation script. They publicly accused other women of "debauching and criminally knowing" their husbands, claimed a property injury from the loss of affection and sexual fidelity, and wielded the resources of the legal system to profit from their husbands' adulteries.[3] At the same time, their lawsuits treated their husbands as passive sexual victims, gave them no opportunity to speak, and treated the adultery as perpetrated solely by the Other Woman, the female defendant. The rhetorical cross-dressing these cases enacted suddenly made the artificiality of the law's story visible, producing an important series of responses.

The Law's New Story

As I have already noted, in the classic criminal conversation case the wife's role in bringing about the act of adultery had no bearing on the husband's right to bring the action. The logic of the tort did not deny that wives might be active seducers; it simply made female sexuality and assertiveness legally irrelevant and therefore outside the parameters of the law's narrative. With little evident strain, courts were able to separate the actual story of the adulterous relationship, with which they were not essentially concerned, from criminal conversation's legal story of the lover's injury to the husband's property rights in the wife. As in a case of statutory rape of a minor, the wife's legal inability to consent (because control of her body for sexual purposes belonged to her husband) meant that the sexual act could be legally imaged as a forcible invasion with the defendant conclusively presumed to be the aggressor. In determining the question of liability, the law's story thus substituted a legal narrative of the adultery for the actual circumstances of the relationship. That the legal story was almost always obviously counterfactual was simply ignored in determining the plaintiff's right to bring his case to trial. A single instance of adulterous intercourse entitled the plaintiff to recover damages.[4]

The key point here is the absolute separation of actual fact from legal fiction. As with the jurisdictional legal fictions discussed in chapter 2, the legal system established a fixed script for the torts, with preestablished roles and dialogue that litigants were required to enact and speak. The script had three roles: plaintiff, defendant, and plaintiff's spouse. Plaintiff and defendant were "human" parts; they spoke and responded, had legal rights and obligations, and had emotions and motives that were "relevant" and therefore narratively *in* the story. In contrast, the plaintiff's spouse, though clearly holding a "character-position" in the story, functioned as an object, not a person. Whoever played this part had no lines to speak; the spouse's inner life was ignored and his or her sexual aggression was irrelevant. In the eighteenth century, the powerful congruence between stereotypical attributes accorded to men and women and their roles in the criminal conversation script made that script's gender dependence so absolutely constitutive that, like G.I. Joe's aggression, it was taken for granted. But when sexually active men were cast in the role of disputed object, a series of gaps opened between the law's new story, the actual facts of the case, and still-entrenched assumptions about male aggression in narratives of seduction and adultery. The congruence had disappeared.

When wives began to bring criminal conversation and alienation of affections cases, courts thus found themselves constrained by what I have been calling the criminal conversation script to treat sexually active men as passive and damaged sexual objects, and to impose financial liability on the husbands' female partners regardless of the circumstances of particular cases. The resulting appellate opinions show clear signs of strain: some courts demonstrated their discomfort by sweeping aside longstanding legal rules without acknowledgment or citation, while others manifested an increasing inability to keep the "actual" and the "legal" stories separate. Yet none of these early cases seriously considered jettisoning either tort, and at least one leading legal theorist characterized the acceptance of female adultery plaintiffs as evidence of the law's progressive adaptability to changing historical circumstances. Nevertheless, as I will argue, the gender-reversed cases, interacting with the larger cultural changes that produced them, played a critical role in the demise of both torts several decades later. By the second half of the twentieth century, widespread acceptance of female autonomy made it untenable to base an action on legal rules that reduced a spouse—male or female—to a manipulated object. While changing attitudes toward women and marriage were part of the story, they contributed to a broader re-imaging of sexual interaction that, except in cases of rape, insisted on the independent decision-making capacity of each partner. As this notion gained cultural acceptance, courts found it increasingly difficult to apply the legal fictions governing criminal conversation and alienation of affections in either male or female cases. Ultimately, the torts became so incongruent with cultural assumptions about marriage and sexuality that they were no longer viable in most states.

In the 1904 case of *Tinker v. Colwell*, discussed in chapter 5, the U.S. Supreme Court readily acknowledged that it was almost "universally the case" that wives voluntarily consented to adultery, yet the court was quite comfortable ruling that consent wholly irrelevant to the question of liability (481). Similarly, proof that the wife "procured" the act, "seduced" the defendant, or "enticed" him into adultery was held by the courts of California, Indiana, and Michigan respectively not to affect the husband's right of action (*Bedan v. Turney*; *Wales v. Miner*; *Egbert v. Greenwalt*). So unequivocal was the husband's right to control his wife's body that his own behavior was equally irrelevant to the defendant's liability. A husband might beat his wife (*Hadley v. Heywood*), treat her so badly that she was forced to swear out a peace warrant against him and leave him (*Johnson v. Allen*), give her just cause to leave because of his cruelty (*Michael v. Dunkle*), be guilty of "open lewdness" with a "vile strumpet" (*Browning v. Jones*), or leave his wife alone for years at a time (*Yundt v. Hartrunft*) and still be able to collect damages from any man who had intercourse with her. As the court noted in *Cross v. Grant*: "If the husband, by his conduct, compels the separation from him of his wife, he may, as to her, have lost his legal right to the solace and comfort of her society, but not as to all the world. His consent is not thereby extended to other men for sexual commerce with her" (686). As Prosser emphatically puts it, "it was considered that [the wife] was no more capable of giving a consent which would prejudice the husband's interests than was his horse" (919).

To some extent, the courts' untroubled ability to separate actual from legal stories may have depended on the law's imaging adultery as an injury to property, but that imaging was itself dependent, I think, on a fundamental congruity between the tort's legal story of male sexual aggression and reigning cultural and literary stories of seduction and betrayal, in which the sexual aggressor was almost universally male. In these powerful, familiar stories—from *Clarissa* to *Charlotte Temple* to *Adam Bede*, and on to *Jennie Gerhardt* and *An American Tragedy*—women are sexual victims, not predators; sexually experienced men prey on young women, and seduction is disastrous for the now unmarriageable girl. In many such stories, the act of sexual violation seems necessarily to cut off any possibility of a future story for the unfortunate young woman: Clarissa, Charlotte Temple, Hetty Sorrel, and Roberta Alden can only die. Dickens's Little Em'ly, seduced and abandoned by the selfish Steerforth, is permitted to emigrate to Australia, but not to marry. The female victim need not be wholly sympathetic: Hetty's weakness, vanity, and general moral and intellectual feebleness make her the passive murderess of her newborn baby, a perpetrator as well as a victim. Yet their catalogue of negative traits, even if it includes a fatally responsive sensuality, does not extend to the kind of sexual aggression that initiates seduction.[5] In the less morally complex genres like popular melodrama, the poor girl and the vile seducer become established stereotypes, familiar figures of warning. The moral lessons for stage audiences were clear and unvarying: men are dangerous villains when sexuality motivates their behavior, so wise women must be careful not to become their prey.[6]

Much more than in the late seventeenth and eighteenth centuries when criminal conversation was invented, the Victorians, as Michael Grossberg has discussed, "stressed the passionlessness of normal women" (47, and see Cott 1983). In his study of breach of promise cases, Grossberg comments on the willingness of late-nineteenth-century American courts to assume that assertive sexuality was a purely male phenomenon, and to see themselves as defenders of female virtue. "The bench appears to have been particularly determined to protect women from seducers. . . . They redefined seduction as victimization that sprang from the passion and deceit of males; the passivity of women was newly emphasized," he notes, citing an Illinois case in which the court declared that "it is possible but hardly probable that a case may arise where the parties are equally guilty" (47, and citing *Tubbs v. Van Kleek*, 12 Ill. 446, 465–66 [1874]). If the familiar stories of victim and seducer assumed a level of female passionlessness at odds with the behavior of some real women, they were consonant with late nineteenth-century cultural assumptions, and the law's male-voiced script comfortably maintained the parallel.

When the genders were reversed, however, the story of active female sexuality, instead of being erased or denied, became the one "written" by the law's requirements. When the facts of the case presented a sexual liaison between a married man and a woman not his wife, the "natural" instinct, as conditioned by traditional story forms, would be to construct a familiar narrative of female violation by a predatory male. Yet the law of criminal conversation asked courts to construct from those facts a story of male violation and marital destruction by an aggressive female. The law's story, though admittedly counterfactual, merely "legal" or formal, nevertheless conflicted so directly with the ghost of the more familiar, culturally congruent story that some courts could "write" it only with difficulty, and others could not write it at all.

In *Kroessin v. Keller* (1895), for instance, the Supreme Court of Minnesota found the gender-switched story so repugnant that it simply refused to construct it. In traditional criminal conversation cases, the court noted, it was no defense that the male defendant had been "enticed" because "the man was always conclusively presumed to be the guilty party":

> From this statement as to the grounds or elements constituting this action, it will be seen that the principal ones cannot possibly exist or be involved in a similar action brought by a wife. And what has been said about the unavailability of the defense that the defendant himself was the victim, and not the seducer, is suggestive of what the courts might have to hold to be the rule of pleading, and what they might have to inquire into, upon an action of this kind. Would it be held, following the old rule we have mentioned, and for which the reason seems well founded, that it was no defense for the female sued to allege and prove that she was the party seduced and that the greater wrong and injury had been inflicted upon her, not upon the plaintiff wife? or would the contrary rule prevail? But we need not consider the subject further, for a moment's reflection will suggest the remarkable results flowing from the adoption of either rule. 60 Minn. 372, 374 (1895)

The *Kroessin* court seems to catch its breath on a precipice of unspeakability; the thought of what it "might have to inquire into" shocks it into euphemism and vagueness. Yet what is most striking is that, were the court to adopt the law's formal narrativizing rules in female-plaintiff cases, the "real facts" are precisely what would *not* have to be "inquired into." The story paradigm would unrebuttably position the woman as the aggressor and the man as the victim, but such a positioning would impute nothing at all about who "really" seduced whom. Apparently able to think of male and female sexuality only in terms of victims and perpetrators, the court is confronted by unpleasant disjunctions whichever way it turns. Either it will be forced to ignore the familiar fiction of female seduction that it clearly wants to write, thereby mislabeling what it wants to call a victim as a perpetrator, or, if the law's story matches the "real facts," it will become complicit in writing a *true* story of female sexual aggression and male victimhood. This latter prospect is so repugnant that it must be denied as what "cannot possibly exist." *Kroessin* is significant not for its display of traditional sexual stereotypes but as powerful evidence that the coming of female plaintiffs stimulated a new awareness of the rigid fictionality of traditional criminal conversation law. That fictionality, with its story-determining presumptions, could not be used to produce comfortably familiar stories about sex in gender-reversed cases. The *Kroessin* court adopted a logically inconsistent but culturally comfortable position: it continued to permit cases brought by men but refused to permit those brought by women.

In *Churchill v. Lewis*, 17 Abb. 226 (N.Y. 1886), a New York court dealt with its discomfort in another way: permitting the case to go forward, it simply changed the law without citation or acknowledgment. While allowing a middle-aged wife's claim against a young unmarried woman (the daughter of the spouses' boarding-house landlady) to go to the jury, the court instructed jurors that the "guilty relations must have been maintained at the solicitations of the defendant." The instructions continued: "The plaintiff's husband is over forty years of age, having been married to the plaintiff nearly twenty years. He was not a young and inexperienced man. If you find that there was this wickedness between the plaintiff's husband and the defendant, but that it originated with the plaintiff's husband, if he enticed the defendant into illicit relations with him, then the plaintiff's case is not made out. To charge the defendant, it must affirmatively appear that she was the seducer and enticer" (229–30). Without citing a single case, the court quietly jettisoned two centuries of well-established legal principles in order to protect the victim status of a young unmarried woman. Further, the court instructed the jury that the case must be "free from doubt," a standard so far beyond the "more probable than not" requirement usually applied in civil actions that it may well have exceeded even the stringency of "beyond a reasonable doubt," the standard applied to criminal cases.

Twelve years later, in *Witman v. Egbert*, 50 NYS 3, 27 App. Div. 374 (1898), another New York appellate court displayed similar confidence, declaring the law to be in full accord with its assumptions about the workings of male and female sexuality. Refusing to cast a woman, particularly a pretty one, in the role of predatory seductress, the court announced that "it was incumbent on the plaintiff to prove that the defendant was blamable for plaintiff's husband's infatuation. Unless the defendant did or said something with the wrongful and willful intent to engage his affections and thereby to seduce him from his fidelity to his wife, she is not liable. The law imputes to her no fault because of her attractiveness, nor because she may have been pleased with the admiration of the plaintiff's husband" (3). *Churchill* and *Witman* are worth noting for what the opinions omit. So convinced are both courts that the applicable law *must* parallel their own assumptions about relationships that they simply declare the law to be what they are confident it is. No cases are cited or distinguished; a reader unfamiliar with the tort law in this area would have no way of knowing that contradictory precedents exist or that a straightforward application of seemingly gender-neutral criminal conversation law to female plaintiffs would produce a radically different set of rules than those enunciated in the opinions. That "correct" application of the law might produce a story profoundly at odds with cultural expectations seems to have been a possibility so outlandish that it was not even considered.

The courts' rigidity is expressed in narrative terms as an inability to write new stories or construct new characters; adultery can only be understood as a wrongful aggressor's seduction of a passive victim, while female defendants must be either stereotypical virgin-victims or naturally sinful "fallen women." Yet the belief that women should be held less responsible for adulterous behavior because they had lower sex drives began to erode significantly by the turn of the century. While the *Witman* court seemed to see the female defendant as little more than a stereotypically attractive sex object, other courts brought a different understanding of sexual interaction to their analyses. In *Hart v. Knapp*, 76 Conn. 135 (1903), for instance, a Connecticut appellate court firmly refused to permit a defense of seduction. While it applied the "traditional" rule that the identity of the aggressor was irrelevant to liability, the court's reasoning represented a radical departure. Instead of basing its conclusion on the plaintiff's property interest in the body of the spouse, the court grounded its denial of the defense on the female defendant's full independence and subjectivity:

> She was a widow of full age, with full knowledge that Hart was the husband of the plaintiff. She admits, hypothetically, that she engaged with him in a great wrong to the plaintiff. She knew that her course of conduct with him would probably lead him to abandon his wife. . . . She now claims, in effect, that because the husband seduced her she is absolved from liability for her own wrongs against the wife. . . . When . . . the defendant says that the husband seduced her, that is merely saying that he first solicited, enticed and persuaded her to adulterous intercourse with him, and that she yielded to his persuasion. . . . Solicitation, persuasion, enticement, temptation, however urgent, powerful or alluring, do not constitute duress. In law, so far as regards the plaintiff, what the defendant did with Hart, she did of her own free will; and she is responsible to the wife for the results of her conduct with the husband, even if it be true that he persuaded her to do what she did and "was the active or aggressive party" in procuring her to do so. (139–40)

Hart's narrative of adultery as a mutual interaction between two responsible, decision-making individuals is a crucial moment in the history of criminal conversation. Like the gradual re-imaging of marriage discussed earlier in chapter 5, the court's new "story" of sexuality makes the female partner a person rather than an object. Indeed, in some ways we might say this new story goes further, for it grounds the defendant's liability not in anyone's sentimental vulnerability or obligation, but in notions of "free will," knowledge, and responsibility. The court explicitly refuses the defendant's attempt to position herself as a sentimental victim, rejecting arguments based on her female weakness and the husband's seductive allure. The court does not deny that the idea "originated with the plaintiff's husband," to use the words of the *Churchill* court. Nevertheless, it insists that when all is said and done, except in the very extreme cases of duress or, presumably, rape, the law may properly assume that a woman is responsible for her choices and for the consequences of her actions, just as a man is.

Significantly, though the holding mimics the "traditional" rule that liability exists regardless of who is the seducer, its logic is anything but traditional. The earlier male-voiced cases made the wife's assertiveness irrelevant because she lacked the legal responsibility to make choices about the sexual use of her own body; a wife could be only object, never subject, within the law. In *Hart*, the husband's dominance or assertiveness doesn't matter because both he and his adulterous sexual partner are fully responsible for the uses they make of their bodies. The same principle underlies the holding ten years later in *Miller v. Pearce*, 86 Vt. 322 (1913) in which, as in *Hart*, the trial court had refused to instruct the jury that it must affirmatively appear that the defendant was the seducer or enticer. Considering whether "it makes any difference in law whether the defendant was the seducer or the seduced," the appellate court concluded that "it does not, for seduction, unlike rape, does not preclude consent, but gains it by persuasion, procurement, and enticement, leaving the seduced a willing participant in the wrong; and the act of adultery itself, subject to all the consequences that the law attaches to it, one of which is, in actions like this, that the loss of *consortium* necessarily results from it, regardless of which party was the seducer" (327). In both *Hart* and *Miller* then, the court concluded that the law, instead of operating to void the female partner's power to consent, would presume it to have been in full operation at all times. Female defendants might thus be accorded subjectivity by the court, but it was plaintiff wives who won cases as a result of this approach. Not at all coincidentally, the court granted wives the same rights-bearing subjectivity as female lovers: *Miller* is also one of the few cases to declare absolutely that "carnal knowledge of the husband is as much a civil injury to the wife, as carnal knowledge of the wife is a civil injury to the husband" (328).[7]

It is important to remember that at the same time that courts began describing adultery as a matter of mutual choice rather than seduction, the structure of the criminal conversation tort still required that a single actor—the defendant—be held fully financially responsible for the affair's adverse consequences to the plaintiff's marriage and family. To the extent that they began to wield a rhetoric of equality and independence in these cases, courts were engaged in a profoundly contradictory undertaking. Female defendants might be grateful to be considered fully responsible human beings, but they were surely less than delighted to find themselves, as a result, financially accountable to the wives of their lovers for whatever damages could be linked to the adultery, while the husband-lovers escaped financial judgment completely. If female defendants were allowed independence and control over their bodies, why wasn't each marital partner entitled to the same privilege? And if they were—that is, if adultery was ultimately a choice made by consenting adults—then on what grounds could a plaintiff—husband or wife—be entitled to damages when a spouse decided to engage in an extramarital affair? The causal link that had made the act of adultery first a direct trespass by the defendant on the husband's sexual property, then an equally direct injury to the plaintiff spouse's feelings, was weakening.

The ultimate inconsistency in seeing female-plaintiff cases as evidence of progress for women can be seen in the series of lectures Benjamin Cardozo gave at Yale in 1923, later published under the title *The Growth of the Law*. In an elegantly reasoned essay, Cardozo argues that a working balance must be struck between the need for consistency and certainty in law, and the equally important need for responsiveness to cultural, scientific, and sociological change. Judicial decision-making must exemplify creativity within constraint, predicting and shaping the future rather than rigidly enshrining the past, Cardozo asserts. As an example of the "true" historical method he advocates, he cites *Oppenheim v. Kridel*, 236 N.Y. 156 (1923), decided earlier that year by the New York Court of Appeals, on which he then sat as a judge. The holding in the case was that a woman, as well as a man, may maintain an action for criminal conversation. Cardozo begins by noting that in ruling against the wife, the court of intermediate appeal had cited precedents back to the time of Coke, when, it was stressed, "a man had a property right in the body of his wife" while a wife had no complementary right in his body and when, moreover, she could not bring a suit without joining him as plaintiff.

> We did not ignore these precedents, but we held them inconclusive. Social, political, and legal reforms had changed the relations between the sexes, and put woman and man upon a plane of equality. Decisions founded upon the assumption of a bygone inequality were unrelated to present-day realities and ought not to be permitted to prescribe a rule of life. The historical method was the organ of judgment in each court, but its application led in each to opposite results. One court, in its interpretation of legal history, was satisfied to treat as finalities the precedents of ancient year books. The other found a stream of thought, a tendency, a movement forward to a goal. Which, then, is the truer use of the historical method? Which exhibits the saner and the sounder loyalty? Shall the significance of events be determined by transporting them to our own time and viewing them as if they were the product of our own day and thought, or by viewing them as of the time of their occurrence, the product of their era, the expression of its beliefs and habits? (105–6)

Cardozo's eloquent self-congratulation is worth a closer look. The "stream" and "tendency" he credits the court with appreciating was apparently the societal and legal movement toward gender equality. The opinion in *Oppenheim*, written by Judge Crane and concurred in by Cardozo, is a splendid amalgam of the sentimental and the scientific. On the one hand, it joins with those opinions discussed earlier that ground the wife's right of action in her feelings: "If he had feelings and honor which were hurt by such improper conduct, who will say to-day that she has not the same, perhaps even a keener sense of the wrong done to her and to the home?" the court asked, insisting that each spouse's rights in the other's body must be understood "in a refined sense worthy of the times" (161). On the other hand, the court bolsters its recognition of the wife's sentimental entitlements by according her an interest in the "bodily and mental health of her children," which parallels the husband's interest in legitimacy and which, "science to-day teaches us," may be threatened by "the dire consequences which sometimes follow promiscuous intercourse by a man" (161).

Yet if *Oppenheim* relies on a forward-looking championship of womanhood and venereal cleanliness for its departure from the "harsh" strictures of earlier rules of procedure, the decision stops short of moving from procedure to substance. Crowing that "the common law is not rigid and inflexible, a thing dead to all surroundings and changing conditions, it does expand with reason" (164), the court overturns unequal rules of pleading that prevented female-plaintiff actions, but it nevertheless continues to administer—and indeed expands—a tort remedy grounded in precisely the same inequality. It does not do so blindly. The defendant-appellant argued in his brief that current equality of the sexes should have no bearing on the case because it was "predicated upon the possessory right of the superior being in the body of the inferior" (160). Refusing to consider whether the tort should therefore be abolished, the court contented itself with declaring that in New York "such an action still exists and we are merely holding that what is law for the man is also law for the woman" (168). By holding that "there is no reason in law against her maintaining such an action to-day so long as the husband may do so" (159), while avoiding the question whether the husband should, in law, continue to be able to do so, the New York court congratulates itself on taking enormous strides forward that are actually half-steps to the side.

Three years later, Jacob Lippman began an influential article on "The Breakdown of Consortium" by asserting that changes in gender relationships "have left no mark on our law. The economic, intellectual and political independence of woman, the breakdown of religion and the vast amount of knowledge concerning sex and contraception have definitely altered the marriage relationship for the parties concerned. But the law has not kept apace. Matrimonial jurisprudence is anachronistic" (651). Tracing the history of criminal conversation and related actions in detail, Lippman was among the first to point out that the logical consequence of spousal equality within marriage would be the abolition, not the extension, of such torts as criminal conversation. Lippman argued that gender inequality is at the substantive heart of the action, not merely a removable procedural accessory. His critique of the widespread acceptance of female plaintiff cases singled out the then-recent case of *Oppenheim v. Kridel.* "In extending to the wife this right of action," argued Lippman, "the Court first preserves the old fictions (under the illusion that it is destroying them), and then proceeds to create new ones. . . . That which previously accrued to the husband alone by reason of his superiority, is extended to the wife who has become his equal. Thus the real basis of the action is ignored. The archaic fiction of property rights in the body of a spouse which is criticized, and justly so, in the *Oppenheim* case, is not destroyed but is given new life" (664). Lippman was ahead of his time. While criticism of "heart balm" torts grew in the 1930s and a movement began to abolish them legislatively, most of the opposition was based on the torts' potential for abuse and their failure to provide reasonable defenses (Kavanagh 330, and see Feinsinger [1935], Kane [1936], and the unsigned "Note" in the *Virginia Law Review* [1935]).

Within the last twenty years, a new round of cases and statutes has abolished one or both torts of criminal conversation and alienation of affections in most, though by no means all, states. Significantly, the new story of female equality within marriage is a key factor. In *Kline v. Ansell,* 287 Md. 585 (1979), the Maryland Court of Special Appeals outlawed criminal conversation in a case in which a husband had won more than $44,000 in damages against his wife's paramour. Detailing the tort's history at length, the court noted its amenability to extortion and abuse, as well as its refusal to permit a reasonable range of defenses. Yet the factor that was "most important" to the court was that "today's sense of the increasing personal and sexual freedom of women is incompatible with the rationale underlying this action" (589). That the tort was "unreasonable and anachronistic" was not enough by itself to "predicate its demise"; what did the trick was the passage of the Maryland ERA, which prohibited imposing "different benefits or different burdens upon the members of a society based on the fact that they may be man or woman" (592). Because only a man could bring a criminal conversation case in Maryland,[8] the tort operated discriminatorily, violating the protections of the ERA. The common law tort "is a vestige of the past," the court declared. "It cannot be reconciled with our commitment to equality of the sexes" (593). Recognizing that the gendered inequality of the tort's fundamental underlying "rationale" could not be canceled out simply by opening litigative doors to women, the court abolished the tort entirely. Interestingly, it did so in a case in which both parties were male. That no female plaintiff was pressing the point was immaterial; the question of the tort's viability raised questions about gender in *every* case. Similarly, in *Irwin v. Coluccio*, 32 Wash. App. 510, 648 P. 2d 458 (1982), the Washington State Court of Appeals reviewed the history of criminal conversation and concluded that the act of adultery "was regarded as an invasion of a husband's property right in the body and services of his wife, an exclusive right reserved to him for his personal enjoyment. . . . This medieval rationale for the viability of the tort of criminal conversation offers the very reason the tort should be abolished. Such concepts as a husband's property right in the body of his wife offend the right of every woman to be treated as an equal member of society" (460).

Let us look back now for a moment to the late-nineteenth-century female-plaintiff cases, which were grounded in a shift from the husband's traditional marital rights in the body and services of his wife to a mutually enforceable spousal entitlement to exclusive love and affection. Read from a position determined by late-twentieth-century cultural assumptions, these cases look quite different. What seemed at the time to be the sharp rejection of a property-based concept of marriage and the recognition of female equality now appears as the perpetuation (only slightly translated) of the same "ownership" model and the reinscription of gender inequalities and stereotypes. "Love" merely replaced "use of wife's body" as the basis of each spouse's rights and obligations. The wives' struggle to be accepted as criminal conversation plaintiffs was, in a very real sense, a quest to make love and affection into a form of spousal property, property that could be stolen or violated, and its loss compensated for by money. If we look closely, the self-congratulatory rhetoric of equality deployed by various courts in permitting the wives' actions coexists quite uncomfortably with the same cases' use of sentimental imaging of women as different, "sensitive," and in need of masculine protection. Where in the eighteenth century, criminal conversation had been welcomed as a "civilized" advance over such violent self-help remedies as the duel, its logic now—even with and especially since the advent of female plaintiffs—seems hopelessly backward looking. Even after the acceptance of wives as plaintiffs, the cases appear as offensive holdovers from a day when marriage created in a spouse a form of property ownership, whether that ownership is understood as a sexual entitlement or as an emotional right.

By the second half of the twentieth century, cultural assumptions about spousal equality had caught up, in most instances, with the earlier courts' merely rhetorical gesturing. New stories of relationships, both marital and adulterous, began to gain ascendancy. The theme of the law's marriage stories followed suit, replacing narratives about emotional interdependence and entitlements with ones that presented marriage as a continuously effortful process for which each partner is fully responsible and in which such matters as sexual fidelity can no longer be assumed. As might be expected, the law's new story has not triumphed everywhere, nor has it avoided resistance. In *Bearbower v. Merry*, 266 N.W. 2d 128 (Iowa 1978), the Supreme Court of Iowa abolished criminal conversation but permitted the tort of alienation of affections to be retained. In upholding the usefulness of the alienation suit, Justice Reynoldson's majority opinion harks back to the model of the law as guardian for vulnerable wards. "The relevant question," he declares, "is whether a family member's interest in the harmony of her or his home is of sufficient magnitude to warrant judicial protection from those who intentionally would interfere with it" (130). An alienation of affections action is thus a deterrent to, not just a means to compensate for, injury. If marriage partners can be shielded from destructive interlopers, the judge suggests, problems can be worked out: "Even a shaky marital edifice ought to be permitted to collapse from its own imperfections, if it will, before a third party is authorized to kick out a cornerstone" (132).

In a frequently cited partial dissenting opinion that would have abolished both torts, Justice McCormick rejected the majority's assumption that a single third party could "cause" and therefore be solely liable for adultery or alienation:

> The disintegration of a marriage is ordinarily as complex a process as is its integration. It is not caused by only one factor or through some imperfection of only one of the spouses. Any third person who kicks at the cornerstone of a shaky marriage will not bring it down without active support from one or

> both of the parties. It is simplistic and unrealistic to suppose the edifice will be held together either so long as or because spouses have the right to obtain vengeance in the form of damage suits against the third person. Although a recovery of damages will punish the third person and soothe the ego while enriching the purse of the plaintiff, it is hardly calculated to be a constructive influence in maintaining or restoring a mature and stable marriage between two individuals with free will and separate identity. (138)

Perhaps the most important consequence of the shift registered in McCormick's opinion is its rejection of the traditional plot paradigm of seduction. McCormick refers approvingly to Homer H. Clark's 1968 treatise on the *Law of Domestic Relations*, which argues for the abolition of alienation of affections cases on the ground that certain of what he calls "psychological assumptions" (and what I would call culturally dominant narratives) have become outdated: "As has been indicated," Clark asserts, "viable contented marriages are not broken up by the vile seducer of the Nineteenth Century melodrama, though this is what the suit for alienation assumes. In fact the break-up is the product of many influences" (267).

In the movement from Reynoldson's defense of tort remedies for interference with the marriage relation to Clark and McCormick's call for abolition, we can see a shift from sentimental and melodramatic narratives of marriage and seduction, with their unambiguous categories of perpetrators and victims, seducing interlopers and helpless prey, toward realist narratives of psychological complexity and independence. In Clark and McCormick's discursive imaging of marital breakdowns, the typical husband and wife are more like Bartley and Marcia Hubbard, the divorcing spouses in William Dean Howells's 1883 *A Modern Instance*, where the stubbornness and moral weakness of the husband finds its match in the jealousy and undisciplined selfishness of the wife; or Maggie Verver and her Italian prince in Henry James's 1904 *The Golden Bowl*, who work out a form of marital compromise that acknowledges adultery, self-indulgence, materialism, and various forms of need.

Interestingly, these realist fictions were presenting complex views of marital interaction and spousal independence at around the same time that appellate courts were appropriating much earlier sentimental formulations of emotional dependence. In a roughly similar manner, the realist reformulation worked its way into the law over several decades, appearing in early cases like *Hart v. Knapp* but only gradually becoming dominant enough in legal narratives to undermine the torts' continued viability. In other areas of law too, new views of marriage produced major legal changes. The emergence of no-fault divorce, for instance, substituted a morally neutral category of "irreconcilable differences" for the at-fault decrees that made public declarations of blame and prevented the "guilty" spouse from remarrying for years, if not for life. By 1976, when the U.S. Supreme Court upheld a statute permitting a wife to obtain an abortion without her husband's consent, the concept of sexual and reproductive autonomy within marriage had become an accepted part of the law's underlying story of marital rights and obligations in many states (see *Planned Parenthood of Central Missouri v. Danforth*, 428 U.S. 52 [1976], cited in Kavanagh 335).

The skeletal story of criminal conversation was being stretched past its breaking point; there seemed to be no way anymore to twist its strands into compatibility with cultural stories and expectations about the ways that husbands and wives should behave. In chapter 5, I discussed how the absolute assumption that a wife's adultery caused injury to her husband helped produce the logic of the criminal conversation narrative. By 1992, that causative link was no longer self-evident. In *Saunders v. Alford*, 607 So. 2d 1214 (1992), for instance, the Supreme Court of Mississippi rejected the plaintiff-husband's argument that abolition of criminal conversation would allow an injury to the cuckolded spouse to go unredressed. "The problem is that he does not identify how he is injured in person, property or reputation," the court declared. "Detached as it is from an actual injury to the marital relation, criminal conversation requires no actual injury at all. It is born of the notion that the cuckold spouse is presumptively injured, or the notion that the spouse has some property interest in the chastity of the other. Such presumptions and notions have no vitality in today's society" (1218–1219). If American society no longer believes that a wife's adultery necessarily inflicts an injury on her husband, then the story written by the tort of criminal conversation loses its logical coherence, its narrative persuasiveness, and consequently its legal viability. McCormick's 1978 opinion, cited earlier, is in an important sense a proclamation of the new marriage story of "free will and separate identity." Significantly, McCormick refers to the acceptance of female-plaintiff cases as the critical moment when the law's story became visibly separated from the reality of modern relationships, a moment when, in his view, the wrong decision was made: "When these torts were perpetuated in Iowa," McCormick asserts, "instead of rejecting the fiction that one spouse owns the love which it is the other spouse's decision to give or deny, this court simply recognized a reciprocal fiction in the case of the wife" (137). The new marriage story, as McCormick writes it, assumes few if any enforceable marital entitlements or obligations between spouses. Equally strikingly, it avoids all discussion of love and affection, speaking instead in terms of psychology ("soothe the ego," "mature and stable") and autonomous individualism ("free will and separate identity"). There is no discussion in the opinion of the differing characters, roles, or needs of men and women; rather, the judge treats the spousal partnership as between virtually interchangeable parties. Yet the opinion stops short of calling for the constitutional protection of adultery as intimate consenting behavior carried on within a protected zone of privacy, as some commentators have done.[9]

Three years after *Bearbower*, a different majority of the Supreme Court of Iowa adopted McCormick's reasoning and abolished the tort of alienation of affections as well in *Funderman v. Mickelson*, 304 N.W. 2d 790 (1981). Though again both parties were male, *Funderman* grounded its rejection of the viability of both torts on the fact that their theory of recovery was "rooted in ideas we have long since renounced, involving wives as property" (794). "We think the action should be abolished because spousal love is not property which is subject to theft," declared the court. "We do not abolish the action because defendants in such suits need or deserve our protection. We certainly do not do so because of any changing views on promiscuous sexual conduct. It is merely and simply because the plaintiffs in such suits do not deserve to recover for the loss of or injury to 'property' which they do not, and cannot, own" (794). This approach was echoed by commentator Kay Kavanagh in a perceptive article on the need to abolish both torts: "the assertion that one person possesses rights to the feelings of another is inherently offensive. . . . Yet the tort actions rest on precisely such a foundation, veiled somewhat by the presence of the third party on whom the change in the marriage is blamed. But if it is hard to imagine a court awarding damages between the parties to a marriage, why award the same damages against a third party?" (338). Perhaps the most precise formulation of the new story is the Supreme Court of South Dakota's. In *Hunt v. Hunt*, 309 N.W. 2d 818, 821 (S.D. 1981), a female-plaintiff case that abolished the tort of criminal conversation, the court simply declared that "wives are not property. Neither are husbands. The love and affection of a human being who is devoted to another human being is not susceptible to theft."

The story of the rise and fall of criminal conversation and alienation of affections helps us understand one way that legal change can be accomplished. Like the use of legal fictions discussed in chapter 2, the shifting appropriation of literary modes and vocabularies had the advantage, for the late-nineteenth-century cases that retained the torts and permitted wives to bring them, of effecting change without requiring that the change be explicitly acknowledged. This approach encouraged a sense of unbroken legal continuity, avoided public or legislative debate about the issues, and maintained the tort law's external consistency.

At the same time, the early female-plaintiff cases were internally inconsistent and in many ways regressive. They may have given women new avenues for redress of injury and strengthened their litigative voice and power, yet they did so at the cost of demonizing female defendants as sexually voracious home-wreckers. More, the all-or-nothing logic of the tort held female lovers financially responsible for the destruction of a marriage and, often, a family, while the husband avoided any legal condemnation by verdict and any imposition of a damage penalty. The cross-dressed female-plaintiff cases, because they deployed the traditional criminal conversation script with its underlying skeletal story of spouse-as-object and defendant-as-seducer, created new story lines that conflicted sharply with the old ones in which women could be only sexual victims, not perpetrators. The female-plaintiff cases came to play an important interim role in the eventual abolition of the torts, partly by giving women a voice and a story, but at least as importantly by bringing the torts' narrative assumptions out into the open, where they could not be ignored. Once seen in the light of day, the cases' property-based claims looked not just atavistic but ridiculous. There was no way to rewrite the adultery story's assumptions to keep it compatible with the law's requirements; instead, with a flourish, many states celebrated the end of "heart-balm" actions. Just as the turn-of-the-century courts complimented themselves on their progressive recognition of women's humanity in permitting them to bring criminal conversation suits, so the courts of the 1980s and '90s sound more than a bit self-congratulatory as they abolish the suits altogether because they are "inherently" offensive to ideas of marital love, female equality, and psychological independence.

Just when it seems that the wheels of legal history have made their final turn and we can say goodbye forever to the torts of criminal conversation and alienation of affections, a highly publicized new case in the summer of 1997 has started those wheels rolling again. On August 5, 1997, a North Carolina jury awarded one million dollars in damages to Dorothy

Hutelmyer, who had sued her ex-husband's new wife for criminal conversation and alienation of affections. The case was covered in many major newspapers, and Mrs. Hutelmyer and her lawyer were interviewed sympathetically on the *Today* show. In the wake of the verdict, the husband's lawyer announced that he was considering an appeal on the ground that the actions are "extremely outdated" and seeking their abolition (*Boston Globe*, 9 August 1997, " 'Storybook Marriage' ends with Record-book Lawsuit"). Perhaps he will be successful. While North Carolina is one of the fourteen or so states that have retained criminal conversation, alienation of affections, and breach of promise to marry as viable torts, the trend is certainly toward abolishing them, either by legislative act or by appellate court decision. Yet in the states that do permit these torts, the number of cases filed appears to be rising. In the fall of 1997, for instance, an investigative report on a national television news magazine show ran an episode about an Illinois case in which a husband was suing his ex-wife's lover for criminal conversation and alienation of affections, charging that the defendant had acted aggressively to destroy a marriage that would otherwise have remained successful and intact. The case was newsworthy precisely because it was so unusual, yet its respectful national coverage suggests that we may see a surge in alienation of affection and criminal conversation suits in the next few years.

If so, appellate courts will be challenged to construct new narratives of marital rights and obligations that will make the suits culturally viable once again. For the torts to work, there must be some form of interest, created in a spouse by virtue of the marriage contract, that is violated by the actions of the other spouse's lover. Certainly, claims based on violations of the plaintiff-spouse's property rights to sexual exclusivity or a propertylike right to the emotional benefits of love and affection are unlikely to be successful. So long as the reign of marriage as a union of independent self-sufficient equals continues, courts are likely to look with disfavor on the idea that, as Prosser and Keeton put it, "one spouse can recover for an act the other spouse has willingly consented to" (917). Yet a closer look at the Hutelmyer case suggests that once again the latest twist in the narrative formulation of spousal entitlements may be based in a borrowing from literary discourse.

Noting the quality and intensity of response that her case had received, *The Boston Globe* asserted that Mrs. Hutelmyer "has been hailed by women from around the nation as the heroine of the First Wives Club," a reference to the successful 1996 movie. In the film, characters played by Bette Midler,

Goldie Hawn, and Diane Keaton scheme successfully for revenge against the husbands who have left them for younger women, as Mrs. Hutelmyer's husband left her to marry his much younger secretary. The popularity of that film led to a series of articles in newspapers and other media about jilted middle-aged wives, their financial difficulties, and their frustrations. What is interesting about the response to both the movie and the case is how different its focus was from the traditional sources of injury in criminal conversation and alienation of affection cases. Neither the husbands' adultery nor the emotional pain of the wives' rejection seemed to be at the heart of the matter. Rather, outrage was directed against the new wives for stepping into a life of luxury and wealth to whose accumulation they had not contributed, and against the husbands for the ease with which they were able to maintain their wealth and to acquire younger and therefore more socially valued partners. The First Wives, like Mrs. Hutelmyer, understood themselves as equal partners in their marriages; while the husbands spent decades rising in their fields and acquiring status, money, and power, the wives contributed time, energy, emotional commitment, mothering, and other intangible assets. Since husband and wife had shared the difficulties and deprivations of life on the way up, it seemed grossly unfair that the husband alone would reap the benefits at the top or shower them on a woman who had done nothing to earn them while the wife was left without money, status, or lover. Yet this story of sudden impoverishment and abandonment—as the coverage of the movie made only too clear—is familiar to Americans from novels, television, and their own lives. What the First Wives' cinematic schemes and Mrs. Hutelmyer's lawsuit did was to write a new ending to the story, a final chapter that provides revenge, financial reward, and a level of empowerment sufficient to cancel out the feelings of worthlessness caused by the husband's departure.

If this narrative works as a basis for reviving—or at least continuing—the torts of criminal conversation and alienation of affections, it will be only the latest in the fairly long line I have been tracing here of essentially nonlegal stories about the substantive basis of marriage that have worked their way into the law. Several ironies are worth noting. First, the level of interest in the sudden financial well-being of the husband's new lover returns the idea of spousal property rights to a tangible form. What the husband owes the wife is not sexual chastity or love and affection but a fair share of the assets that have been accumulated through the joint, though different, efforts of both husband and wife. If a third person interferes with the marriage so that the wife's interests are damaged, she can sue to vindicate them. If the wife's property interest is thus the most old-fashioned possible, the use of the lawsuit to vindicate it also harks back to earlier eras. Just as the very earliest English cases conceptualized the injury of adultery in property terms, in order to qualify for the money-based remedies accessible through the king's law courts but not through the ecclesiastic courts that had traditional jurisdiction over adultery, so the use of the tort by Mrs. Hutelmyer seems designed to remedy a perceived inability of the divorce courts to provide an equitable division of assets. Far from being a new or radical use of the tort, such manipulation of remedies, narratives, and avenues for relief is surprisingly traditional.

Finally, both the First Wives and the Hutelmyer suit take a palpable pleasure in vengeance. Wrongdoers suffer publicly while virtuous plaintiffs gloat; domestic revenge becomes legitimate and even fashionable. One of the primary factors leading to the abolition of the torts in many states was the courts' belief that it was not the government's task to enforce morality or use moral judgments as the basis for distributing burdens and rewards. No-fault divorce ended the centuries-old restriction under which a marriage could only be terminated through a finding that one partner was at fault; the decriminalization in many states of private sexual behavior, including adultery, prevents the government from judging or punishing acts now described as matters of consent and choice. To hold a third party wholly liable for the breakup of a marriage was to reject a typically complicated reality in which all parties shared responsibility and replace it with what Homer Clark called "the vile seducer of Nineteenth Century melodrama" (267). Yet the next wave of narratives, if they do emerge, might revel in the construction of victims and perpetrators and ensure that the bad guys are made to suffer for their immoral acts while the virtuous plaintiffs garner nationwide support.

As a final note, I'd like to return briefly to my earlier argument that the substance of spousal entitlements and obligations was defined by late-nineteenth-century appellate courts through a discourse originating in sentimental literary fiction. While lawyers' arguments to juries at trials have, from Aristotle onward, been understood to require and justify the use of emotion in order to maximize persuasion, the "purely" legal pronouncements made in appellate court opinions have traditionally been assumed to be the quintessence of rationality. Law, the nature of legal rights, and the texts that announce them have all been understood to be characterized by objectivity, rationality, and impersonal abstract analysis. Much of the recent wave of law and literature writing has attacked legal discourse on precisely the ground that it emphasizes "rationality, abstraction, a preference for statistical and empirical proofs over experiential or anecdotal evidence, [and] universal and objective thinking" (Lucinda Finley, "Breaking Women's Silence in Law," 886, 893–94). Feminists like Finley complain that some things cannot be said using "the legal voice" because it lacks emotion (903–4); "outsider" scholars like Richard Delgado call for the legal establishment to make room for and listen closely to "storytelling" by minority speakers because only such voices can capture the actual experiences of women and minorities.[10]

Yet the creation of two categories of legal discourse, one personal, emotional, and grounded in the experience of disempowered outsiders of all kinds and the other white, male, abstract, and non-narrative, rests on a somewhat oversimplified dichotomy. As we have seen, even the seemingly super-rational discourse of appellate courts sometimes relies on such supposedly antirational rhetorical forms as literary sentimentality. This is not to say that the late-nineteenth-century judiciary, which was universally white and male, was undercutting its own position of power by creating and deploying sentimental narratives. Similarly, appellate court decisions that drew comfortably on a fictional discourse privileging emotion over intellect did not produce a generally "feminized" jurisprudence. Yet the ability of such courts to absorb and deploy sentimental rhetoric to serve their own needs surely suggests a permeability and interaction among legal and literary discourses and those who wield them. When a court uses a moving description of a "sensitive wife's" pitiful "anguish" as the basis for establishing a legally enforceable right to bring a lawsuit, it becomes very difficult to characterize either the substance or the rhetorical form of law as entirely cut off from emotion and experience. In moments such as this, many nonlegal voices, the sentimental prominent among them, can be heard within the law's authoritative speech.

NOTES

PART I. INTRODUCTION AND HISTORICAL FOUNDATION

PROLOGUE: Telling Stories in the Courtroom

1. Judge Merlin's prediction that Mrs. Walsh will contest the suit "in vain" because "the law always gives the father possession of the children, unless he is morally, mentally, or physically incapable of taking care of them" is historically accurate for the antebellum period in which the novel is set. In *Governing the Hearth*, Michael Grossberg details the legal assumption of paternal rights in the early nineteenth century, its gradual yielding to those of the mother, and, by the end of the century, to the doctrine of the "best interests of the child" (234–85).

2. For a good survey of the classic debunking texts, including Brown, Pattee, Papashvily, Habegger, and Douglas, as well as the recent change in critical attitudes toward Southworth and her colleagues, see Susan K. Harris, *Nineteenth-Century American Women's Novels*, 1–13. Southworth's supposed relation to the "true" (inevitably male) writers is found in such comments as Ann Douglas's description of the "hothouse language of exaggeration" in Melville's *Pierre* as a possible "parody of the legendary and tempestuous best-sellers cranked out by women like E.D.E.N. Southworth" (*The Feminization of American Culture* 312).

3. Joanna Dobson has written on *The Hidden Hand*, Susan K. Harris on *The Deserted Wife* (*Nineteenth-Century American Women's Novels* 128–51). In 1988 Rutgers University Press reissued *The Hidden Hand; or, Capitola the Madcap*, edited by Dobson.

4. Frank Luther Mott has declared that "for overall sales" Southworth was the greatest publishing success in nineteenth-century America" (Nina Baym, *Woman's Fiction*, 114, relying on Mott). While noting that "the extent of her popularity is difficult to gauge," Baym generally agrees, and emphasizes her longevity as a popular writer, "widely known and widely read in America for some forty years" (114).

5. Though they were refused admission to the bar in Wisconsin (1875), Massachusetts (1881) and Virginia (1890s), by 1900 women had been admitted to the legal profession in thirty-four states. The numbers of women lawyers practicing law and appearing in courts remained extremely low, however (D. Kelly Weisberg, "Barred from the Bar," 232). In 1898 Utah became the first state to permanently permit women to serve on state juries (they had been admitted briefly earlier in

Wyoming). In 1879 the U.S. Supreme Court ruled that states could confine jury duty to males (*Strauder v. West Virginia*, 100 U.S. 303 [1879]). As late as 1966, Alabama, Mississippi, and South Carolina excluded women entirely from juries. The Civil Rights Act of 1957 ensured that women could serve on federal juries; a series of cases in the 1960s made the right available in state courts. See Leo Kanowitz, *Women and the Law*, 28–30.

6. Mary Kelley makes a similar point when she notes that Ishmael "devote[s] his life as a lawyer to defending wronged women in court and to seeking to amend laws that discriminate against them. Ishmael has male ambitions, but he pursues female gains" (*Private Woman, Public Stage* 324).

7. "Under the inspiration of the hour," Southworth tells us, Ishmael "spoke truths new and startling then, but which have since resounded through the senate chambers of the world, changing the laws of the nations in regard to woman" (*Ishmael* 472). Southworth was deserted by her own husband when she was pregnant with her second child. Although her supporters passed a bill in Connecticut that would have enabled her to obtain a legislative divorce, she never pursued divorce, which she considered a sacrilege (Kelley, *Private Woman, Public Stage*, 238).

8. Vivian, the comic lawyer, relies on *Joe Miller's Jests*, an eighteenth-century joke book that continued to be reissued through the nineteenth century. It includes such stories as one in which "a woman once prosecuted a Gentleman for a Rape: Upon the trial, the Judge asked if she made any Resistance. I cry'd out, an please you, my Lord, said she: Ay, said one of the witnesses but that was Nine Months after" (Miller 44–45). Another is: "Second Thoughts, we commonly say, are best; and young Women who pretend to be averse to Marriage, desire not to be taken at their Words. One asking a Girl, if she would have him? Faith, no, John, says she, but you may have me if you will" (65). Both jokes are premised on the assumption that women's words are not credible, that women in fact desire the sex they seem to refuse, and that even their sworn testimony in court should not be taken at face value.

9. In *Ravishing Maidens: Writing Rape in Medieval French Literature and Law*, Kathryn Gravdal notes that in the pastourelle, rape is presented as acceptable, pleasurable, and funny, while the woman's resistance is trivialized or presented as a mask for her real sexual desire, which, after the rape, is expressed in thanks and requests for more of the same (104–22). She then juxtaposes fourteenth-century French court records of rape cases with contemporary pastourelles and songs. Parallels between these texts lead Gravdal to ask whether the literary songs and stories "offer the linguistic paradigm for attitudes toward sexual violence," authorizing and legitimating official victimization of women (135). See also Gravdal's "Poetics of Rape Law in Medieval France," a revised version of *Ravishing Maidens*'s final chapter. As Gravdal notes, the majority of the pastourelles "legitimizes a view of the shepherdess as an unreliable character—greedy, ambitious, deceitful or unfaithful"

(*Ravishing Maidens* 115). As a consequence, all of the woman's vocal expressions, whether cries of pain or articulated refusals to submit, may be dismissed.

1. Criminal Conversation and the Conversational Process of the Law

1. Andrew L. Shapiro, "Reading O.J." *The Nation* 6 March 1995, 297. Dershowitz was employed by the defense team at the time, and was actively involved in the conduct of the case. Dershowitz's talk was later revised, expanded, and published with others from the conference in *Law's Stories: Narrative and Rhetoric in the Law*, edited by Peter Brooks and Paul Gewirtz.

2. Michael Riffaterre's *Fictional Truth* uses narratology to analyze the complicated ways that texts produce an effect of verisimilitude. Reversing the traditional assumption that literary realism depends on an accumulation of mimetic detail and a strong positive correlation with a referential world of experience familiar to readers, Riffaterre argues that realism is achieved wholly within the text, by such strategies as the satisfaction of textual expectations and use of apodeictic assertion.

3. See Nancy Pennington and Reid Hastie, "A Cognitive Theory of Juror Decision Making" (storytelling model by which jurors impose a narrative organization on evidence); the semiotic analyses of Bernard Jackson in *Law, Fact and Narrative Coherence*; Kathryn Holmes Snedaker, "Storytelling in Opening Statements"; W. Lance Bennet, "Storytelling in Criminal Trials"; W. Lance Bennet and Martha Feldman, *Reconstructing Reality in the Courtroom*; Kim Lane Scheppele, "Finding Facts in Legal Interpretation"; and Robert Hariman, *Popular Trials.*

4. Robert Ferguson has been a leading scholar in this field, as his work "Story and Transcription in the Trial of John Brown" and recent essay in Brooks and Gewirtz, *Law's Stories*, demonstrate. Ferguson is one of a small group who have looked closely at the issue of genre in litigative storytelling. Others include Susan Staves, whose "Money for Honor" reads eighteenth-century criminal conversation narratives as specific contests of interpretation between tragedy and farce; Claire Dalton, whose "Essay in the Deconstruction of Contract Doctrine" includes a revealing study of the gendered literary stereotypes that underlie judicial characterization of parties; Anthony Amsterdam and Randy Hertz, whose detailed "Analysis of Closing Arguments to a Jury" invokes classic narrative forms; Philip N. Meyer, whose "Desperate for Love" reads a closing argument in a criminal case through the cinematic influences at work in it; Richard K. Sherwin, whose "A Matter of Voice and Plot" has analyzed courtroom narration in terms of what he calls "belief and suspicion"; and Kathryn Gravdal, whose work connecting medieval rape cases to pastourelle is cited in the Prologue discussion of *Ishmael.*

5. In his famous preface to *The House of Seven Gables*, Nathaniel Hawthorne distinguishes the Romance from the Novel by claiming for the former "a certain lattitude" to depart from depicting with "minute fidelity" the "probable and ordinary course of man's experience." While an author may appropriately introduce

even supernatural elements into a romance, Hawthorne declares, such a work "sins unpardonably so far as it may swerve aside from the truth of the human heart" (1).

6. In a carefully controlled experiment, Pennington and Hastie analyzed jurors' processing of evidence at trials, and concluded that jurors put together a mental narrative of the case as the evidence was presented, a narrative frequently revised to account for new and seemingly inconsistent facts. "A Cognitive Theory of Juror Decision Making," 519–57.

7. Dershowitz argues that the universe is comprised of random and unpredictable facts and events. He uses Chekhov's famous remark, that if a gun is hung on the wall in act 1 it must be discharged by the end of the play, to assert that many facts claimed in court to be relevant are in fact extremely poor predictors of subsequent events and only seem so because of audience familiarity with literary narratives ("Life Is Not a Dramatic Narrative" 100). In many ways, his argument is similar to mine; we both agree that familiar story forms significantly affect jurors' assessment of evidence. Yet where Dershowitz believes that the "importation" of narrative into the courtroom can be eliminated, I do not. The jury's job is to make inferences about the occurrence or nonoccurrence of an event (the defendant did or didn't kill the victim) from whatever predictive evidence is presented (he was seen in the area, he bought a gun, etc.). Whenever inferences must be made, what Riffaterre calls "consecution," the "proceeding from one proposition or fact to another that follows from it" is an issue (*Fictional Truth* 126). Narratives that aim to justify inferences must rely on the predictive valence of certain facts in connection to other facts. As randomness increases, all forms of causation erode, and an inference of guilt from any circumstance or past behavior (because Simpson beat his wife, he probably killed her) becomes harder and harder to make. In general, defense attorneys want to undercut systems of predictability, while prosecutors want to reaffirm them.

8. Aristotle's treatise, "The Art of Rhetoric," devotes a long section to the connections among emotion, proof, and character.

9. In part III, chapters 5 and 6, my analysis of female-plaintiff cases also includes the tort of alienation of affections, an American tort that developed out of criminal conversation.

10. For an analysis of the historical origins and development of the tort of criminal conversation, see chapter 2.

11. These definitions and references can be found in the O.E.D. under "conversation." The place where one lives or dwells, def. 1, Hampole, *Psalter* xviii (1340); consorting or having dealings with others, def. 2, Parsons, *A conference about the next succession to the crowne of England* (1594); sexual intercourse, def. 3. *The first Three English books on America. [1511]–1555. Being chiefly Translations, Compilations &c, by Richard Eden.* Edward Arber, ed. Birmingham, 1885, xxvii; an occupa-

tion or study, def. 4, Bacon, *Words* (a. 1626); manner of conducting oneself, def. 6, *Book of Common Prayer* (1552).

12. Before 1857, divorce was available in England only by way of a private Act of Parliament directed at the particular marriage in question, and only granted on the ground of the wife's adultery, attested to by two witnesses. Such acts were both rare (there were never more than fifty-five a year and usually fewer than twenty) and so prohibitively expensive that only the very rich could even consider them. See Lawrence Stone, *Road to Divorce*, 301–47.

13. Exactly when the first case of criminal conversation appeared is impossible to tell because, as legal historians note, most of the court records for the seventeenth century have now disappeared. See J. S. Cockburn, *History of English Assizes*, 139; J. H. Baker, *An Introduction to English Legal History*, 519; Stone, *Road to Divorce*, 233.

14. In *Commonwealth v. Stowell*, 389 Mass. 171 (1983), the Supreme Judicial Court of Massachusetts rejected a claim that the state's criminal adultery statute violates an adult's constitutional right to privacy when that adult engages in private consensual extramarital sex. For a cogent critique of the decision, see Anne W. Hulecki, "Limitations on the Scope of the Privacy Doctrine in Making Decisions Concerning Adultery," 83–90.

15. In early modern England, adultery was also understood as a sin against the law of God, and was therefore properly dealt with by the ecclesiastical rather than the royal courts. Because only royal, or civil, courts awarded damages, the early history of criminal conversation is shaped by the attempts of litigants to frame the wrong in terms that civil courts would redress (see chapter 2).

16. Another striking example is insanity law. Within the past 150 years, five different tests for criminal insanity have been administered by American courts. From the point of view of a defense attorney preparing a final argument, the applicable definition will vitally affect the way his client's actions are discursively connected to his mental illness. In one jurisdiction, the story will be about a person so vicitimized by illness that his behavior is beyond his control, rendering him the pawn of powerful destructive emotional forces ("irresistable impulse" test, excusing behavior if "because of mental illness, the defendant could not exercise proper control over his unlawful actions"). In another jurisdiction, or in the same jurisdiction at another time, the story will be about a person who is intellectually dissociated from reality, who misinterprets or simply cannot understand the true nature of his own actions (the "McNaghten" rule, which established a cognitive test, excusing behavior only if the actor "did not know the nature and quality of the act, or did not know it was wrong"). Obviously, expert psychiatric testimony and the particular facts will play a role, but we should not underestimate how responsively courtroom narratives are shaped to legal requirements. On the history of insanity defenses, see Ingo Keilitz, "Researching and Reforming the Insanity Defense"; R. D. Mackay, "Post-Hinckley

Insanity in the U.S.A."; and Robert F. Schopp, "Returning to *M'Naghten* to Avoid Moral Mistakes."

2. The Transformative Magic of Legal Fictions

1. *Hide v. Cyssell* is listed by both Baker, *Introduction* (519) and Jeremy D. Weinstein, "Adultery, Law and the State" (217, *sub nom Hyde v. Scyssor*); both historians identify the case as an adultery action brought for "loss of consortium" in the early seventeenth century.

2. Lon Fuller's *Legal Fictions* is the best, and almost the only, extended treatment of the subject. He discusses typical fictions, including the trover and corporation examples, on pages 12–14. As Fuller notes, "the austere science of jurisprudence has not found it possible to dispense with fictions. The influence of the fiction extends to every department of the jurist's activities" (1–2).

3. Fuller's definition of a fiction is "a statement propounded with a complete or partial consciousness of its falsity, or a false statement recognized as having utility" (ibid. 9).

4. Henry Sumner Maine advocates "pruning away the legal fictions," assuming that their verbal content can be easily dispensed with (*Ancient Law* 27). William Blackstone sees them as utilitarian conveniences (*Commentaries* 3:43). Fuller, *Legal Fictions* pays close attention to their content, dividing them into "live" and "dead" fictions and discussing their metaphorical workings, but he sees them as purely linguistic, not as bringing about changes in the real world.

5. For a good historical discussion of the property relations that underlay marriage from medieval to modern times, see Lawrence Stone, *The Family, Sex and Marriage in England 1500–1800.* Carol Pateman, *The Sexual Contract* analyzes the legal contract of marriage in feminist terms; Nancy Armstrong, *Desire and Domestic Fiction* links the rise of the English middle class to reformulation in domestic fiction of earlier cultural assumptions about the relation of marriage to property, birth, and class.

6. Fuller declares that fictions are "the cement that is always at hand to plaster together the weak spots in our intellectual structure," that they are necessary to express premises or assumptions: "a premiseless law would be a fictionless law" (*Legal Fictions* 52). In addition to "live" and "dead" fictions, he categorizes legal fictions on the basis of their content and form as assertive and assumptive (36–37), historical and nonhistorical (56), scientific (71), abbreviatory (81), apologetic (83), fanciful and habitual (85), general and specific (87), procedural (89), and statutory (90).

7. The process of pleading changed over the centuries from a flexible oral challenge and response to a written set of documents, and from Latin to law-French to (in 1731) English. See Baker, *Introduction,* 90–103, 244–45.

8. The English court system was reformed in 1853 by an act that eliminated all

fictions, as well as legal or formal phrases like "force and arms." The process of reform as a whole took much longer, of course. See ibid., 107–10. For the similarly slow and not at all steady process in the United States, see Lawrence Friedman, *A History of American Law*, 391–412. As these discussions show, the much-touted process of simplification created a new set of requirements neither simple nor straightforward, and was not particularly successful at eliminating the mystifying legal speech that justified the monopoly of a priestly class of lawyers.

9. The use of the word "fiction" derived from the Roman *fictio*, a false averment of fact that could not be traversed (Maine, *Ancient Law*, 24–25). The absoluteness of legal fictions in general and of coverture in particular has been persuasively challenged by both recent historians like Baker and classic apologists like Frederick Pollock and Frederick Maitland (*The History of English Law*). Both stress the many ways that courts could take the actual circumstances of a case into account, particularly through the equity side of the law. For example, equity policy permitted a wife whose husband had absconded to make contracts in her own name. Similarly, the eminent eighteenth-century judge, Lord Mansfield, declared (in a probable overstatement) that fictions of the law "hold only in respect to the ends and purposes for which they were invented; when they are urged to an intent and purpose not within the reason and policy of the fiction, the other party may show the truth." *Morris v. Pugh*, (1761) 3 Burr. 1242, 1243, cited in Fuller, *Legal Fictions*, 51*n*6. The frequency with which such fictions were actually and successfully challenged, however, was probably not very great.

10. In "Poetic Diction and Legal Fiction," A. O. Barfield declares that "life varies, law is of its nature unvarying. Yet at the same time it is the function of law to serve, to express, and indeed partly to *make* the social life of the community. That is the paradox, the diurnal solution of which constitutes the process called society. One solution is legislation, the other is fiction. Legislation is drastic, *a priori*, and necessary. Fiction is flexible, empirical and also necessary. 'Without the Fiction of Adoption,' says Maine in his *Ancient Law*, 'it is difficult to understand how Society would ever have escaped from its swaddling-clothes' " (122–23). As later chapters, particularly chapters 5 and 6, demonstrate, I do not share Barfield's confidence in the generally "unvarying" nature of law.

11. Bentham lamented "the necessity of which we are subjected by the imperfection of the instrument for the purposes of discourse, the necessity of mixing falsehood with truth, on pain of being without ideas, as well as without conversation, on some of the most interesting of the subjects that lie within the pale of our cognizance" (*Works* 8:129). But if he reluctantly accepted the utility of fictions in "ordinary" discourse, Bentham refused to admit that they could be anything but pernicious in legal discourse, and he, like Locke, called repeatedly for their total elimination.

12. All citations to Donne's poetry can be found in *The Complete English Poems*:

"The Ecstasy" (53); "The Canonization" (47); "Valediction: Forbidding Mourning" (84).

13. Theodore Redpath, *The Songs and Sonnets of John Donne*, for instance, notes that the "Valediction: Forbidding Mourning" and other related poems "express such deep satisfaction that it seems reasonable to suppose that they arise out of Donne's marriage or the relationship that led up to it" (4). "The Canonization," which some have thought extramarital, he attributes to Donne's desire "to emphasize that romantic love is not the exclusive property of unauthorized liaisons; and also that this marriage for which he was in disgrace and which for some people savored of the extra-marital, was an assertion of the value of love against all competing worldly values" (5). "The Ecstasy" he attributes to courting (14). See also J. B. Leishman, *The Monarch of Wit*, 182–83; R. C. Bald, *John Donne: A Life*, 146, 242.

14. Interestingly, the recent fad for describing male business executives or presidential advisers as "suits," though it reduces men to a category of fungible objects and is certainly used disparagingly, also carries a complimentary resonance, as the suit is thought to bring with it no-nonsense economic or business expertise.

15. Pollock and Maitland express outrage at the suggestion that the wife could be thought a form of chattel, preferring to image coverture as a benign form of guardianship ("We do not treat the wife as a thing or as somewhat that is neither thing nor person; we treat her as a person," *The History of English Law* 406). Weinstein, "Adultery, Law and the State," 214, critiques careless analysts like Jacob Lippman for ignoring this distinction and asserting as legal fact the popular misconception that a husband "owned" his wife as a chattel.

16. Baker calls this a "legal rather than a factual fiction," implying that only the law's characterization of the action as forcible is fictional (*Introduction* 518). Yet the insistence of the allegations of force, especially as they frequently involve descriptions of property damage and physical battery, seem to me to involve quite as much "factual" fictionalization as the other aspects of the legal fictions.

17. In certain circumstances, especially in very early cases, a defendant could apparently defeat an action *vi et armis* by proving that no force had been used. Weinstein describes a 1261 case in which allegations that defendant had broken into plaintiff's house by force and begat a son on his wife were defeated by a jury finding that the defendant had entered at the wife's invitation ("Adultery, Law and the State" 213). Yet Baker also describes a 1308 case in which the plaintiff recovered despite an express jury finding that the abduction was not forcible (518–19).

18. See also the cases cited in ibid. 519*n*51 and Weinstein, "Adultery, Law and the State," 217*n*159. The court in *Guy v. Livesey*, Cro. Jac. 501 (79 Eng. Rep. 428 [K. B. Mich 1619]), said: "The action is not brought in respect of the harm done to the wife, but it is brought for the particular loss of the husband, for that he lost the company of his wife, which is only a damage and loss to himself, for which he shall

have this action, as the master shall have for the loss of his servant's services" (cited in ibid. 217*n*159).

19. The Latin term *consortium*, Englished without alteration, came to include a bundle of rights arising out of the marital relationship. As the *Restatement of the Law of Torts* defines it: "the legally protected marital interests of one spouse include the affections, society and companionship of the other spouse, sexual relations and the exclusive enjoyment of them, services in the home and support" (ch. 32 sec. 683, comment c). Noting that the word "consortium" is frequently used "to indicate any or all of those interests of the husband or wife in the marriage relation that receive legal protection by rules of law," the Restatement rejects it as "ambiguous" and declines to use it. In the English loss of services cases, the award of damages was explicitly keyed to the plaintiff's ability to show a loss of service, however trivial. So once a typical aristocratic plaintiff had shown that his wife formerly made his evening tea, the jury was freed to award enormous damages, clearly intended to compensate the emotional, not the service injury (Weinstein, "Adultery, Law and the State," 217).

20. In the 1904 U.S. Supreme Court case of *Tinker v. Colwell*, 193 U.S. 473 (1904), for instance, the court discussed the "assault *vi et armis*" as a "fiction of the law" (481), the historical framing of adultery as "an actual trespass on the marital rights of the husband" (483), and included citations to Blackstone and half a dozen early English cases, all in the course of adjudicating whether a declaration of bankruptcy under U.S. federal law wiped out an unpaid damage judgment against the bankrupt for criminal conversation. I discuss this case in detail in chapter 5.

PART II. THEODORE TILTON VS. HENRY WARD BEECHER

PROLOGUE: Crisis of Confidence in the Courtroom

1. On Beecher's cultural importance, see generally William G. McLoughlin, *The Meaning of Henry Ward Beecher*; Paul A. Carter, *The Spiritual Crisis of the Gilded Age*; Clifford E. Clark Jr., *Henry Ward Beecher*; and Altina E. Waller, *Reverend Beecher and Mrs. Tilton.* While it is important to my argument to recognize Beecher as a national symbol of religious virtue, it is not my purpose to analyze his doctrines in detail. Though historians agree that Beecher was an enormously important moral and religious figure whose fall triggered a national crisis of confidence in the values he represented, they disagree sharply about just what those values were. To Clark, Beecher symbolized "the Victorian cultural ethos." At a time "when industrialization and the growth of cities were changing the face of the nation, he had reaffirmed the morality of an earlier, more rural America" (225). People who were "frightened by the rapid and chaotic social change" had found Beecher reassuring;

consequently, if the leading spokesman for Victorian morality was unmasked as "a fraud and a charlatan, then how could anyone still believe in the cultural system he espoused?" (198). Altina Waller's book-length examination of the case makes Beecher a champion not of old-fashioned values but of "freedom from the rigidity of traditional institutions—family, church, or town"; an advocate of love and "affinity" over obligations to family; a believer in the value of social mobility and material success; the perfect preacher for "a congregation of young men whose chances for survival in a changing world required a geographic, economic, and intellectual departure from the past" (67, 109). To Waller, the trial called into question not "the morality of an earlier, more rural America" but Beecher's radical doctrines of emotional "affinity," raising fears that Beecher's "Doctrine of Love" might be the first step down a slippery slope that would end in promiscuous and irreligious cohabitation.

2. See Carter, *The Spiritual Crisis of the Gilded Age*, 115. As the scandal grew, a number of quickly published books appeared on the market, reprinting the "documents" in the case and offering biographies of the people involved. A large number appeared between the time that Tilton filed his complaint (August 1874) and the beginning of the trial (January 1875). Typical titles include: Charles F. Marshall, *The True History of the Brooklyn Scandal: Being a Complete Account of the Trial of Henry Ward Beecher, of Plymouth Church, Brooklyn, Upon Charges Preferred by Theodore Tilton, Including All the Original Letters, Documents, and Private Correspondence With Biographies of the Leading Actors in the Great Drama* (1874); Francis P. Williamson, *Beecher and His Accusers: A Complete History of the Great Controversy, Including the Life of Henry Ward Beecher, Together With Pen and Ink Sketches of the Persons Prominently Involved, A Full Record of All the Facts, Leading Comments, Choice Extracts, Characteristic Anecdotes and Important Revelations From Reliable Private Sources* (1874); "A classmate of H. W. Beecher," *The Veil Removed; or, Henry Ward Beecher's Trial and Acquittal Investigated, Love Demonstrated in Plain Dealing, The Congregational Council Reviewed* (1874).

3. E. L. Godkin, letter to James Russell Lowell, 30 July 1874 (William Armstrong, ed., *The Gilded Age Letters of E. L. Godkin*, 212).

4. On July 22, 1874, the *Chicago Tribune* published five columns on "The Beecher Explosion." On August 13, in a "major and highly sensational scoop," nearly five pages, twenty-two full columns, were devoted to the publication of the Tiltons' letters, which were then picked up and published in the New York papers (Lloyd Wendt, *Chicago Tribune*, 248–50). Robert Shaplen reports that "with the case taking whole pages, national and world news was often reduced to one or two lines," and discusses international coverage (*Free Love and Heavenly Sinners* 206–14).

5. Although the name of the common law tort is criminal conversation, this was a civil, not a criminal case. Criminal conversation is a husband's suit for money

damages from his wife's lover. For an introduction to the tort and its history, see chapter 2. The distinction between civil and criminal was, perhaps understandably, blurred or lost completely in both the forensic and the media discourse surrounding the scandal and trial. Newspapers focused on the alleged acts of adultery at the heart of the case and, disregarding legal niceties, described Beecher as "under the suspicion of a dark crime" (*The Beecher Trial: A Review of the Evidence* 33). Even such generally well-informed modern historians as Altina Waller have mischaracterized the case as criminal (*Reverend Beecher and Mrs. Tilton* 11). The law's circumscribed civil story was simply overpowered by the universal sense that something much larger was profoundly at stake.

Beecher was never indicted on criminal charges, but a wealth of lawsuits surrounded the case. In 1872, Victoria Woodhull was briefly imprisoned at the request of morality warden Anthony Comstock on federal charges of sending obscene materials through the mails, the "materials" at issue being the *Woodhull & Claflin's Weekly* article that began the scandal (Shaplen, *Free Love and Heavenly Sinners*, 162–64). In October 1874, before the criminal conversation trial began, Beecher swore out a criminal complaint that led to indictments against Tilton and his friend Frank Moulton on charges of malicious libel. When the criminal conversation case ended inconclusively, Moulton "clamored to be tried" on the libel charges, knowing that Elizabeth Tilton "would be subpoenaed and both she and the pastor would be rigorously cross-examined." The suit was dismissed, whereupon Moulton sued Beecher for malicious prosecution, a charge that was also eventually dismissed (Shaplen 260; Marshall, *The True History*, 606–9).

6. Tilton's complaint alleged, in the verbal formula required for the torts of criminal conversation and alienation of affections, that Beecher's adultery with his wife had caused the alienation of her affections from him, by reason of which "the plaintiff has wholly lost the comfort, society, aid and assistance of his said wife," causing "great distress in body and mind to the damage of the plaintiff one hundred thousand dollars" McDivitt, *Tilton versus Beecher*, 1:2–3. (The transcript, recorded by newspaper reporters in the courtroom, was published in small booklets as the trial proceeded, and issued later in the year in three bound volumes by two different publishers. Hereafter, transcript references will be made in the text by parenthetical reference to volume and page number in the McDivitt edition.) The amount of damages sought was highly unusual even for such cases. When it became apparent that the public was reacting with horror and distaste to the idea that Tilton sought to profit financially from his wife's disgrace, he withdrew all claims for money damages, declaring that he wanted only vindication and truth. See the closing argument for Tilton (3:907), asserting that he "disdains the idea of touching the gold" of Beecher and wants only the impartial hearing he couldn't get from Beecher's church council.

7. Although Elizabeth Tilton's reputation and future life were very much at

stake, she had no part in the lawsuit. A verdict for Tilton would not have rendered her liable to pay damages, nor would it have served as a legally binding judgment against her in a criminal prosecution for adultery. The case was carried on between the two men; it is in this sense that her "interests" were not involved. For a fuller discussion of her role in the case, see chapter 4. The longstanding ban on spouses testifying for or against each other in any litigation disqualified her from appearing as a witness. Simon Greenleaf justified the ban on public policy grounds in his 1854 *Treatise on the Law of Evidence*, declaring: "It is essential to the happiness of social life that the confidence subsisting between husband and wife should be sacredly protected and cherished in its most unlimited extent; and to break down or impair the great principles which protect the sanctities of that relation would be to destroy the best solace of human existence" (sec. 334–35, 495–96). See also William Bowdesley Best, *Principles of the Law of Evidence*, sec. 127. Yet even Beecher's attorneys called Elizabeth "the true defendant in the cause—she whose lips are sealed and whose hands are tied, while the battle is waging over her body" (2:5). For strategic reasons, Tilton offered to waive the spousal privilege if his wife wished to testify for Beecher. As he no doubt expected, however, the trial judge refused the offer of waiver (3:313–14).

8. See, for example, testimony of Theodore Tilton, 2:391, 396–98 (recitation of Mrs. Tilton's "confessions of guilt to her husband"); 2:402 (Beecher had told Tilton that "their sexual commerce had been through love and not through lust"); 2:454–57 (series of questions to Tilton about Elizabeth's character, "pride in woman's chastity," reading habits, religious opinions, "the delicacy of her behavior toward the other sex," and whether she was "of a sympathetic and affectionate nature"). During the opening and closing arguments, lawyers for both sides commented freely on her "middle age" and "gray hairs" (3:649, 826). Beecher's lawyers characterized her as a "child" an "unhappy little woman" engaged in a "violent and protracted struggle between her passion and her sense of duty, which had destroyed her health and unsettled her reason" (2:49, 48). Tilton's attorneys refused to agree that she had an "exalted and perfect character" (3:887), stressing instead her "shame and infamy," her "weakness" and her "fall" (3:889–92).

9. For descriptions of the carnival atmosphere of the trial, see daily reporters' commentaries in the transcript, especially day 19 ("a stranger might have thought himself in a place of amusement," 1:459); Shaplen, *Free Love and Heavenly Sinners*, 216; Milton Rugoff, *America's Gilded Age*, 207–8. In "An Afternoon at the Beecher Trial," an *Overland Monthly* reporter describes the trial as a "matinee" and "reviews" it as drama. Samuel Leland Powers, *Portraits of a Half Century*, provides a description of both the trial and Beecher's Sunday sermons during the trial from the point of view of a very young lawyer. For the delivery of floral arrangements see Walter Earle, *Shearman and Sterling 1873–1973*, 117–19. E. L. Godkin, who was disgusted by the scandal and considered Beecher a fraud, likened the flowers in the courtroom

to "wreaths round the man-hole of a sewer." Quoted in Clark, *Henry Ward Beecher*, 227. On the scalping of tickets, see the *Overland Monthly* article and Rugoff, *The Beechers*, 496.

10. Complete trial transcripts were published daily in several New York newspapers, including the *New York Tribune* and *The New York Times*. The *Tribune's* reporter became an important functionary in the courtroom; Judge Neilson occasionally asked him to read back testimony (1:171). His daily transcripts became the basis for McDivitt and Campbell's three-volume edition of the trial, *Tilton versus Beecher, Action for Crim. Con.* See also advertisements for the "Pictorial History of the Beecher-Tilton trial" for sale "at all news depots price 30 cents," and classified ads for "agents wanted for the True History of the Brooklyn Scandal" in *Frank Leslie's Illustrated Newspaper.*

11. Mrs. Tilton's letter to her legal adviser was reprinted in most American newspapers. In it, she declared that "the charge of adultery between myself and the Reverend Henry Ward Beecher was true, and that the lie I had lived so well the last four years had become intolerable to me." Even three years after the trial, *The New York Times* devoted four columns on page 1 to the story of Mrs. Tilton's letter, Beecher's denials, and the comments of family, friends, and lawyers (16 April 1878, 1).

3. The Maintenance of Mutual Confidence

1. The Beecher scandal has received a substantial amount of critical attention. Though reaching sharply different assessments of the famous preacher's personal virtue, biographers such as Clark, McLoughlin, and Hibben see the scandal as critical evidence for the project of understanding the Gilded Age through its most "representative" figure. The introduction to Paxton Hibben's 1927 biography, *Henry Ward Beecher: An American Portrait*, attributes Beecher's significance to his representative capacity: he is "a prodigious figure not by blazing a path in any wilderness, but by the fact that his inner experience was identical with that of millions of his fellow countrymen" (xiv). Clifford E. Clark Jr.'s biography, *Henry Ward Beecher: Spokesman for a Middle-Class America*, attributes Beecher's popularity to his having "articulated the attitudes and values of a new urban middle class that emerged at mid-century," while his life "provides new insight into the relationship between religion and Victorian culture in America during the crucial middle decades of the nineteenth century" (3, 4). Social historians, reading the scandal through such situating specifics as the demographics of membership in Beecher's church, the political affiliations of his attorneys, and the editorial slants of the media coverage, argue that it elicited widespread expressions of anxiety about spirituality (Carter), intimacy (Fox), and political and religious rivalries between different denominations and political parties (Waller). Significantly, none of these major studies analyzes the trial or its rhetoric closely. There are two notable exceptions to this communal dismissal of the trial as subject: Cheree Carlson, "The Role of Character in Public

Moral Argument: Henry Ward Beecher and the Brooklyn Scandal," and Ann Douglas, *The Feminization of American Culture.* Carlson's article uses Douglas's "feminization" thesis to analyze Beecher's defense strategy. Douglas considers the trial briefly and disdainfully, mocking Elizabeth Tilton's intimacy with Beecher rather than analyzing it.

2. There is a lively critical literature on narrative and storytelling in the courtroom. Recent examples include Brooks and Gewirtz's excellent collection of essays, *Law's Stories*; Robert Weisberg and Guyora Binder, *Literary Criticism of Law* (1996); essays collected in *Vermont Law Review* 18 (1994); Robin West, *Narrative, Authority and the Law* (1993); Dennis R. Klink, *The Word of the Law* (1992); "Symposium: Legal Storytelling," *Michigan Law Review* 87 (1989). Earlier work by Bennett and Feldman, Hariman, Schuetz and Snedaker, and Bernard Jackson, among others, continues to be useful (see list of works cited for full citations).

3. The jury's verdict, while it provides a formal moment of closure at the end of the trial, may well not be the last narrative in the case. On appeal, a new set of oppositional stories will be told, narratives that will include the "story" of the trial and the alleged errors that were committed there. One or more appeals court decisions will supply additional narrative framings of the case, each with a different emphasis. It is worth noting, however, that because the jury is officially denominated the "finder of fact," questions about events antecedent to the trial that have been settled by the verdict are not technically open on appeal. This gives the jury a special authoring power within the realm of fact. As Kim Lane Scheppele has persuasively argued, however, the distinction between fact and law is often more apparent than real, as fact and law are "mutually constituting, not simply hard to tell apart" ("Finding Facts in Legal Interpretation" 62).

4. A similar interactive drama is the long-running Boston production of the murder mystery *Shear Madness.* Audience members are permitted to question the character-actors directly, as actors improvise responses. The audience then votes on the murderer, after which a final scene validates their choice. "You have to make the audience important," says Bruce Jordan, the show's producer. "Their input must be cherished." (Patti Hartigan, "*Madness* Cuts It for 10 Years," B33).

5. This is not to imply that all stories fit neatly into preexisting genres or that, once labeled, they will inevitably follow predictable patterns. Much of the pleasure of reading involves being surprised by the unexpected (see Stanley Fish, *Surprised by Sin*). While Wolfgang Iser has argued that "expectations are scarcely ever fulfilled in truly literary texts" because their confirmation suggests a didactic purpose and a reductive clarity, readers often report that their greatest enjoyment in reading such genres as melodrama and romance is tied to the security of their discursive expections, their confidence that the rules will be followed in a satisfying way (see Janice Radway, *Reading the Romance*).

6. In most popular sentimental fiction, sympathetic victims and heroines ulti-

mately succeed in worldly terms, winning marriage, money, and, presumably, personal salvation (see Warner's *The Wide, Wide World*, Cummins's *The Lamplighter*, Evans's *St. Elmo*). Some, like Eva and Tom in *Uncle Tom's Cabin*, "succeed" by going to heaven. Yet even where the sufferings of characters like Tom, or various minor characters in Dickens novels (Jo in *Bleak House*, Smike in *Nicholas Nickleby*) remain unrelieved and unavenged, the novel's inability to "solve" such problems within the confines of its fictional world is consistent with sentimentality's reader-centered strategy, since if the characters' pain is effective it will elicit in readers a determination to relieve suffering wherever they encounter it.

7. In their recent analysis of the Rodney King beating trial, Kimberlé Crenshaw and Gary Peller use this approach effectively, describing the battle for narrative control at the trial as a larger ideological struggle that would determine the meaning of race in the trial context. "This very struggle over meaning is precisely what the intense contestations about race in the law are really about," they argue ("Reel Time/Real Justice" 64). They identify a defense strategy of "disaggregation," a "narrative technique that narrows the perception of the range of illegitimate racial power by divorcing particular episodes from their larger social context," and compare it to a "counternarrative" of insurrection that "implies a focus on the power relations and dynamics that exist between the 'rioters' and the 'police'," conceiving of the uprising "as a communal response to a much larger set of issues of social power" (68).

8. In his closing for Beecher, for instance, Porter dealt with the highly sentimentalized language of one of Elizabeth Tilton's letters both affirmatively and defensively. First, he exploited sentimentality as a guarantor of sincerity and a tool for making determinations of credibility when he noted that the letter was written "by the side of the cradle and on the evening of the Sabbath day" by a "mother loyal to her husband" (3:576). Then, in an attempt to co-opt the sneering response such letters had elicited, he blamed their availability on Theodore Tilton, who betrayed his wife by "sending forth this letter to the world to encounter the scoffs and the derision of those who despise sentimentalism" (3:576). Earlier, he had invited the jurors to blame the letters' artificiality on Theodore: "You marvel at the sentimental form of the letters of Mrs. Tilton. Now bear in mind, gentlemen, she had an excuse, this man required it. It was he that dictated how her letters were to be written" (3:573). This double attitude, both accepting and mocking the emotional intensity of sentimental rhetoric, especially in letters, ran throughout the trial.

9. Beecher's counsel made a delayed opening statement beginning on the thirty-seventh trial day, after Tilton had presented his affirmative case.

10. The complaint that sentimentality's insistence on eliciting sympathetic, even tearful, responses from readers is fraudulent and that it parades false and inauthentic emotion, received its most famous formulation in James Baldwin's attack on *Uncle Tom's Cabin*, "Everybody's Protest Novel." Similar attacks were also made at

the time of the Beecher trial, as when *The Nation* issued a "lesson for sentimentalists" before the trial started, warning that the "letters, 'statements' and other documents of the parties to the affair" exhibited a use of sentimental language that "seems almost to lose the character of an instrument for the expression of definite propositions—or, in other words, for the communication by one human being to another of formulated thought—and becomes a mere mode of indicating certain states of feeling, like the noises made by the lower animals" (Editorial, 3 September 1874, 150). While lawyers for both sides indulged in melodramatic sentimentalized rhetoric without fear of mockery, readings from certain letters and documents elicited vociferous amusement in the courtroom, which the lawyers often exploited. In his summing up for Beecher, for instance, Mr. Porter's reading of "supposed expressions" from the letters was reported as having "stirred up a breeze of merriment in the audience" (3:557).

11. Not to be outdone, defense counsel, in their delayed opening statement on the thirty-seventh day, assured the jury that "the magnitude and importance of the questions here involved cannot be over-estimated, for they go down to the very foundations of our social, moral and religious life," and concluded by assuring the jury that the trial "will loom larger in history than any which has taken place for eighteen centuries" (2:6, 92). Jurors were warned that they would have to answer for their verdict at the Last Judgment, and that "strangers from distant climes" would one day make pilgrimages to the courtroom to see the place "from which was given back to the world freed from cloud or passing shadow, the name of Henry Ward Beecher" (2:1, 92). Though the contesting parties themselves treated the matter as a grudge match between public men over personal betrayal, the attorneys never tired of asserting that all of civilization hung fire on the success of their efforts. Much of this rhetorical grandstanding was obviously aimed at the almost one hundred reporters who attended court daily, writing up each day's "high points" and turning well-known lawyers into nationally lionized heroes, but it also reveals the extraordinary notion participants had at the time of the case's current and imagined future historical significance.

12. Under modern rules of civil procedure, either party can obtain summary judgment if "there is no genuine issue . . . as to any material fact" and the moving party is entitled to a judgment as a matter of law (Fed. R. Civ. Pro. 56[c]). For a history of the gradual adoption of summary judgment procedures, see Charles E. Clark and Charles U. Samenow, "The Summary Judgment" (1929). The intense factual disputes that characterized the Beecher case would have precluded summary judgment, of course, even if it had been available in New York in 1875. To say that there are no conflicts "as to any material fact" does not mean, however, that there is nothing to argue about. Where both parties stipulate to a set of facts, they may nevertheless engage in intense and protracted disputes about how to interpret the facts and about applicable law.

13. This argument does not mean to ignore the often profoundly blurred line between misperception and bias. The unreliability of eyewitness testimony is notorious, and has been for more than a century. See *United States v. Wade*, 388 U.S. 218, 228–43 (1967). The "suggestibility" that troubled the Supreme Court in lineup situations applies to other areas as well, including witness unreliability and jurors' difficulty in assessing the credibility of eyewitness testimony. Many studies have shown that a witness's sincere recollection can be significantly affected by the "unconscious transference" of memories that preexisted the event and by postevent suggestions. See Gary L. Wells and Elizabeth Loftus, eds., *Eyewitness Testimony*, 1–11, 31–33; Paul Ekman, *Telling Lies*, 162. These unreliabilities have led to the adoption of various safeguards, including expert testimony intended to sensitize the jury to factors that affect memory and perception. See Elaine D. Ingulli, "Trial by Jury," and *Law and Human Behavior*'s "Special Issue: The Ethics of Expert Testimony." Nevertheless, it is still possible to distinguish between the inherent unreliability of individual perception and the construction of intentionally false testimony.

14. The line between sincerity and bias can be a fine one. Without intentionally falsifying their characterizations of data or their conclusions, expert witnesses are often influenced by their own ideological, political, and personal agendas. See Barton L. Ingraham, "The Ethics of Testimony," 178–99; and "Special Issue: The Ethics of Expert Testimony." As Gordon Bermant has noted, experts "do not knowingly speak falsely," but debates about the propriety of expert testimony may "camouflage arguments about the strength of psychological knowledge" and the scientific certainty of such expert testimony ("Two Conjectures" 97–98).

15. For a provocative discussion of the increasing use of circumstantial evidence in the nineteenth century and its relation to the rise of the realist novel, see Alexander Welsh, *Strong Representations.*

16. One of the trial's credibility problems was that Elizabeth Tilton's continual assertions and denials of guilt led to "such a bewildering series of recantations that in the end nothing she said was fully believed" (Rugoff, *America's Gilded Age*, 204). Because Mrs. Tilton could not testify, her role in the relationship had to be constructed indirectly, through letters and conversations; such texts were not merely ambiguous, they were directly inconsistent. See discussion in chapter 4.

17. In *Fictional Truth*, Riffaterre argues that the believability or "truthfulness" of a literary fiction is a textual effect rather than a function of the relation between text and external world. This argument seems to me equally persuasive when applied to courtroom narratives, in which the "external world," though very much at issue, can only be represented through the narratives of testimony or, on occasion, the "speaking" narratives of "real" evidence.

18. On the impact of immigration to urban areas on Americans' sense of security and "place," see Robert H. Wiebe, who argues in *The Search for Order* that the rush to the cities "brought a constant influx of inexperienced newcomers" whose

"sense of belonging" was disrupted and who shared little more than a "common sense of drift. . . . Fearful of each other's competition and ignorant of each other's ways, they lived in mutual suspicion, as separated into groups of their own kind as they could manage" (12–14).

19. Halttunen's somewhat oversimplified "rise and fall" trajectory has been critiqued by, among others, William R. Leach, who notes that fears of hypocrisy and prescriptions offered to assuage them both predated and outlasted the years Halttunen assigns. "If middle-class anxieties were as intense and troubling as Halttunen claims, how could they have disappeared so quickly?" he asks ("Review of *Confidence Men and Painted Women*" 56). Leach argues, and I agree, that the "tensions between authenticity and charlatanism" were never resolved and have persisted into our own time (56). The hearings on Justice Clarence Thomas's confirmation for the Supreme Court are a modern case in point. Much of the defensive analysis insisted, as did Beecher's defenders in the 1870s, that the judge's life of public virtue constituted strong evidence that he could not possibly have been a hypocrite hiding a corrupt private life. But while fears about hypocrisy never really disappear, the decade of the 1870s does seem to have been an especially anxious period, a high point of concern.

20. In a September editorial in *The Nation*, E. L. Godkin declared that "people do not know what to believe" and were looking to the trial to settle the vexing questions of the scandal. Godkin also predicted presciently that the trial would present "questions of veracity, between three or four persons whose credit is already greatly shaken, or, in other words, the very kind of questions on which juries are most likely to disagree" (24 September 1874, 201).

21. The jury need not agree that the winning side's narrative version is unqualifiedly "true," or that the losing party's is "false," nor need they agree with each other about what exactly happened to give rise to the lawsuit. Jurors may formulate inconsistent factual narratives, reject the insistent binarism of adversaries by formulating a third factual narrative drawn from both parties' facts, or discount large chunks of either side's version, yet still concur as to which side has the better case overall. Many juries attempt to "split the difference" by such strategies as awarding the plaintiff the verdict but minimal damages or, in criminal cases, by returning a verdict for a lesser included offense. By referring to the verdict as "triumphantly" labeling narratives truth or fiction, I mean to describe their formal effect. Ordinarily, jury verdicts are not accompanied by detailed findings of fact, and each juror's personal narrative does not become part of the record. Yet once the verdict is returned, it retroactively affects the "truth-value" of all witness and party narratives in any subsequent discussion of the case, whether in or out of court. The winner's story is no longer described as "alleged" but as proven, while the loser's story must fight the ineradicable shadow of rejection.

22. As a decade, the 1870s seemed to major in scandal, especially in New York.

In 1873, "Boss" Tweed was convicted of corruption in public office after a sensational trial. A few years earlier, the McFarland-Richardson affair of 1869 combined sex, divorce, and murder to spectacular effect: when actress Abby McFarland left her alcoholic husband and obtained an Indiana divorce, her now ex-husband shot her lover, Richardson, in the offices of the *New York Tribune.* Before Richardson died, Henry Ward Beecher married him to Abby McFarland, and the resulting scandal was of national scope. *The New York Times* publicly doubted "whether a more disgraceful outrage on public morals has ever been committed in this community than is involved in the open scorn of the marriage tie and the total disregard of all principles of justice, which professed ministers of religion and public writers have managed to display" (4 December 1869, quoted in Nelson Manfred Blake, *The Road to Reno,* 102). That Beecher had already been connected in the public mind with sexual scandal may have intensified the interest when his own behavior came under scrutiny a few years later. In *America's Gilded Age,* Milton Rugoff examines the Beecher case as one among a series of sexual scandals during this period, including the Sickles-Key affair, in which a congressman murdered his wife's lover and was acquitted on grounds of temporary insanity, and the Fisk-Stokes affair, featuring blackmail, corruption, and adultery (183–229).

23. For a good discussion of Evarts's important role in nineteenth-century American law and politics, see Brainerd Dyer, *The Public Career of William Maxwell Evarts.* Evarts's eloquence during his long career—in court and out—is collected in three volumes in Sherman Evarts, ed., *Arguments and Speeches of William Maxwell Evarts.*

24. See also Jane Tompkins, *Sensational Designs,* 122–46; Janet Todd, *Sensibility,* ch. 1; S. Clark, *Sentimental Modernism,* 19–41; and Shirley Samuels, ed., *The Culture of Sentiment.* The essays collected in Samuels capture quite well the current critical debates about the political effect of sentimental works (subversive and empowering, or an education in passivity?) and a glimpse of the broad cultural backdrop against which the sentimental synthesis was played out (*Godey's Lady's Book,* murder trials, educational manifestos, abolitionist rhetoric, etc.).

25. Tompkins sees radical action as a consequence of successful sentimentality, particularly a religious re-vision that makes its bid for power by "positing the kingdom of heaven on earth as a world over which women exercise ultimate control" (141). Philip Fisher, however, insists that sentimental texts evoke a sense of powerlessness and helplessness in readers (*Hard Facts*). I see sentimental texts as always crucially pushing toward real-world response, including the possibility of action in contexts broader than those presented only by religious and domestic issues. My argument therefore aligns more closely with Tompkins's and intends to challenge Fisher's.

26. Beecher's counsel compared him, explicitly and implicitly, to Jesus (2:91, 3:557, 651). While they noted the stress on him caused by the scandal, they also took

care to emphasize the outpourings of support he had received, declaring that he was "in this supreme emergency of his life, girded by millions of faithful hearts and walled to heaven by the unfaltering love and confidence of his people" (2:7). Counsel also described happy evenings spent in the Beecher home during the trial, encouraging the jury to envision the "light and joy" in his home where the family was "fused together in one spirit of kindliness and love" (3:562).

27. See Robyn R. Warhol's *Gendered Interventions*, which studies this phenomenon in useful detail.

28. The enormous difference in response to such passages is, I believe, responsible for the widely varying judgments of Stowe's "authenticity" and success as a writer. Some readers resent being "manipulated" by her narrative, but Stowe's assaultive engagement should be recognized as part of her political strategy. All texts are arguably empty until "made" by reading, but Stowe's novel, more than most, is quite literally incomplete until an involved reader constructs its potentialities. As a mother of young children, I should and do read *Uncle Tom's Cabin* differently from the unmarried college students to whom I have taught it. This is not a sign of the text's inadequacy, but of its very particular brand of openness. The emotional depth of my maternal experience is anticipated by and necessary to Stowe's text. It is to her credit that she not only intervenes to create bridges to as many different readers as she does ("generous and noble-minded men and women of the South," "strong-hearted sailors and ship-owners of Maine") but also manages to draw in readers whose experiences do not include parental love.

29. For a similar forensic reading of the licentious body of one accused of a sexual offense, see Ed Cohen, "Typing Wilde: Construing the 'Desire to Appear to Be a Person Inclined to the Gravest of All Offenses.'" Cohen analyzes the way that the media coverage of Oscar Wilde's sodomy trial contrasted Wilde's "feminized," "soft," and "grotesque" body with the Marquis of Queensbury's stalwart masculine appearance and "implacable" gaze, a contrast that "came both to personify the structures of difference through which the newspapers articulated their narratives and to represent the differences in question as the negation of middle-class male norms" (18, 15–20). Beach's "reading" of Beecher's body, like the newspaper's characterization of Wilde's, intended to prove that "abnormal" sexuality was visible, inherent, and transparent. It also aimed, by presenting "undeniable" physical evidence of licentiousness, to demonstrate to jurors that Beecher was different than they were, outside the "middle-class male norms" that, up until the scandal, he had seemed quintessentially to represent.

30. Justin Kaplan's introduction also links *The Gilded Age* to the Credit Mobilier scandal, while Bryant Morey French's book-length study of the novel persuasively reads it as a parody of the 1872 San Francisco murder trial of Laura Fair (*Mark Twain and the Gilded Age* 96–116). It is also true, however, that Warner and Twain were friends of Beecher. Beecher had written the introduction to Warner's *My*

Summer in a Garden, and both were members of Nook Farm, the Hartford social group that included Beecher's sister, Isabella Beecher Hooker. In *Nook Farm: Mark Twain's Hartford Circle*, Kenneth R. Andrews asserts that "nothing else in the years between 1870 and 1875 loomed so large in Nook Farm's experience as the disaster befalling Henry Ward Beecher," and describes in detail the involvement of Twain and Warner in the unfolding scandal and the trial (35, 33–41). It is quite likely, therefore, that the scandal was very much on their minds as they co-wrote the novel at breakneck speed.

31. Though he does not analyze the novel, Paul Carter also notes its parallels to the Beecher-Tilton case, commenting briefly that "the real people in *Tilton v. Beecher* talked like the fictitious people involved in the Laura trial in volume 2 of *The Gilded Age*, published two years earlier. Perhaps it was another case of life imitating art" (*The Spiritual Crisis of the Gilded Age* 116).

32. On the connection between *The Gilded Age* and Twain's attitudes toward juries and insanity pleas, see French, *Mark Twain and the Gilded Age*, 96–116. For a reading of the novel as an attack on sentimental literature in general, see Susan K. Harris, "Four Ways to Inscribe a Mackerel," 138–53. Twain's words are taken from a March 10, 1873 letter to the editor of the *New York Tribune* (p. 5), describing the "ideal criminal juror" (cited in French 100).

33. Twain's confidence that his text demonstrates the outrageousness of the temporary insanity plea may be seriously misplaced. The satirical treatment of the Hawkins verdict and Twain's well-known disdain for such pleas make it clear that he expected readers to agree that Laura's was an act of premeditated murder, committed by a wholly sane, morally corrupt woman who should be held responsible both for the murder and for her sexual "fall." This conclusion is undercut, however, by the earlier sections of the book, which construct Laura as an assemblage of sentimental topoi—a sympathetic character abused, betrayed, and irremediably damaged by her seducer. At bottom, the pretrial narrative of her life and lawyer Braham's sentimental formulation are not very different. Many sympathetic modern readers will reasonably connect Laura's sexual victimization to her later loss of control and resort to violence, especially since Twain never accords her an inner life or an autonomous "rational" decision-making independence. A more serious attack on the gendered insanity defense would have required imaging Laura *outside* the stereotypes of female irrationality that produced the defense in the first place. See Edward Berenson's *The Trial of Madame Cailloux*, which connects legal concepts of insanity at the turn of the twentieth century to the gendered, stereotypical literary and scientific discourses of the day about women and sexuality.

34. For a novel that presents the empathic bonds of sentimentality as the ideal forensic mode for courtroom argument, see E.D.E.N Southworth's *Ishmael*, discussed in the prologue to part 1.

35. By referring to the unambiguous moral field in which sentimental fiction is

explicitly enacted, I do not mean to deny the power of such fictions to implicitly subvert their surface simplicity. Like sensationalist fictions of the 1860s, sentimental novels often subtly invite different alliances than those explicitly claimed by the text. In particular, they offer female readers images of sexual and social empowerment, however necessary it may be to "punish" such independence by the novel's end. For explorations of this complexity, see Tompkins, *Sensational Designs*; Baym, *Woman's Fiction*; and Lyn Pykett, *The 'Improper' Feminine*; and my discussion in chapter 4 of Elizabeth Tilton's sentimental response to *Griffith Gaunt*, a sensationalist novel.

36. The distinction I am getting at here can best be understood in the context of criminal behavior. Sentimental villains—Stowe's Simon Legree; Dickens's Murdstone, Bill Sykes, and Wackford Squeers—may have sketchy, unloved childhoods, but are not permitted to become genuinely sympathetic or to be seen as less than responsible for their own evil. Realist fiction, however, has as a central trope the protagonist who is both murderer and victim, from Clyde Griffiths in *An American Tragedy* to Bigger Thomas in *Native Son* to Joe Christmas in *Light in August*. These novels invite us to see criminal behavior in a larger context of racial, class, and cultural oppression, forcing us to rethink such notions as moral judgments of "character," individual responsibility, and free will. Both Dreiser and Wright use climactic trials to contrast the morally ambiguous world created by the novel's narrative with the criminal law's reductive drive to fix all blame on a single, stereotypically "evil" defendant. Their fictional trials can in turn be contrasted to an actual trial like Beecher-Tilton, at which the drive for a single "answer" became diffused into multiple and competing versions of events and interpretations of documents until the possibility of fixing the "blame" definitively was thoroughly undercut.

4. Silent Woman, Speaking Fiction

1. The day after the trial ended, the *Times* printed a lengthy analysis of the evidence, later published separately as a pamphlet (see discussion at end of chapter 3, above). Although the trial ended without a verdict, the *Times* judged Beecher unequivocally guilty of adultery and condemned Tilton as self-interested and corrupt. While it did censure both of the male parties to the case, the *Times* judged Elizabeth Tilton most harshly, declaring that "a city full of such women would not be worth the trouble and misery which this one has occasioned" (34).

2. Theodore Tilton testified for fourteen days, from the sixteenth to the twenty-ninth trial day. See transcript, 1:385–693. Beecher also testified for fourteen days, from the fifty-sixth to the sixty-ninth trial day. See 2:728–902; 3:1–136.

3. On the wife's exclusion from criminal conversation litigation, see note 7, prologue to chapter 3.

4. The description of Mrs. Tilton is from the Reporter's notes to the day's testimony. The Reporter also included Mrs. Tilton's statement in full, so while the jury did not hear it, it appears in the published transcript and, of course, in the various

newspapers covering the trial. The statement, an assertion of her innocence, is discussed in detail later in this chapter.

5. For an excellent history of criminal conversation in England, see Stone, *Road to Divorce*, 231–300 ("The wife, as one whose legal personality was absorbed into that of her husband, was not permitted to play any part in it; she was denied the opportunity to call witnesses or testify in her own defense" 234). Other useful discussions include Staves, "Money for Honor"; Weinstein, "Adultery, Law and the State"; and Jacob Lippman, who in "The Breakdown of Consortium" concentrates on American cases. In using the term "homosocial," I invoke Eve Sedgwick, who in turn relies on Rene Girard, Claude Levi-Strauss, and Gayle Rubin for the model of homosocial triangulation of relationships in which two men attain intimacy through their complex sharing of a woman who, as the object of their exchange, is denied subjectivity.

6. On the irrelevance of the wife's consent, see the historical discussion in chapter 2 and the narrative analysis in my discussion of female-plaintiff cases in chapter 5. As the U.S. Supreme Court declared in *Tinker v. Colwell*, 193 U.S. 473, 481 (1904): "the husband has certain personal and exclusive rights with regard to the person of his wife which are interfered with and invaded by criminal conversation with her; that such an act on the part of another man constitutes an assault even when, as is almost universally the case as proved, the wife in fact consents to the act, because the wife is in law incapable of giving any consent to affect the husband's rights as against the wrongdoer."

7. In addition to criminal conversation cases, divorce cases that named a husband's alleged lover as correspondent also accused women of the reputation-destroying crime of adultery while the structure of the litigation prevented them from entering the case or defending themselves. In an unusual 1880 divorce case, *Clay v. Clay*, 21 Hun. (N.Y.) 609 (1880), A New York appellate court responded to the petition of Isabella D. Lyon, who had been named as the adulterous correspondent in a divorce case. Miss Lyon protested that unless she could intervene as a party in the action, her good name and character were liable to be destroyed by a public trial at which the plaintiff could introduce supposed evidence of her adulterous behavior that she was powerless to contradict. While holding that it did not have the legal power to permit the intervention, the court nevertheless did its best to assure her full participation in the case, ordering that notice be given to her counsel of all proceedings, that she be allowed through counsel to cross-examine all witnesses, and that she was entitled to testify herself and to have compulsory process for the production of witnesses in her own behalf.

8. See testimony of Tilton, 2:391, 396–98 (recitation of Mrs. Tilton's "confessions" of guilt to her husband), 402 (Beecher told Tilton that "their sexual commerce had been through love and not through lust"), 443 (Beecher never denied the "criminal intercourse" with Elizabeth, but insisted that he should be blamed for it), 452 (asked

"what estimate do you put on the intellectual powers of your wife?" Tilton replied "she has more than common brain"), 454–57 (series of questions to Tilton about her character, "pride in woman's chastity," reading habits, religious opinions, "the delicacy of her behavior toward the other sex," whether she was "of a sympathetic and affectionate nature?"). A complete list of such references would go on for many pages.

9. The opening and closing arguments are so permeated with references to Elizabeth Tilton's character and to her involvement in the adultery that specific references would have to include most of the text. The lawyers for both sides felt free to comment on her "middle age" and "gray hairs" (3:649, 826). Beecher's lawyers characterized her as "like a child," an "unhappy little woman" with a "shattered mind" (2:44) and suggested that her "passion" and "dangerous affection" for Beecher led her to "imagine that the object of her love had solicited her affections" (2:44–47) while maintaining—with perhaps obvious over-protestations—that she was "pure as gold, chaste as snow, pious as a saint" (3:658). Tilton's attorneys refused to agree with either party's assertions that she had "an exalted and perfect character" (3:887), stressing instead her "shame and infamy," her "weakness," and her "fall" (3:889–92) as a woman who betrayed her marriage vows (3:817).

10. Judge Neilson ruled that the confidential communications between husband and wife could not be admitted (2:387); moreover, without Elizabeth's available testimony, a recitation of her words was clearly hearsay. Positioning the recital as a narrative from Tilton to Beecher made the conversation admissible because it showed the information that Tilton had given to Beecher, and thus explained Beecher's motives and actions. It was not admitted as evidence of the truth of Elizabeth's recital, but only of the fact that such a recital took place. Of course, the jury heard the testimony in full, regardless of how they were instructed to receive it.

11. In his opening for Beecher, Benjamin Tracy argued that Tilton's "facility at scheming" made him the "true source of most of the scandals" about Beecher (2:20). He accused Tilton of having coaxed and threatened his wife into writing her "retraction" (2:23), suggested that Beecher's so-called "Apology" had been deviously obtained by Tilton (2:44), that various letters consisted of "words that are manufactured and put into the mouth of Henry Ward Beecher on occasion after occasion" (2:52). Summing up later for Beecher, John Porter described Theodore Tilton's letters as "a sham" (3:567), rejected the testimony of Elizabeth's brother, Joe Richards, as not credible because he was a "dastard . . . tutored by Theodore Tilton" who made "a theatrical exhibition of himself which no one could have devised without the aid of Theodore Tilton's acquaintance with the histrionics of all sham" (3:583). Describing Beecher as "true but simple-hearted," he accused Tilton and Moulton of having Beecher "under their control as the hour hand of the watch is under the control of the manufacturer who put together the machinery that made it" (3:597). Beecher's confessional statements were full of expressions of which he was absolutely incapable; Beecher's real words "come leaping, living burning from

the heart," while these words were obviously "Tiltonian," betraying their "incongruous ideas with rhetorical charm" (3:606).

12. In felony cases in the mid-eighteenth century in England, the prosecution was permitted to have counsel, but the defense was not. There was no privilege against self-incrimination. The accused might consult with a lawyer outside the courtroom, as Catherine Gaunt did, but the in-court examination of witnesses and address to the jury were performed by the defendant on his or her own behalf (John H. Langbein, "The Criminal Trial Before the Lawyers," 307–14). This rule was gradually relaxed beginning with isolated cases in the 1740s and 1750s, but it was not until the Prisoners Counsel Act of 1836 that felony defendants were at last given the right "to make full answer and defense thereto by counsel learned in the law" (Baker, *Introduction*, 418).

13. See M. E. Braddon, *Lady Audley's Secret* (1863), in which the scheming, aggressive heroine, a bigamist, arsonist, and attempted murderer, is finally institutionalized as insane; Braddon's *Aurora Floyd* (1863), in which the heroine, a wild, tomboyish child, marries her father's groom to satisfy an obvious sexual passion, horsewhips a man for maltreating a dog, and commits bigamy; and Wilkie Collins's *No Name* (1862), in which the exploits of the sexually aggressive heroine, Magdalen Vanstone, "include running away from home, working as an actress, appearing in disguise as her governess, taking a job as a parlour-maid, marrying under a false name, and setting up a partnership to deceive with a disreputable rogue" (Reynolds and Humble, *Victorian Heroines*, 120).

14. My comparison of sensational and sentimental fiction is not meant to ignore the current critical debate about the subversive potential of sentimental fiction. Where Ann Douglas (*The Feminization of American Culture*) famously dismissed sentimental fiction as a fake, "rancid," escapist education in submissiveness, Jane Tompkins (*Sensational Designs*) and Nina Baym (*Woman's Fiction*), among others, have fought back by re-imaging sentimental fiction as producing its own form of power. For Tompkins especially, sentimental fiction takes into account the fact that "women could neither own property, nor vote, nor speak at public meeting if both sexes were present," offering to women in such situations "a way of defining themselves which gave them power and status nevertheless in their own eyes and in the eyes of the world" (160–61). "While outwardly conforming to the exigencies of her social role," declares Tompkins, "inwardly the heroine becomes master of her fate and subject to no one outside herself" (165). It is precisely this *un*worldly power that Elizabeth Tilton found in *Griffith Gaunt.*

15. Letter, Charles Dickens to Wilkie Collins, 20 February 1867 (Paroissien, ed., *Selected Letters*, 358–59).

16. *Griffith Gaunt* seems to have had a striking affinity for the courtoom. Reade, a trained (though nonpracticing) lawyer who delighted in litigation, sued both *The Round Table* and *The London Review.* According to Frank Luther Mott, the novel

was introduced into evidence in Reade's *Round Table* suit and half of it was read to the jury by a well-known elocutionist (*Golden Multitudes* 92). Reade had the unsatisfactory pleasure of winning the case but obtaining a verdict for only six cents in damages. Some consolation was no doubt provided, however, by the fact that the trial publicity caused the novel to sell "like hot cakes" (92).

17. Modern reviewers include Burns, Elwin, and Hughes. It is worth noting in this context that while *Griffith Gaunt* is not only Reade's best book but also a splendid example of the transgressive, female-empowering sensation novel of the 1860s, it has been roundly ignored by feminist critics of the genre like Pykett, Garrison, and Showalter, whose investigations have been limited to novels by women writers. Yet it is Reade's complex rendering of female psychology that makes him "nearly alone among the mid-Victorians, for once on a level with his rival George Eliot, in his perceptive creation of women as full, intelligent, sexual beings" (Winifred Hughes, *The Maniac in the Cellar*, 103).

18. This group of critics includes Garrison, Hughes, Pykett, Cvetkovich, Showalter, and Reynolds. Reynolds confidently refers to the "modern critical consensus that sensation fiction represents a radical, socially disrupive literary form" (*Victorian Heroines* 104).

19. My analysis has of course assumed what the letter never asserts—that the "sin" referred to is the sin of adultery. While that assumption seems to me justified by my own study of the transcripts and related historical materials, we should not forget that it was the central fact at issue in the case. I believe and write on the assumption that Elizabeth Tilton did in fact have a sexual affair with Beecher. The adultery was never proved in court, nor did Beecher admit it. Biographers and historians are split. While my arguments about reading would still be valid in the absence of an affair, I do not take the position that whether or not the relationship was consummated is irrelevant.

20. This spiritual cleansing should not be attributed exclusively to the "ministry" of Catherine Gaunt, however. It should also be read as more evidence of the complex generic intertextuality that characterizes Elizabeth Tilton's reading experience: her sudden access to moral purity after penitent contemplation of "sin" suggests that, along with sentimental and sensational fiction, her response may have been influenced by familiarity with Christian conversion narratives.

21. A very incomplete list of explicit literary references made in the opening and closing arguments alone includes detailed discussions of biblical episodes (Sermon on the Mount 1:336, David and Uriah 3:931, the Last Supper 2:34–35, the Day of Revelation 2:92, the crucifixion 3:651, Samson and Delilah 3:658), Emerson's *Essays* (3:717), Moliere's *School for Scandal* (3:695), Dickens's *Our Mutual Friend* (2:32), Byron's "the Giaour" (3:934), Macauley's *Life of Bacon* (3:885), Scott's *Heart of Midlothian* (3:947), Burns's "epistle to a young friend" (3:942), Josephus' *Antiquities of the Jews* (3:947), Whittier's "Ichabod" (3:1017), Shakespeare's *Othello* (3:604).

22. The devotion and purity of the character were based on Elizabeth, Theodore Tilton said, and "I know it is good because I made it up from Elizabeth's letters, and my heart was cleft in twain to find in these letters some of the same sentences that crept into this chapter." His aim, he added, was to paint their relationship for the public: "it would be a very thorough answer, as coming from me, to the scandals in the community, and people would say, 'Theodore respects his wife,' as I do today" (see text of Tilton's cross-examination in *The Great Brooklyn Scandal* 66). As at the trial, both a novel and Elizabeth's letters were offered as evidence of her "real" character. The twist in the Church investigation was that instead of the letters recording a response to fiction, they apparently stimulated its creation.

23. For a useful discussion of this phenomenon see John Henry Raleigh, who begins by declaring that "one of the least understandable appeals of Scott's novels is what was thought to be their great realism, of which, in the context of the conventional novel of the day (Austen, of course, excepted), they were prize examples" ("What Scott Meant to the Victorians" 100). Raleigh details the "ring of authenticity" in Scott's history novels, their ability to convince readers that, as Raleigh quotes Nassau Senior asserting in a review, "though the details presented to us never existed, yet they must resemble what really happened; and that while the leading persons and events are as remote from those of ordinary life as the inventions of Scuderi, the picture of human nature is as faithful as could have been given by Fielding or Le Sage" (105).

24. It was a central tenet of Beecher's theory of the case that Tilton had manufactured evidence, put words into the mouths of witnesses, dictated the form in which his wife's letters were written, and otherwise been "the true source" of all the scandals (2:20, and see 2:37, 52; 3:557, 563, 567, 574, 583, 593, 641, 711, 713–18, 775). In return, Tilton's attorneys accused John Porter and Benjamin Tracy (Beecher's attorneys) of being "theatric" and a "facile, versatile performer" (3:816, 1011), declared that Mrs. Beecher's presence in the courtroom had a "theatric air" intended to influence the jury (3:882), accused a witness against Tilton of being a theatric sham (3:991), and charged that Beecher's defense aimed to "curry up a crime" against Tilton, while Beecher's rhetoric was full of sophistries (1:299, 3:939).

25. The counteractive effect of witnessing decreases, though, if X is a disfavored witness—a prostitute, say, or a person with a criminal record—whose narrative will be vulnerable to attack regardless of its verisimilitude.

26. At one point, for instance, Evarts excoriates Tilton for having published the letter as if it were a confession of adultery when he "knew perfectly well that there was no adultery on the part of the wife Catherine in 'Griffith Gaunt,' he knew there was an abundance of the part of Griffith, the husband" (3:743).

27. Other instrumental distortions of the novel's plot, though not as egregious, were made to further Evarts's forensic strategy of painting Tilton rather than Beecher as the corrupt adulterer. Reade describes Griffith as an essentially unspiri-

tual, unintellectual man whose fiery jealousy is grounded on resentment of his wife's obvious preference for and attraction to the priest. Yet Evarts characterized Griffith as jealous of the "greater intellect, and the greater piety, and the greater aspirations and the greater labors" of the "holy man," a clear reference not to the novel, but to the defense contention that Tilton's suit was motivated by jealousy of the "greater" Beecher. Similarly, Griffith's relationship with the altogether admirable Mercy Vint is presented by Reade not as adulterous, but as bigamous—that is, he accepts her love, engages in a pristine, gentle courtship, and only commences sexual relations after their marriage. In other scenes, he virtuously resists the temptations to adultery offered by the maid Ryder. Yet Evarts characterizes the adverse "consequence" of the novel's marital discord to be its "driving the husband into actual adultery" and the false jealousy of the husband as "plunging him into actual guilt" (3:741–42), and refers to the "abundance" of adultery on the part of Griffith (3:743). Here again, the interpretive characterization of the book was intended not to explicate the novel but to emphasize Tilton's sexual infidelities and failures as a husband.

28. If Elizabeth Tilton's smothered selfhood can be read as typically Victorian, we should also note that both she and her husband were involved in the women's suffrage movement (Theodore was president of the Union Suffrage Association), and that both were friends of such strong and reformist women as Susan B. Anthony and Laura Curtis Bullard. The proximity of Elizabeth to women like Anthony and Bullard is one more piece of evidence that the unique convergence of each person's circumstances, rather than cultural generalities, determines her character and behavior.

29. See note 13.

30. In submitting their marital correspondence to the press for publication, Theodore Tilton abridged the "Catherine Gaunt" letter by omitting the line "I know not that you will ever be able to say this to *me*." He was cross-examined at length about this omission, with the suggestion that the letter, far from demonstrating a consciousness of the wife's adultery, referred quite explicitly to the husband's. From a textual point of view, the transformations, alterations, and interpretations of the letter intensify its referential insufficiency—its inability to be permanently captured by any one particular, definitive, or unambiguous meaning.

PART III. FEMALE-PLAINTIFF CRIMINAL CONVERSATION CASES

5. Rethinking the Law's Story of Marriage

1. The first wave of opposition to the actions did not come until the 1930s, when public resentment over their possible abuse led to the legislative abolition of the

"heart balm" torts of alienation of affections, criminal conversation, seduction, and breach of promise in Indiana, New York, and Illinois (Nathan Feinsinger, "Legislative Attack," 979; Kay Kavanagh, "Alienation of Affections and Criminal Conversation," 330). As of 1994, thirty-four states and the District of Columbia had abolished alienation of affections, while thirty-seven states and the District of Columbia had abolished criminal conversation. In most states, abolition was accomplished by statutory acts of the state legislature; in a significant number, however, the state's courts abolished either or both of the torts by decision. See *Thomas v. Siddiqui*, 869 S.W.2d 740, 743–44 (Mo. banc 1994).

2. As the discussions in chapters 2 and 4 detail, criminal conversation is historically a commercial claim for deprivation of the husband's property interest in the exclusive use of his wife's body and services (see generally Stone, *Road to Divorce*, 231–346). It is a classically homosocial story in which the wife functions as a silent object whose sexuality is given a money value to be paid by one man to another. In using the term "homosocial" I intend to invoke Eve Sedgwick, who proposes a model of homosocial triangulation of relationships in which two men attain intimacy through their complex sharing of a woman who, as the object of the exchange, is denied subjectivity. The wife could not be a witness because spouses were disqualified from testifying either for or against each other, on the ground that "it is essential to the happiness of social life that the confidence subsisting between husband and wife should be sacredly protected and cherished in its most unlimited extent" (Greenleaf, *Treatise*, secs. 334–35).

3. While the husband obtained a form of ownership of, or a property right in, his wife's body, "a wife did not acquire a similar property right over the body of her husband despite the mutual exchange of vows at the wedding ceremony" (Stone, *Road to Divorce*, 243). As Prosser declares in his *Handbook of the Law of Torts*, "the wife, at common law, had no actions analogous to those of the husband for interference with the domestic relation" (C.19, sec. 101:927).

4. On coverture in general, see Blackstone 1:442; Stone, *Family*, 136–42. On the legal preclusions, see Baker, *Introduction*, 550–57. The absoluteness, in practical terms, of these legal preclusions has been challenged in recent years by writers on English (Baker) and American (Norma Basch, *In the Eyes of the Law*) legal history. In the female-plaintiff cases discussed below, defendants sometimes raised on appeal the wife's failure to join the husband as plaintiff. In *Foot v. Card*, for instance, the Supreme Court of Connecticut ruled that spousal joinder was unnecessary in such a case, because it was "the pith and marrow of the complaint that in alienating the husband's conjugal affection from the wife . . . the defendant . . . has inflicted upon the plaintiff an injury by which from the nature of the case it is impossible for the husband to suffer injury; for which it is impossible for him to ask redress either for himself or for his wife" (58 Conn. 1, 10 [1889]).

5. On the domestic ideal of nineteenth-century American womanhood, see

Carroll Smith Rosenberg, *Disorderly Conduct*; Nancy F. Cott, *The Bonds of Womanhood*; Barbara Welter, "The Cult of True Womanhood." While the ideal woman was happily homebound, it is important to remember that women in this era also ventured into the public spaces of authorship, political agitation, and the professions, though often in the face of vehement opposition. See, e.g. Mary Kelley, *Private Woman, Public Stage* (female authors); Katherine Kish Sklar, *Catherine Beecher* (the public life of Catherine Beecher); Deborah L. Rhode, *Justice and Gender* (female lawyers and feminist activists).

6. Female plaintiff criminal conversation cases were never brought in Great Britain because the Matrimonial Causes Act of 1857 abolished criminal conversation as a separate cause of action at approximately the same time that women would first have been able to bring such suits. The suit for damages was incorporated as an option into the suit for divorce, until its final elimination in 1970. The 1857 act established the British divorce courts and ended almost two centuries of Parliamentary divorce (Stone, *Road to Divorce*, 290–95).

7. In a 1930 law review article, "The Breakdown of Consortium," Jacob Lippman discussed the cases briefly in analytical terms, and they have been acknowledged in modern tort treatises such as Prosser's and by law review authors considering the continued viability of "heart balm" torts (Kavanagh, "Alienation of Affections and Criminal Conversation"; Feinsinger, "Legislative Attack"). Yet no recent work that I am aware of has taken up these cases in detail, from either a legal or a narrative perspective.

8. In these cases, the text of the applicable Married Women's Property Acts, for instance, varied widely from state to state. Some acts spoke in broad terms about giving married women vastly expanded substantive rights, while others were narrowly drawn to apply only in specifically enumerated contexts. As Elizabeth Bowles Warbasse notes, the acts were often badly drafted, ambiguous, and confusing. Passed to remedy particular perceived problems, they often "corrected minor abuses but left major ones unchanged" (*The Changing Legal Rights of Married Women* 300–301). Significantly too, the preexisting law of criminal conversation, though fairly consistent among states, did contain variations. Massachusetts, for instance, did not permit a separate action for alienation of affections, allowing the claim only as an element of the damages in a suit for criminal conversation (*Houghton v. Rice*, 174 Mass 366 [1899]).

9. Some areas of the law are more statute-dependent than others. For instance, the Uniform Commercial Code and the federal tax code contain myriad specific rules and subrules that govern transactions. Even in these areas, however, the applicability of the provisions of the relevant code to a particular fact situation often requires interpretation by courts, opening the way for the same kind of narrative delineation of the law that takes place in any traditionally common law field.

10. Though issued by a single author, appellate texts may inscribe a variety of

dialogues; sometimes issued "per curiam," they are usually written by and issued under the name of a single judge, whose opinion a majority of the bench joins. Majority opinions may be followed by concurring or dissenting opinions from other members of the appellate court that challenge the logic, approach, or results adopted by the majority. Even when such intracourt challenges are not embodied in separate opinions, they may nevertheless be reflected in the text of the majority opinion, the terms of which are often negotiated to obtain needed votes. In the cases at issue here, opinions also frequently conform to, quote, or argue with decisions of lower courts or courts in other jurisdictions. In addition, the opinions also inevitably participate in ongoing cultural dialogues about issues that impinge on the legal questions addressed, dialogues carried on in other venues such as newspapers, scientific treatises, and literary fiction.

11. The best analysis of the interrelation of law and fact is Kim Lane Scheppele's. As she notes, "the practice of judging simultaneously engages both [fact and law] in an ongoing project of meaning making, producing a single opinion in which fact and law are woven together in one coherent whole" ("Finding Facts" 60). In producing that opinion, appellate courts have a freedom to rewrite or substitute new or allegorical fact constellations as a way of getting at the legal principles they wish to analyze. Because appellate opinions have as an explicit aim the formulation of general legal principles that can be applied in a variety of contexts, the specific facts of the case can be subordinated to a paradigmatic or didactic set of facts.

12. The New York appellate court in *Bennett v. Bennett*, for instance, framed its discussion of applicable statutes and precedents by asking whether "the wife" has "such a legal right to the conjugal society of her husband as to enable her to recover against one who wrongfully deprives her of that right?" (588), a question it then answered in the affirmative.

This is not to suggest that appellate court opinions are able to delineate with certainty the applicable rule to be followed in future, different circumstances than those in the case before them. Even the most seemingly determinate opinion can provide only the starting point for a future process of interpretation. The open-ended indeterminacy of appellate law is the subject of much scholarly writing and dispute. See Stanley Fish, *Doing What Comes Naturally*; Richard A. Posner, *Law and Literature*; Steven Mailloux, "Rhetorical Hermeneutics"; Sanford Levinson, "Law as Literature"; Ronald Dworkin, "Law as Interpretation."

13. Much of the explosion of "law and literature" writing in recent years has been devoted to explicating or challenging this principle. See, for instance, the interchanges between Stanley Fish on one hand and Owen Fiss, Richard Posner, and Ronald Dworkin on the other. Fish's essays, "Working on the Chain Gang: Interpretation in Law and Literature," "Wrong Again," "Fish vs. Fiss," and "Don't Know Much About the Middle Ages: Posner on Law and Literature," are collected in *Doing What Comes Naturally*. See also Fiss, "Objectivity and Interpretation" and

Posner, *Law and Literature.* Dworkin, "Law as Interpretation" and "My Reply to Stanley Fish" are in *The Politics of Interpretation,* W.J.T. Mitchell, ed. In an attempt to restrict the applicability of its decision beyond the unique constellation of circumstances upon which it has based its ruling, appellate courts will occasionally go so far as to limit their holdings explicitly to "the facts of the case." Yet even when a court does its best to carve a very narrow niche, its decision will be available as a form of law and therefore open to the full process of interpretation and argument. As Charles W. Hedrick says about parables, language that aims at clarity is just as subject to ambiguity and interpretation as language that is deliberate or self-conscious about its linguistic indeterminacy (*Parables as Poetic Fictions*).

14. On characterization in parable, see ibid.; Angus Fletcher, *Allegory*; Louis Macneice, *Varieties of Parable.*

15. Here the court narratives function as parables did for audiences contemporary with their construction. Hasidic parables and Jesus' parables recount familiar events and types from the culture of the people intended to read and hear them. The symbolic dimension of killing a fatted calf is more visible to us now that most Americans don't fatten calves for food; similarly, the medieval court cases discussed in chapter 2, with their narratives about broken hedges and stolen headdresses, seem more obviously referential and parable-like than they would have to the community for which they were intended.

16. The tort of alienation of affections permits a plaintiff to sue based on any acts intended to induce an emotional and physical separation between the plaintiff and the spouse. Adultery is presumed to be such an act, but nonsexual interferences will also support a claim, and in-laws frequently appear as defendants (Prosser, *Handbook of the Law of Torts,* 920–21).

17. The court's absolute deletion of the facts of the case is not typical. Most appellate opinions do include statements of facts that contextualize the law and that the court returns to for justificatory "evidence" to support its conclusions. Even where the facts are narrated, however, they are meant to represent a class of replicable situations and interactions, so their function always pulls away from the specific and toward the generic.

18. The American Law Institute's *Model Penal Code* (*MPC*) notes that at common law, robbery was "specific aggravated behavior occurring in the course of committing a theft," and distinguishes robbery from ordinary larceny "by the presence of the victim and the use or threat of violence" (Intro. Note to sec. 222.95). The current ALI definition of robbery is: "A person is guilty of robbery if, in the course of committing a theft, he: (a) inflicts serious bodily injury upon another; or (b) threatens another with or purposely puts him in fear of immediate serious bodily injury; or (c) commits or threatens immediately to commit any felony of the first or second degree." An act shall be deemed "in the course of committing a theft" if it occurs in an attempt to commit theft or in flight after the attempt or commission (222.1).

At common law, the crime of burglary "consisted of a breaking and entering of a dwelling house of another at night with the intent to commit a felony therein" (221.1) The current definition "proscribes as burglary an unprivileged entry into a building or occupied structure with intent to commit a crime therein" (Intro. Note to sec. 221.1). The current ALI definition of burglary is: "A person is guilty of burglary if he enters a building or occupied structure, or separately secured or occupied portion thereof, with purpose to commit a crime therein, unless the premises are at the time, open to the public or the actor is licensed or privileged to enter. It is an affirmative defense to prosecution for burglary that the building or structure was abandoned" (221.1).

19. See Sherry Hamburg Flax, "Note: Judicial Abrogation," 206 ("Although the cause of action was regarded as an intentional tort, the elements were only a valid marriage and an act of sexual intercourse between the defendant and the plaintiff's wife"); *Restatement of the Law of Torts* sec. 685; *Prosser and Keeton on the Law of Torts* sec. 124 at 917.

20. Kim Lane Scheppele uses the familiar turtle story to describe the interconnectedness of fact and law in any lawsuit or judicial opinion ("Finding Facts" 69*n*14). She attributes it to Clifford Geertz, who tells the Indian tale of "an Englishman who, 'having been told that the world rested on the back of an elephant which rested on the back of a turtle, asked. . . . What did the turtle rest on? Another turtle. And that turtle? "Ah, Sahib, after that, it is turtles all the way down" ' " (*The Interpretation of Cultures* 29).

21. For a fuller discussion of this principle, see chapter 2.

22. See Aristotle, *Poetics,* 7. A whole is that which has a beginning, middle and end.

23. In "Money for Honor: Damages for Criminal Conversation," Susan Staves explores the class implications of a lawsuit premised on "what was sometimes felt to be the fundamental impropriety of exhanging honor for money" (279), in which, while denigrating the equation of honor and money, upper-class plaintiffs were not only willing to take cash but also insisted on taking more of it for the same injury than "humbler men in the professions or in trade" (280).

24. For a good analysis of the changing status of women in relation to the law in nineteenth-century America, see Norma Basch, "The Emerging Legal History of Women in the United States." See also Warbasse, *The Changing Legal Rights of Married Women*; Basch, *In the Eyes of the Law*; and Linda K. Kerber, *Women of the Republic.*

25. Recent scholarship has depicted the acts as the ratification of a "silent revolution" that brought women into the economic and commercial marketplace, making it in both men's and women's interest to remove archaic disabilities that kept married women from managing their own property (Rhode, *Justice and Gender,* 24–26; Basch, *In the Eyes of the Law,* 225–31).

26. Martha Minow expands this point with relation to gender by explaining that "legal rules effectively defined the functions and powers of women both within and outside the family by reinforcing social roles, and yet women used these very roles to sustain function and powers beyond those contemplated by legal rules." She then suggests "that their creative use of social roles allowed women periodically to challenge not only particular legal rules, but also the conception of rights and individual autonomy implicit in the legal system" (" 'Forming Under Everything That Grows' " 837–38). While Minow does not explicitly consider the role of literary culture in shaping roles and expectations, she does analyze legal rules as interacting with a broad range of cultural structures.

27. While state law governs both substance and procedure of tort actions, tort cases can be brought in federal courts when there are grounds for federal jurisdiction. *Tinker* presented questions of federal bankruptcy law, specifically whether a money judgment for criminal conversation was wiped out when the defendant declared bankruptcy (as a commercial debt), or survived the bankruptcy (as a matter of moral turpitude). The court found that the debt did survive: "The injury for which it was recovered is one of the grossest which can be inflicted upon the husband, and the person who perpetuates it knows it is an offense of the most aggravated character . . . and we think Congress did not intend to permit such an injury to be released by a discharge in bankruptcy" (489–90).

28. Maine courts were especially wary of female-plaintiff cases. In *Roe*, the court feared permitting wives to bring such cases because "such a power would furnish them with the means of inflicting untold misery upon others, with little hope of redress for themselves" (82 Me. at 504). Eight years later, in *Morgan v. Martin*, the Supreme Court of Maine again rejected female plaintiffs, worrying that "impulsive and emotional women" who could initiate adultery suits whenever they liked would be highly destructive, especially to wealthy women against whom the suits might be brought abusively. Indeed, Maine courts continued to forbid female-plaintiff adultery suits outright until forced to take them by a 1913 statute, after which they interpreted the statute so narrowly as to prevent many claims from succeeding. See *Howard v. Howard*, 120 Me. 479 (1921), which construed the statute to preclude an alienation of affections claim by a wife against her father-in-law, because the defendant was male.

29. When, in the early twentieth century, scientific interest in sexuality and disease entered into legal decision making, a few courts found that the risk of a wife's contracting venereal disease from an unfaithful husband was an appropriate counterbalance to the dangers of illegitimacy produced by a wife's infidelity. In *Nolin v. Pearson*, 191 Mass. 283 (1906), the Massachusetts Supreme Judicial Court declared that the "loss of fellowship" to the wife when her husband is seduced by another woman "is an injury as tangible and from which she may suffer as acutely and with more disastrous consequences to herself" than from loss of reputation (191 Mass. at

288–89). Seventeen years later, the New York Court of Appeals explicitly equated the husband's right to beget his own children with the wife's interest in "having a clean man and healthy children," holding that the interest of the husband in the legitimacy of his children "may be offset by the interest which the wife has in the bodily and mental health of her children when they are legitimate" and that can be threatened by "the dire consequences which sometimes follow promiscuous intercourse by a man" (*Oppenheim v. Kridel*, 236 N.Y. 156, 161 [1923]).

30. On the historical origins and modern "breakdown" of consortium, see Lippman. He defines consortium generally as "the mutual right of the parties to the society, companionship and affection of each other, and the right of the husband to the services of the wife" ("The Breakdown of Consortium" 651).

31. See discussion in chapter 2, and see Baker, *Introduction*, 517–21, who argues that torts for loss of services began with suits for procuring or enticing a servant to depart from his service, and were "matched" in an analogous way by actions for an interference with the marital relationship, usually grounded in adultery. It is this historical connection to master-servant cases that accounts for the verbal formulation of criminal conversation in terms of a loss of the wife's services.

32. Citing Stone, Wadlington, and Trumbach, Minow observes: "these works locate the shift from patriarchal to egalitarian families in England and Europe during the eighteenth century, while the American story tends to focus the shift in the nineteenth century (" 'Forming Under Everything That Grows' " 830*n*32). On companionate marriage in America in the nineteenth century, see Kerber, *Women of the Republic*; Cott, *The Bonds of Womanhood*; and Elaine Tyler May, *Great Expectations.*

33. See Halttunen, who discusses the "sentimental synthesis" in fashion, funeral arrangements, and etiquette books (*Confidence Men and Painted Women*); Tompkins, who wrote the first full analysis of literary sentimentality (*Sensational Designs*); and the essays collected in Samuels, *The Culture of Sentiment*, which examine the use of sentimentality in cultural practices as far-ranging as the government's handling of Native American children.

34. See Fisher, who calls the sentimental novel "the most radical popular form available to middle-class culture," grounding his analysis in the claim that sentimentality "depends on an inward and empathic emotional bond" (*Hard Facts* 91, 92); and Tompkins, whose section on "Pain" in her discussion of *The Wide Wide World* (*Sensational Designs* 172–85) emphasizes the sentimental heroine's continual and necessary sufferings as she progresses toward spiritual perfection and emotional self-discipline.

35. "Separate spheres" ideology and sentimentalism countered assumed female inferiority, irrationality, and impulsiveness with an inherent superiority of spirituality and feeling, which gave women the power to "save" and inspire their men and so to be the central redemptive force in society. See in general Tompkins,

Sensational Designs; Rhode, *Justice and Gender*; Welter, "The Cult of True Womanhood"; Cott, *The Bonds of Womanhood.* For a court's use of the seeming moral "superiority" of women as a cover for enforcing their exclusion from the litigative arena, see the *Duffies* case discussed above, at 131–34.

36. On sentimentality's resistance to "humanizing" its villains, see Fisher, *Hard Facts*, 116–17. The gallery of prototypical sentimentalized victims is large; it includes such familiar children as Dickens's Little Nell, street sweeper Jo, abused boy Smike, Oliver Twist, and David Copperfield, along with Stowe's Little Eva, Warner's Ellen Montgomery, and Cummins's Gertie. *Uncle Tom's Cabin* is obviously a prime source of slave-victims, from Prue to Topsy ("I've seen this child whipped with a poker, knocked down with a shovel or tongs, whichever came handiest") to Tom himself. And we should not forget Anna Sewell's equine victim, Black Beauty, imaged in emotionally all-too-human terms and suffering such horrifying mistreatment that the novel triggered major outcries against the victimization of animals.

37. Rose Clark, the eponymous heroine of Fanny Fern's second novel, and Edna Earl, the protagonist of Augusta Evans's best-selling *St. Elmo*, begin in the unloved, socially dislocated state that characterizes so many sentimental heroines. Rose especially is abused by cruel relatives and teachers in a manner reminiscent of Jane Eyre's early years.

38. Anger is a major problem for such heroines as *The Wide Wide World*'s Ellen Montgomery; Edna Earl in *St. Elmo* is a studious, actively publishing scholar in the field of ancient and arcane myths and philosophies.

39. At this point it is significant to note that the tort of alienation of affections was first introduced in the 1860s (Prosser 920–21). Claims for alienation of affections were often joined with criminal conversation, and this chapter considers them together, but the former made the destruction of marital intimacy a compensable violation of spousal rights *by definition.* Obviously, there is a strong correlation between the reconceptualization of adultery as an injury to emotion rather than property, and the invention of a tort that makes "alienating" or destroying marital love a redressable injury.

40. In 1898 an appeals court in California asserted, as if it were indisputable, that if one compared the injury in cases where a spouse had been "enticed" away, "ordinarily, the injury is greater to the wife than to the husband" (*Humphrey v. Pope*, 122 Cal. 253, 256 [1898]).

41. See *Nolin v. Pearson, Turner v. Heavrin.*

42. *Bennett* is an interesting counterpoint to *Duffies*, the Wisconsin case discussed in the first section of this chapter. Using a version of the same sentimentalized, pure, and sensitive wife that other courts deployed to grant women an enforceable right to their husband's "society," the *Duffies* court denied women such rights on the ground that while women's domesticity kept them in the home, men's commercial exigencies legitimately kept them away from it. The employment of

similar stereotypes to opposite ends is a good illustration of the serviceability of literary modes, the ways that they can be bent to produce different effects and tell different stories.

43. In 1873, the U.S. Supreme Court rejected Myra Bradwell's claim that the privileges and immunities of state citizenship included the right to apply for membership in the bar. In a famous concurrence, Justice Bradley grounded the "necessary" exclusion of women from public and professional life on the natural, even divine separation of spheres, which makes women timid and delicate and "unfits" them for "the occupations of civil life," arousing a natural repugance at the very idea (*Bradwell v. Illinois*, 83 U.S. 130, 141 [1873] [Bradley J. concurring]).

44. See Baym, *Woman's Fiction*, xxxix (Barbara Welter's "true woman" is virtually absent from "woman's fiction"), and Harris's excellent outline of the critical condemnation of women's writing, from Pattee, Brown, and Papashvily to Douglas (*Nineteenth-Century American Women's Novels* 3–8).

45. In 1872 Southworth was the author whose work was most in demand at public libraries (Kelley, *Private Woman, Public Stage*, 26). Mary Kelley asserts that her sales were the greatest of any female author in American history; in large measure this is a function of both the quantity of her output and the continual reissue of her many novels, most of which were originally serialized in magazines. The Union Catalogue lists more than 100 separate titles for Southworth. In the three decades from 1880 to 1910, the Catalogue lists over 175 editions of various Southworth novels, including many multiple editions of the same novel.

6. Consequences of Change

1. This is not to say that Barbie's identity hasn't changed. Her professional interests have gone from stewardess in the 1960s to doctor in the 1980s ("doctor by day, glamorous date by night!" the "literature" that accompanied her white coat and stethoscope proclaimed). So far as I know, however, she has not yet appeared with a gun.

2. A good example of the current sensitivity to gender-based scripts occurred when the phrase "math class is tough!" was included among "Teen talk" Barbie's comments. An uproar over sex stereotyping and role models ensued, and Mattel responded promptly by eliminating the offending comment from the doll's repertory (see "Mattel Muzzles Grumbling Barbie," *Los Angeles Times* 22 October 1992, D2; "Mattel Subtracts Comment on Math From Barbie's Doll," *Wall Street Journal* 21 October 1992, b10[E]).

3. See, e.g., *Breiman v. Paasch*, 17 Abb. N.C. 249 (1879), in which a wife alleged that the defendant "willfully, wickedly, and maliciously gained the affections of the said Breiman, induced him to have carnal intercourse with her . . . willfully and maliciously debauched him, and is now, and has been since the 14th day of December, 1877, living with him in open and notorious adultery, without the priv-

ity or consent of this plaintiff, and in opposition to her most peaceable efforts to gain him from the defendant's influence and control" (250). As late as 1951, a Pennsylvania court refused to find allegations insufficiently specific for criminal conversation when a wife alleged that the defendant "wrongfully, wickedly and unjustly debauched and carnally knew the said George Hoopert then and there still being the husband of the said plaintiff." *Hoopert v. Obenstine*, 77 D & C (PA) 409, 412 (1951).

4. The complexities of both the marital and adulterous relationships were not entirely irrelevant to the lawsuit, however; once liability was established, they were central to determining the amount of damages to be awarded. If the defendant could show, for instance, that he could not have debauched the wife because he was only the latest in a long line of lovers, he could minimize the damages although he could not obtain the dismissal of the suit. Though they were no bars to liability, the facts that the plaintiff had also engaged in adulterous behavior, that the plaintiff's spouse was unchaste and had a reputation for unchastity, and that the marriage was loveless or stormy were all admissable to mitigate the extent of damages incurred by the adultery or alienation (Prosser, *Handbook of the Law of Torts*, sec. 101:924; Lippman, "The Breakdown of Consortium," 658–60).

5. See George Watt, *The Fallen Woman in the Nineteenth-Century English Novel*, and Kimberley Reynolds and Nicola Humble, *Victorian Heroines*. One category of fiction, however, the sensationalist novels of the 1860s, did sometimes present gleefully wicked heroines whose transgressions included an active, even predatory sexuality, such as Magdalene Vanstone, the heroine of Wilkie Collins's 1862 *No Name*, or the heroine of M. E. Braddon's eponymous 1863 novel *Aurora Floyd*. These novels, while wildly popular, were generally dismissed as immoral and improper by the literary and cultural establishment (see Hughes, *The Maniac in the Cellar*; Cvetkovich, *Mixed Feelings*; and the discussion of Reade's *Griffith Gaunt* in chapter 4). Interestingly, in the cases I've examined, the figure of the female defendant as sexual predator rarely appears. The allegations of the complaint may accuse the woman formulaically of "debauching and criminally knowing" the plaintiff's husband, but even cases that rely on detailed sentimental descriptions of the wife in legitimating her suit tend to avoid parallel descriptions of the female defendant. A basically conservative state judiciary's discomfort with the notion of offensively predatory women may have influenced the rhetoric of its decisions permitting the cases as well as those denying them.

6. On seduced daughters and fallen women as "clearly established stereotypes" who "had little hope of rising once [they] had sinned," see Gilbert Cross, *Next Week—East Lynne*, 211, 214. Michael Booth's *English Melodrama* begins with a good discussion of stock characters, plots, and moral lessons, 13–39; Frank Rahill's *The World of Melodrama* covers seduction plots and stereotypical characters in American and English melodrama; and David Grimsted's *Melodrama Unveiled* traces moral lessons to be learned from heroines threatened by "vile passions," 204–48.

7. For a contrary view, see *Keen v. Keen*, 49 Or. 362 (1907). The judge's comment that "a woman is not liable to be seduced without she contributes a little in some way to the general purposes of the case" held reversible error because it imputes liability based on husband's seduction rather than defendant's actions.

8. Although it had permitted female-plaintiff alienation of affections cases since *Wolf v. Frank*, 92 Md. 138 (1900), over time the court had construed Maryland's Married Women's Property Act as narrowly as possible, and had refused wives the right to bring criminal conversation actions. See *Kline v. Ansell*, 287 Md. 585 at 593*n*4.

9. In this regard, see Hulecki, "Limitations of the Scope of the Privacy Doctrine," critiquing the Massachusetts Supreme Judicial Court's reasoning in *Commonwealth v. Stowell*, 389 Mass. 171 (1983), which upheld the constitutionality of criminal statutes prohibiting adultery. Hulecki supports defendant's argument that private, consensual extramarital sex should be within the First Amendment's protected zone of privacy, like decisions about marriage, procreation, contraception, and child rearing: "The framework of privacy logically includes the rights of individuals to make moral judgments and, therefore, should bar the government from policing adultery" (89). A constitutional "right to adultery," like a right to commit sodomy or other "deviant" sexual acts, has thus far won only limited judicial acceptance. Judge Reynoldson (author of *Bearbower*), in his *Fundermann* dissent, complained that the majority's rule would "be hailed by those who believe extramarital conduct sould be accorded a constitutional right of privacy, and those who support the increasing amoralization of public policy" (304 N.W. at 797).

10. For feminist analyses, see Lucinda Finley, "Breaking Women's Silence in Law"; Patricia Williams, *The Alchemy of Race and Rights*; West; Margaret Jane Radin, "The Pragmatist and the Feminist." Racial approaches include Mari J. Matsuda, "Public Response to Racist Speech"; Richard Delgado, "Storytelling for Oppositionists and Others"; Derrick Bell, "The Final Report." Similar approaches have been taken by gay scholars such as William Eskridge ("Gay Legal Narratives").

Works Cited

Abrams, M. H. *A Glossary of Literary Terms.* 3d ed. New York: Holt, Rinehart and Winston, 1971.

"A Classmate of H. W. Beecher." *The Veil Removed; or, Henry Ward Beecher's Trial and Acquittal Investigated, Love Demonstrated in Plain Dealing, The Congregational Council Reviewed.* New York: n.p., 1874.

Alger, Horatio. *Ragged Dick and Struggling Upward.* 1868; reprint, New York: Penguin, 1985.

American Law Institute. *Model Penal Code and Commentaries.* Philadelphia: ALI, 1980.

Amsterdam, Anthony G. and Randy Hertz. "An Analysis of Closing Arguments to a Jury." *New York Law School Law Review* 37 (1992): 55–122.

"An Afternoon at the Beecher Trial." *Overland Monthly* (August 1875): 182–94.

"An Indecent Publication." Unsigned. *The Round Table* 28 July 1866.

Andrews, Kenneth R. *Nook Farm: Mark Twain's Hartford Circle.* Seattle: Washington University Press, 1969.

"Annotation: Punitive or Exemplary Damages in Action for Alienation of Affections or Criminal Conversation." *American Law Reports* 16:1316–1322.

Armstrong, Nancy. *Desire and Domestic Fiction: A Political History of the Novel.* Oxford: Oxford University Press, 1987.

Arthur, T. S. *Anna Lee: The Maiden, The Wife, The Mother.* London: T. Nelson, 1871.

Austin, J. L. *How to Do Things With Words.* Cambridge: Harvard University Press, 1962.

Baker, J. H. *An Introduction to English Legal History.* 3d ed. London: Butterworth, 1990.

Baker, J. H. and Milsom, S. F. C. *Sources of English Legal History: Private Law to 1750.* London: Butterworth, 1986.

Bald, R. C. *John Donne: A Life.* 1970; reprint, Oxford: Clarendon, 1986.

Baldwin, James. "Everybody's Protest Novel." *Partisan Review* 16 (June 1949): 578–85.

Barfield, A. O. "Poetic Diction and Legal Fiction." In C. S. Lewis, ed., *Essays Presented to Charles Williams.* London and New York: Oxford University Press, 1947, 106–27.

Basch, Norma. "The Emerging Legal History of Women in the United States:

Property, Divorce, and the Constitution." *Signs: Journal of Women in Culture and Society* 12 (1986): 97–117.
——. *In the Eyes of the Law: Women, Marriage and Property in Nineteenth-Century New York.* Ithaca: Cornell University Press, 1982.
——. "Relief in the Premises: Divorce as a Woman's Remedy in New York and Indiana, 1815–1870." *Law and History Review* 8 (1990): 1–24.
Baym, Nina. *Woman's Fiction: A Guide to Novels by and About Women in America 1820–1870.* Ithaca: Cornell University Press, 1984.
Beecher, Henry Ward. *Seven Lectures to Young Men, on Various Important Subjects; Delivered Before the Young Men of Indianapolis, Indiana During the Winter of 1843–4.* Indianapolis: Thomas B. Cutler, 1844.
The Beecher Trial: A Review of the Evidence, Reprinted From The New York Times of July 3, 1875 With Some Revisions and Additions. New York: The New York Times, 1875.
Bell, Derrick. "The Final Report: Harvard's Affirmative Action Allegory." *Michigan Law Review* 87 (1989): 2382–2410.
Bennet, W. Lance. "Storytelling in Criminal Trials: A Model of Social Judgment." *Quarterly Journal of Speech* 64 (1978).
Bennet, W. Lance and Martha Feldman. *Reconstructing Reality in the Courtroom: Justice and Judgment in American Culture.* New Brunswick: Rutgers University Press, 1981.
Bennets, Leslie. "In 'Drood,' the Cast Gives Clues and the Audiences Give Clues." *New York Times* 5 Jan. 1986, 2:1.
Bentham, Jeremy. *Works.* John Bowring, ed. 11 vols. (1838–1843) New York: Russell and Russell, 1962.
Berenson, Edward. *The Trial of Madame Caillaux.* Berkeley: University of California Press, 1992.
Bermant, Gordon. "Two Conjectures About the Issue of Expert Testimony." *Law And Human Behavior* 10 (1986): 97–100.
Best, William Bowdesley. *Principles of the Law of Evidence; With Elementary Rules for Conducting the Examination and Cross-examination of Witnesses.* Albany: Weare C. Little, 1875.
Bigelow, Melville M. *Elements of the Law of Torts.* Boston: Little, Brown, 1886.
Blackstone, William. *Commentaries on the Law of England.* 4 vols. London: 1768.
Blake, Nelson Manfred. *The Road to Reno: A History of Divorce in the United States.* New York: Macmillan, 1962.
Booth, Michael R. *English Melodrama.* London: Herbert Jenkins, 1965.
Boyle, Thomas. *Black Swine in the Sewers of Hampstead: Beneath the Surface of Victorian Sensationalism.* London: Hodder and Stoughton, 1990.
Brooks, Peter. *The Melodramatic Imagination.* New York: Columbia University Press, 1985.

Brooks, Peter and Paul Gewirtz, eds. *Law's Stories: Narrative and Rhetoric in the Law.* New Haven: Yale University Press, 1996.
Brown, Herbert Ross. *The Sentimental Novel in America, 1789–1860.* Durham: Duke University Press, 1940.
Burns, Wayne. *Charles Reade: A Study in Victorian Authorship.* New York: Bookman Association, 1961.
Camfield, Gregg. "The Moral Aesthetics of Sentimentality: A Missing Key to *Uncle Tom's Cabin.*" *Nineteenth-Century Literature* 43 (1988): 319–45.
Cardozo, Benjamin. *The Growth of the Law.* New Haven: Yale University Press, 1924.
Carlson, Cheree. "The Role of Character in Public Moral Argument: Henry Ward Beecher and the Brooklyn Scandal." *Quarterly Journal of Speech* 77 (1991): 38–52.
Carter, Paul A. *The Spiritual Crisis of the Gilded Age.* DeKalb: Northern Illinois University Press, 1971.
Clark, Charles E. and Charles U. Samenow. "The Summary Judgment." *Yale Law Journal* 38 (1929): 444–56.
Clark, Clifford E. Jr. *Henry Ward Beecher: Spokesman for a Middle-Class America.* Urbana: University of Illinois Press, 1978.
Clark, Homer Harrison. *Law of Domestic Relations.* St. Paul, Minn.: West, 1968.
Clark, Suzanne. *Sentimental Modernism: Women Writers and the Revolution of the Word.* Bloomington: Indiana University Press, 1991.
Cockburn, J. S. *A History of the English Assizes 1558–1714.* Cambridge: Cambridge University Press, 1972.
Cohen, Daniel A. "The Murder of Maria Bickford: Fashion, Passion, and the Birth of a Consumer Culture." *American Studies* 31 (1990): 5–30.
Cohen, Ed. "Typing Wilde: Construing the 'Desire to Appear to Be a Person Inclined to the Commission of the Gravest of All Offenses.'" *Yale Journal of Law and the Humanities* 5 (1993): 1–49.
Cott, Nancy F. *The Bonds of Womanhood: "Woman's Sphere" in New England 1780–1835.* New Haven: Yale University Press, 1977.
——. "Passionless: An Interpretation." *Signs* 4 (1979): 219–36.
Cover, Robert. "The Supreme Court, 1982 Term—Foreword: *Nomos* and Narrative." *Harvard Law Review* 97 (1983): 4–68.
——. "Violence and the Word." *Yale Law Journal* 95 (1986): 1601–1629.
Crenshaw, Kimberle and Gary Peller. "Reel Time/Real Justice." In Robert Gooding-Williams, ed., *Reading Rodney King/Reading Urban Uprising.* New York: Routledge, 1993.
Cross, Gilbert B. *Next Week—East Lynne: Domestic Drama in Performance 1820–1874.* Lewisburg: Bucknell University Press, 1977.
Culler, Jonathan. "Literary Competence." In Jane P. Tompkins, ed., *Reader-Response Criticism: From Formalism to Post-Structuralism.* Baltimore and London: Johns Hopkins University Press, 1980.

Cummins, Maria Susanna. *The Lamplighter.* Edited and introduced by Nina Baym. New Brunswick: Rutgers University Press, 1988.

Cvetkovich, Ann. *Mixed Feelings: Feminism, Mass Culture, and Victorian Sensationalism.* New Brunswick: Rutgers University Press, 1992.

Dalton, Claire. "An Essay in the Deconstruction of Contract Doctrine." *Yale Law Journal* 94 (1985): 997–1221.

Davidson, Cathy N. *Revolution and the Word: The Rise of the Novel in America.* New York: Oxford University Press, 1986.

Deland, Margaret. *Philip and his Wife.* Boston and New York: Houghton Mifflin, 1894.

Delgado, Richard. "Storytelling for Oppositionists and Others: A Plea for Narrative." *Michigan Law Review* 87 (1989): 2411–2441.

Dershowitz, Alan M. "Life Is Not a Dramatic Narrative." In Peter Brooks and Paul Gewirtz, eds., *Law's Stories: Narrative and Rhetoric in the Law.* New Haven: Yale University Press, 1996.

Dickens, Charles. *Selected Letters of Charles Dickens.* Ed. David Paroissien. London: Macmillan, 1985.

Dimock, Wai Chee. "Criminal Law, Female Virtue and the Rise of Liberalism." *Yale Journal of Law and the Humanities* 4 (1992): 209–47.

——. *Residues of Justice: Literature, Law, Philosophy.* Berkeley: University of California Press, 1996.

Dobson, Joanne. "The Hidden Hand: Subversion of Cultural Ideology in Three Mid-Nineteenth-Century American Women's Novels." *American Quarterly* 38 (1986): 223–42.

——. Introduction to E.D.E.N. Southworth, *The Hidden Hand, or Capitola the Madcap.* New Brunswick: Rutgers University Press, 1988, xi–xlii.

Donne, John. *The Complete English Poems.* Ed. A. J. Smith. Harmondsworth: Penguin, 1971.

Douglas, Ann. *The Feminization of American Culture.* New York: Knopf, 1988.

Dworkin, Ronald. "Law as Interpretation." In W.J.T. Mitchell, ed., *The Politics of Interpretation.* Chicago, University of Chicago Press, 1982, 249–70.

——. "My Reply to Stanley Fish (and Walter Benn Michaels: Please Don't Talk About Objectivity Anymore." In W.J.T. Mitchell, ed., *The Politics of Interpretation.* Chicago, University of Chicago Press, 1982, 287–313.

Dyer, Brainerd. *The Public Career of William Maxwell Evarts.* Berkeley: University of California Press, 1933.

Earle, Walter. *Shearman and Sterling 1873–1973.* New York: n.p., 1973.

Ekman, Paul. *Telling Lies: Clues to Deceit in the Marketplace, Politics, and Marriage.* New York: Norton, 1985.

Elwin, Malcolm. *Charles Reade: A Biography.* London: Jonathan Cape, 1931.

Eskridge, William. "Gay Legal Narratives." *Stanford Law Review* 46 (1994): 607–46.

Evans, Augusta Jane. *St. Elmo.* New York: Grosset and Dunlap, 1866.
Evarts, William Maxwell. *Arguments and Speeches of William Maxwell Evarts.* Ed. Sherman Evarts. 3 vols. New York: Macmillan, 1919.
Feinsinger, Nathan. "Legislative Attack on 'Heart Balm.' " *Michigan Law Review* 33 (1935): 979–1009.
Ferguson, Robert A. "Story and Transcription in the Trial of John Brown." *Yale Journal of Law and the Humanities* 6 (1994): 37–73.
Fern, Fanny (Sarah Parton). *Rose Clark.* New York: Mason Brothers, 1855.
——. *Ruth Hall and Other Writings* (1852). New Brunswick: Rutgers University Press, 1986.
Finley, Lucinda M. "Breaking Women's Silence in Law: The Dilemma of the Gendered Nature of Legal Reasoning." *Notre Dame Law Review* 64 (1989): 886–910.
Firestone, David. "While Barbie Talks Tough, G.I. Joe Goes Shopping." *New York Times* 31 Dec. 1993, A12.
First English Book on America (of newe landes and of the people found by the messengers of the kynge of portyngale named Emanuel). c. 1511. Birmingham: Arber, 1885.
Fish, Stanley. *Doing What Comes Naturally: Change, Rhetoric and the Practice of Theory in Literary and Legal Studies.* Durham and London: Duke University Press, 1989.
——. *Is There a Text in This Class? The Authority of Interpretive Communities.* Cambridge: Harvard University Press, 1980.
——. *Surprised by Sin: The Reader in Paradise Lost.* London: Macmillan, 1967.
Fisher, Philip. *Hard Facts: Setting and Form in the American Novel.* Oxford: Oxford University Press, 1987.
Fiss, Owen. "Objectivity and Interpretation." *Stanford Law Review* 34 (1982): 739–63.
Flax, Sherry Hamburg. "Note: Judicial Abrogation of the Civil Action for Adultery." *University of Baltimore Law Review* 10 (1980): 205–14.
Fletcher, Angus. *Allegory: The Theory of a Symbolic Mode.* Ithaca: Cornell University Press, 1964.
Fluck, Winfried. "The Power and Failure of Representation in Harriet Beecher Stowe's *Uncle Tom's Cabin.*" *New Literary History* 23 (1992): 319–38.
Fox, Richard Wightman. "Intimacy on Trial: Cultural Meanings of the Beecher-Tilton Affair." In R. W. Fox, ed., *The Power of Culture: Critical Essays in American History.* Chicago: University of Chicago Press, 1993, 103–32.
French, Bryant Morey. *Mark Twain and the Gilded Age.* Dallas: Southern Methodist University Press, 1965.
Friedman, Lawrence M. *A History of American Law.* New York: Simon and Schuster, 1973.
Fuller, Lon L. *Legal Fictions.* Stanford: Stanford University Press, 1967.

Garrison, Dee. "Immoral Fiction in the Late Victorian Library." In Daniel Walker Howe, ed., *Victorian America.* Philadelphia: University of Pennsylvania Press, 1976, 141–59.

Geertz, Clifford. *The Interpretation of Cultures: Selected Essays.* New York: Basic Books, 1973.

Godkin, E. L. *The Gilded Age Letters of E. L. Godkin.* Ed. William Armstrong. New York: SUNY Press, 1974.

Grant, Robert. *Unleavened Bread.* New York: Charles Scribner's, 1900.

Gravdal, Kathryn. "Poetics of Rape Law in Medieval France." In Lynn A. Higgins and Brenda R. Silver, eds., *Rape and Representation.* New York: Columbia University Press, 1991, 207–26.

——. *Ravishing Maidens: Writing Rape in Medieval French Literature and Law.* Philadelphia: University of Pennsylvania Press, 1991.

The Great Brooklyn Scandal: All The Documents in the Famous Beecher-Tilton Case, Unabridged. New York: J. H. Paxon, 1874.

Greenleaf, Simon. *A Treatise on the Law of Evidence.* Boston: Little, Brown, 1854.

Grimsted, David. *Melodrama Unveiled: American Theater and Culture 1800–1850.* Chicago: University of Chicago Press, 1968.

Grossberg, Michael. *Governing the Hearth: Law and the Family in Nineteenth-Century America.* Chapel Hill: University of North Carolina Press, 1985.

Habegger, Alfred. *Gender, Fantasy, and Realism in American Literature.* New York: Columbia University Press, 1982.

Halem, Lynne Carol. *Divorce Reform: Changing Legal and Social Perspectives.* New York: Collier Macmillan, 1980.

Halttunen, Karen. *Confidence Men and Painted Women: A Study of Middle-Class Culture in America 1830–1870.* New Haven: Yale University Press, 1982.

Hariman, Robert, ed. *Popular Trials: Rhetoric, Mass Media and the Law.* Tuscaloosa: University of Alabama Press, 1990.

Harris, Susan K. " 'But is it any *good*?': Evaluating Nineteenth-Century American Women's Fiction." *American Literature* 63 (1991): 43–61.

——. "Four Ways to Inscribe a Mackerel: Mark Twain and Laura Hawkins." *Studies in the Novel* 21 (1989): 138–53.

——. *Nineteenth-Century American Women's Novels: Interpretive Strategies.* Cambridge: Cambridge University Press, 1990.

Harrison, Ross. *Bentham.* London: Routledge, 1983.

Hartigan, Patti. " 'Madness' Cuts It For 10 Years." *Boston Globe* 28 Jan. 1990, B33.

Hawthorne, Nathaniel. Preface to *The House of the Seven Gables.* Centenary Edition of the Works of Nathaniel Hawthorne, William Charvat, Roy Harvey Pearce, Claude Simpson, General eds. Columbus: Ohio State University Press, 1962.

Hedrick, Charles W. *Parables as Poetic Fictions: The Creative Voice of Jesus.* Peabody, Mass.: Hendrickson, 1994.

Hibben, Paxton. *Henry Ward Beecher: An American Portrait.* New York: Doran, 1927.

Hicks, Frederick C., ed. *Famous American Jury Speeches: Addresses Before Juries and Fact-Finding Tribunals.* St. Paul, Minn.: West, 1925.

Howells, William Dean. *A Modern Instance.* 1882; reprint, London: Penguin, 1984.

Hughes, Winifred. *The Maniac in the Cellar: Sensation Novels of the 1860's.* Princeton: Princeton University Press, 1980.

Hulecki, Anne W. "Note—Limitations on the Scope of the Privacy Doctrine in Making Decisions Concerning Adultery." *Suffolk University Law Review* 18 (1984): 83–90.

Ingraham, Barton L. "The Ethics of Testimony: Conflicting Views on the Role of the Criminologist as Expert Witness." In Patrick Anderson and L. Thomas Winfree, eds., *Expert Witnesses: Criminologists In The Courtroom.* New York: SUNY Press, 1987.

Ingulli, Elaine D. "Trial by Jury: Reflections on Witness Credibility, Expert Testimony and Recantation." *Valparaiso Law Review* 20 (1986): 145–85.

Iser, Wolfgang. *The Implied Reader: Patterns in Communication in Prose Fiction from Bunyan to Beckett.* Baltimore: Johns Hopkins University Press, 1974.

Jackson, Bernard. *Law, Fact and Narrative Coherence.* London: D. Charles, 1988.

——. "Narrative Theories and Legal Discourse." In Christopher Nash, ed., *Narrative in Culture: The Uses of Storytelling in the Sciences, Philosophy and Literature.* London and New York: Routledge, 1990, 23–50.

Jakobson, Roman with Morris Halle. "Two Aspects of Language and Two Types of Aphasic Disturbances." *Fundamentals of Language.* New York: Mouton, 1956.

Kanowitz, Leo. *Women and the Law: The Unfinished Revolution.* Albuquerque: University of New Mexico Press, 1969.

Kaplan, Justin. Introduction to Mark Twain and Charles Dudley Warner, *The Gilded Age: A Tale of Today.* Seattle: University of Washington Press, 1964, v–xxiv.

Kavanagh, Kay. "Alienation of Affections and Criminal Conversation: Unholy Marriage in Need of Annulment." *Arizona Law Review* 23 (1981): 323–40.

Keilitz, Ingo. "Researching and Reforming the Insanity Defense." *Rutgers Law Review* 38 (1987): 289–322.

Kelley, Mary. *Private Woman, Public Stage: Literary Domesticity in Nineteenth-Century America.* Oxford: Oxford University Press, 1984.

Kerber, Linda K. *Women of the Republic: Intellect and Ideology in the American Revolution.* Chapel Hill: University of North Carolina Press, 1980.

Kete, Mary Lou. *Sentimental Collaboration: Mourning and Middle-Class Identity in Nineteenth-Century America.* Durham: Duke University Press, 1999.

Klinck, Dennis R. *The Word of the Law.* Ottawa: Carleton University Press, 1992.

Lakoff, George and Mark Turner. *More Than Cool Reason: A Field Guide to Poetic Metaphor.* Chicago: University of Chicago Press, 1989.

Langbein, John H. "The Criminal Trial Before the Lawyers." *University of Chicago Law Review* 45 (1978): 263–316.

Leach, William R. "Review of *Confidence Men and Painted Women: A Study of Middle-Class Culture in America*." *New England Quarterly* 56 (1983): 599–603.

Leishman, J. B. *The Monarch of Wit: An Analytical and Comparative Study of the Poetry of John Donne*. London: Hutchinson, 1965.

Lempert, Richard. "Telling Tales in Court: Trial Procedure and the Story Model." *Cardozo Law Review* 13 (1991): 559–75.

Levinson, Sanford. "Law as Literature." *Texas Law Review* 60 (1982): 373–403.

Levinson, Sanford and Steven Mailloux, eds. *Interpreting Law and Literature: A Hermeneutic Reader*. Evanston: Northwestern University Press, 1988.

Lewis, R. W. B. *Edith Wharton: A Biography*. New York: Harper & Row, 1975.

Lippman, Jacob. "The Breakdown of Consortium." *Columbia Law Review* 30 (1930): 651–73.

Locke, John. *Second Treatise of Government*. 1690; reprint, Indianapolis: Hackett, 1980.

Mackay, R. D. "Post-Hinckley Insanity in the U.S.A." *Criminal Law Review* (1988): 88–96.

McLoughlin, William G. *The Meaning of Henry Ward Beecher: An Essay in the Shifting Values of Mid-Victorian America*. New York: Knopf, 1970.

Macneice, Louis. *Varieties of Parable*. Cambridge: Cambridge University Press, 1965.

Mailloux, Steven. "Rhetorical Hermeneutics." *Critical Inquiry* 11 (1985): 620–41.

Maine, Henry Sumner. *Ancient Law: Its Connection With the Early History of Society and Its Relation to Modern Ideas*. 1864; reprint, Tucson: University of Arizona Press, 1986.

Marshall, Charles F. *The True History of the Brooklyn Scandal: Being a Complete Account of Plymouth Church, Brooklyn, Upon Charges Preferred by Theodore Tilton, Including All the Original Letters, Documents and Private Correspondence, with Biographies of the Leading Actors in the Drama*. Philadelphia/Chicago/St. Louis: National Pub. Co., 1874.

Matsuda, Mari J. "Public Response to Racist Speech: Considering the Victim's Story." *Michigan Law Review* 87 (1989): 2320–2381.

Matsuda, Mari J., Charles Lawrence III, Richard Delgado, and Kimberle Crenshaw. *Words That Wound: Critical Race Theory, Assaultive Speech and the First Amendment*. Boulder: Westview, 1993.

"Mattel Muzzles Grumbling Barbie." *Los Angeles Times* 22 Oct. 1992, D2.

"Mattel Subtracts Comment on Math From Barbie Doll." *Wall Street Journal* 21 Oct. 1992, b10(E).

May, Elaine Tyler. *Great Expectations: Marriage and Divorce in Post-Victorian America*. Chicago: University of Chicago Press, 1980.

Meyer, Philip N. "Desperate for Love: Cinematic Influences Upon a Defendant's Closing Argument to a Jury." *Vermont Law Review* 18 (Spring 1994): 721–49.
——. "Will You Please Be Quiet Please? Lawyers Listening to the Call of Stories." *Vermont Law Review* 18 (Spring 1994): 567–579.
Miller, Joseph. *Joe Miller's Jests: or the Wit's Vade-mecum.* London: T. Read, 1739.
Milton, John. *Doctrine and Discipline of Divorce.* London: Goldsmith's Alley, 1643.
——. *Tetrachordon: Expositions Upon The Foure Places in Scripture which Treat of Mariage, or nullities in Mariage.* London: 1645.
Minow, Martha. " 'Forming Under Everything That Grows': Toward a History of Family Law." *Wisconsin Law Review* (1985): 819–98.
Mott, Frank Luther. *Golden Multitudes: The Story of Best-Sellers in the United States.* New York: Macmillan, 1947.
O'Barr, William M. *Linguistic Evidence: Language, Power, and Strategy in the Courtroom.* New York: Academic, 1982.
Ogden, C. K. *Bentham's Theory of Fictions.* New York: Harcourt Brace, 1932.
O'Neill, William. *Divorce in the Progressive Era.* New Haven: Yale University Press, 1967.
Papashvily, Helen Waite. *All the Happy Endings: A Study of the Domestic Novel in America, the Women Who Wrote It, in the Nineteenth Century.* New York: Harper, 1956.
Papke, David Ray. *Narrative and the Legal Discourse.* Liverpool: D. Charles, 1990.
Pateman, Carol. *The Sexual Contract.* Stanford: Stanford University Press, 1988.
Pattee, Fred Lewis. *The Feminine Fifties.* New York: D. Appleton-Century, 1940.
Pennington, Nancy and Reid Hastie. "A Cognitive Theory of Juror Decision Making: The Story Model." *Cardozo Law Review* 13 (1991): 519–57.
Pollock, Frederick and Frederick William Maitland. *The History of English Law.* 2nd ed. 1898; reprint, Cambridge: Cambridge University Press, 1968.
Posner, Richard A. *Law and Literature: A Misunderstood Relation.* Cambridge: Harvard University Press, 1988.
Powers, Samuel Leland. *Portraits of a Half Century.* Boston: Little, Brown, 1925.
Prosser, William L. *Handbook of the Law of Torts.* St. Paul, Minn.: West, 1941.
Prosser, William L. and W. Page Keeton. *Prosser and Keeton on the Law of Torts.* General Editor W. Page Keeton. St. Paul, Minn.: West, 1984.
Pykett, Lyn. *The "Improper" Feminine: The Women's Sensation Novel and the New Woman Writing.* London and New York: Routledge, 1992.
Radin, Margaret Jane. "The Pragmatist and the Feminist." *Southern California Law Review* 63 (1990): 1699–1726.
Radway, Janice. *Reading the Romance: Women, Patriarchy and Popular Literature.* Chapel Hill: University of North Carolina Press, 1984.
Rahill, Frank. *The World of Melodrama.* University Park and London: Pennsylvania State University Press, 1967.

Raleigh, John Henry. "What Scott Meant to the Victorians." *Time, Place and Idea: Essays on the Novel.* Carbondale: Southern Illinois University Press, 1968.

Reade, Charles. *Griffith Gaunt; or Jealousy.* Boston: Ticknor and Fields, 1866.

——. *Readiana: Comments on Current Events.* London: Chatto and Windus, 1883.

Redpath, Theodore. *The Songs and Sonnets of John Donne.* 2nd ed. New York: St. Martins, 1983.

Restatement of the Law of Torts (2d). Washington: American Law Institute, 1976.

Reynolds, Kimberley and Nicola Humble. *Victorian Heroines: Representations of Femininity in Nineteenth-Century Literature and Art.* New York: New York University Press, 1993.

Rhode, Deborah L. *Justice and Gender: Sex Discrimination and the Law.* Cambridge: Harvard University Press, 1989.

Riffaterre, Michael. *Fictional Truth.* Baltimore: Johns Hopkins University Press, 1990.

Rugoff, Milton. *America's Gilded Age: Intimate Portraits from an Era of Extravagance and Change, 1850–1890.* New York: Henry Holt, 1989.

——. *The Beechers: An American Family in the Nineteenth Century.* New York: Harper & Row, 1981.

Samuels, Shirley, ed. *The Culture of Sentiment: Race, Gender and Sentimentality in Nineteenth-Century America.* Oxford: Oxford University Press, 1992.

Scheppele, Kim Lane. "Finding Facts in Legal Interpretation." In Robert Post, ed., *Law and the Order of Culture.* Berkeley: University of California Press, 1991.

——. "Foreword: Symposium on Legal Storytelling." *Michigan Law Review* 87 (1989): 2073–2098.

Schopp, Robert F. "Returning to *M'Naghten* to Avoid Moral Mistakes: One Step Forward, or Two Steps Backward for the Insanity Defense?" *Arizona Law Review* 30 (1988): 135–53.

Schuetz, Janice and Kathryn Holmes Snedaker. *Communication and Litigation: Case Studies of Famous Trials.* Carbondale: Southern Illinois University Press, 1988.

Sedgwick, Eve Kosofsky. *Between Men: English Literature and Male Homosocial Desire.* New York: Columbia University Press, 1985.

Shapiro, Andrew L. "Reading O.J." *The Nation* 6 March 1995, 297.

Shaplen, Robert. *Free Love and Heavenly Sinners: The Story of the Great Henry Ward Beecher Scandal.* New York: Knopf, 1954.

Sherwin, Richard K. "A Matter of Voice and Plot: Belief and Suspicion in Legal Storytelling." *Michigan Law Review* 87 (1988): 543–612.

——. "The Narrative Construction of Reality." *Vermont Law Review* 18 (Spring 1994): 681–719.

Showalter, Elaine. "Family Secrets and Domestic Subversion: Rebellion in the Novels of the 1860s." In Anthony S. Wohl, ed., *The Victorian Family: Structure and Stresses.* London: Croom Helm, 1978, 101–16.

——. *A Literature of Their Own.* Princeton: Princeton University Press, 1977.

Sicherman, Barbara. "Sense and Sensibility: A Case Study of Women's Reading in Late-Victorian America." In Cathy N. Davidson, ed., *Reading in America: Literature and Social History.* Baltimore: Johns Hopkins University Press, 1989, 201–25.

Sklar, Kathryn Kish. *Catherine Beecher: A Study in American Domesticity.* New York: Norton, 1976.

Smith-Rosenberg, Carroll. *Disorderly Conduct: Visions of Gender in Victorian America.* New York: Knopf, 1985.

Snedaker, Kathryn Holmes. "Storytelling in Opening Statements: Framing the Argumentation of the Trial." *American Journal of Trial Advocacy* 10 (1986–87): 15–45.

Southworth, Emma D. E. N. *Ishmael, or In The Depths.* 1876; reprint, New York: Grosset and Dunlap, n.d.

"Special Issue: The Ethics of Expert Testimony." *Law and Human Behavior* 10 (1986): 1–181.

Staves, Susan. "Money for Honor: Damages for Criminal Conversation." *Studies in Eighteenth-Century Culture* 11 (1982): 279–97.

Stone, Lawrence. *The Family, Sex and Marriage in England 1500–1800.* New York: Harper and Row, 1979.

——. *Road to Divorce: England 1530–1987.* Oxford: Oxford University Press, 1990.

Stowe, Harriet Beecher. *Uncle Tom's Cabin.* 1852; reprint, London: Penguin Classics, 1981.

Strindberg, August. *The Stronger* (1888–89). In *August Strindberg: Selected Plays,* trans. Evert Sprinchorn. Minneapolis: University of Minnesota Press, 1986, 327–37.

"Symposium: Legal Storytelling." *Michigan Law Review* 87 (1989): 2073–2494.

Tanner, Tony. *Adultery in the Novel: Contract and Transgression.* Baltimore: Johns Hopkins University Press, 1979.

Taylor, John Pitt. *A Treatise on the Law of Evidence.* 7th ed. London: Wm Maxwell & Son, 1878.

Thomas, Brook. *American Literary Realism and the Failed Promise of Contract.* Berkeley: University of California Press, 1997.

——. *Cross-examinations of Law and Literature: Cooper, Hawthorne, Stowe, and Melville.* Cambridge: Cambridge University Press, 1987.

Tillotson, Kathleen. "The Lighter Reading of the Eighteen-Sixties." Introduction to Wilkie Collins, *The Woman in White.* Boston: Houghton Mifflin, 1969.

Tilton versus Beecher, Action for Crim. Con. 3 vols. New York: McDivitt, 1875.

Todd, Janet. *Sensibility: An Introduction.* New York: Methuen, 1986.

Tompkins, Jane. *Sensational Designs: The Cultural Work of American Fiction 1790–1860.* New York: Oxford University Press, 1985.

Trilling, Lionel. *Sincerity and Authenticity.* Cambridge: Harvard University Press, 1971.

Twain, Mark and Charles Dudley Warner. *The Gilded Age: A Tale of Today.* Hartford: American, 1873.

Waller, Altina L. *Reverend Beecher and Mrs. Tilton: Sex and Class in Victorian America.* Amherst: University of Massachusetts Press, 1982.

Warbasse, Elizabeth Bowles. *The Changing Legal Rights of Married Women, 1800–1861.* New York: Garland Press, 1986.

Warhol, Robyn R. *Gendered Interventions: Narrative Discourse in the Victorian Novel.* New Brunswick: Rutgers University Press, 1989.

Warner, Susan. *The Wide, Wide World.* New York: The Feminist Press, 1987.

Warren, Joyce W., ed. *The (Other) American Traditions: Nineteenth-Century Women Writers.* New Brunswick: Rutgers University Press, 1993.

Watt, George. *The Fallen Woman in the Nineteenth-Century English Novel.* London: Croom Helm, 1984.

Weinstein, Jeremy D. "Adultery, Law and the State: A History." *Hastings Law Journal* 38 (1986): 195–238.

Weisberg, D. Kelly. "Barred from the Bar: Women and Legal Education in the United States 1870–1890." In D. Kelly Weisberg, ed., *Women and the Law: A Social Historical Perspective.* Vol. 2. Cambridge: Schenkman, 1982.

Weisberg, Richard H. *The Failure of the Word: The Protagonist as Lawyer in Modern Fiction.* New Haven: Yale University Press, 1984.

Weisberg, Robert. "The Law-Literature Enterprise." *Yale Journal of Law and the Humanities* 1 (1988): 1–68.

Wells, Gary L. and Elizabeth Loftus, eds. *Eyewitness Testimony: Psychological Perspectives.* Cambridge: Cambridge University Press, 1984.

Welsh, Alexander. *Strong Representations: Narrative and Circumstantial Evidence in England.* Baltimore: Johns Hopkins University Press, 1992.

Welter, Barbara. "The Cult of True Womanhood: 1820–1860." *American Quarterly* 18 (1966): 151–74.

Wendt, Lloyd. *Chicago Tribune: The Rise of a Great American Newspaper.* Chicago: Rand McNally, 1979.

West, Robin. "Jurisprudence and Gender." *University of Chicago Law Review* 55 (1988): 1–72.

——. *Narrative, Authority, and the Law.* Ann Arbor: University of Michigan Press, 1993.

White, James Boyd. *When Words Lose Their Meaning: Constitutions and Reconstitutions of Language, Character, and Community.* Chicago: University of Chicago Press, 1984.

Wiebe, Robert H. *The Search for Order 1877–1920.* New York: Hill and Wang, 1967.

Williams, Patricia. *The Alchemy of Race and Rights: Diary of a Law Professor.* Cambridge: Harvard University Press, 1991.

Williamson, Francis P. *Beecher and his Accusers: A Complete History of the Great Controversy, Including the Life of Henry Ward Beecher, Together with Pen and Ink Sketches of the Persons Prominently Involved, A Full Record of the Facts, Leading Comments, Choice Extracts, Characteristic Anecdotes and Important Revelations from Reliable Private Sources.* Philadelphia: Flint & Co., 1874.

Woodhull, Victoria. *Woodhull and Claflin's Weekly.* 2 November 1872.

Table of Adultery Cases

Following is a group of 120 criminal conversation and alienation of affections cases that formed the textual basis for the arguments and citations in chapters 5 and 6. They fall mostly between 1870 and 1910, but also include some more recent cases. The list includes cases brought by both male and female plaintiffs, and appellate decisions from more than 35 states.

Adams v. Main. 3 Ind. 232 (1891).
Ash v. Prunier. 105 F. 722 (2d Cir. 1901).
Baker v. Baker. 16 Abb. N.C. (N.Y.) 293 (1885).
Bassett v. Bassett. 20 Ill. App. 543 (1886).
Beach v. Brown. 20 Wash. 266 (1898).
Bearbower v. Merry. 266 N.W. 2d 128 (Iowa 1978).
Bedan v. Turney. 99 Cal. 649 (1893).
Bennett v. Bennett. 116 N.Y. 584, 23 N.E. 17 (1889).
Betser v. Betser. 186 Ill. 537 (1900).
Bigaouette v. Paulet. 134 Mass. 123 (1883).
Boues v. Steffens. 62 Hun. 619, 16 N.Y.S. 819 (1891).
Bowersox v. Bowersox. 115 Mich. 24, 72 N.W. 986 (1897).
Breiman v. Paasch. 17 Abb. N.C. (N.Y.) 249 (1879).
Brown v. Brown. 124 N.C. 19 (1899).
Browning v. Jones. 52 Ill. App. 597 (1894).
Callis v. Merrieweather. 98 Md. 361, 57 A. 201 (1904).
Churchill v. Lewis. 17 Abb. N.C. (N.Y.) 226 (1886).
Clark v. Harlan. 1 Cin. Super. Ct. R. 418 (Ohio Sup. 1871).
Clay v. Clay. 21 Hun. (N.Y.) 609 (1880).
Clow v. Chapman. 125 Mo. 101, 28 S.W. 328 (1894).
Colwell v. Tinker. 169 N.Y. 531 (1902).
Cook v. Wood. 30 Ga. 891 (1860).
Cornelius v. Hambay. 150 Pa. 359, 24 Atl. 515 (1892).
Crose v. Rutledge. 81 Ill. 266 (1876).
Cross v. Grant. 62 N.H. 675, 13 Am. St. Rep. 607 (1883).
Dalton v. Dregge. 99 Mich. 250, 58 N.W. 57 (1894).
Deitzman v. Mullin. 108 Ky. 610 (1900).

Dodge v. Rush. 28 App. D.C. 149 (1906).
Doe v. Roe. 82 Me. 503, 20 Atl. 83 (1890).
Dow v. Bulfinch. 192 Mass. 281, 78 N.E. 416 (1906).
Duffies v. Duffies. 76 Wis. 374 (1890).
Eagon v. Eagon. 60 Kan. 697 (1899).
Egbert v. Greenwalt. 44 Mich. 245, 6 N.W. 654 (1880).
Eliason v. Draper. 25 Del. 1, 77 Atl. 572 (1910).
Evans v. O'Connor. 174 Mass. 287, 5 N.E. 557 (1899).
Foot v. Card. 58 Ct. 1, 18 Atl. 1027 (1889).
Fratini v. Caslini. 66 Vt. 273 (1894).
Frederick v. Morse. 88 Vt. 126 (1914).
Fundermann v. Mickelson. 304 N.W. 2d 790 (Iowa 1981).
Gahagan v. Church. 239 Mass. 558 (1921).
Gernerd v. Gernerd. 185 Pa. 233 (1897).
Hadley v. Heywood. 121 Mass. 236 (1876).
Hart v. Knapp. 76 Conn. 135, 55 Atl. 1021 (1903).
Hartpence v. Rogers. 143 Mo. 623, 45 S.W. 650 (1898).
Hawk v. Mann. 86 D.& C. (Pa.) 58, (1952).
Higham v. Vanosdol. 101 Ind. 160 (1885).
Hodge v. Wetzler. 69 N.J.L. 490 (1903).
Hodgkinson v. Hodgkinson. 43 Neb. 269 (1895).
Hoggins v. Coad. 58 Ill. App. 58 (1894).
Holmes v. Holmes. 133 Ind. 386, 32 N.E. 932 (1892).
Hoopert v. Obenstine. 77 D. & C.(Pa.) 409 (1951).
Houghton v. Rice. 174 Mass. 366 (1899).
Howard v. Howard. 120 Me. 479 (1921).
Hoye v. Hoye. 824 S.W. 2d 422 (Ky. 1992)
Humphrey v. Pope. 122 Cal. 253 (1898).
Hunt v. Hunt. 309 N.W. 2d 818 (S.D. 1981).
Irwin v. Coluccio. 32 Wash. App. 510, 648 P. 2d 458 (1982).
Jacobsen v. Siddal. 12 Or. 280, 7 P. 108 (1885).
Jaynes v. Jaynes. 39 Hun. (N.Y.) 40 (1886).
Johnson v. Allen. 100 N.C. 88 (1888).
Johnston v. Disbrow. 47 Mich. 59, 10 N.W. 79 (1881).
Karchner v. Mumie. 398 Pa. 13, 156 A. 2d 537 (1959).
Keen v. Keen. 49 Or. 362 (1907).
Kline v. Ansell. 287 Md. 585, 414 A 2d. 929 (1979).
Knapp v. Wing. 72 Vt. 334 (1900).
Knighten v. McClain. 227 N.C. 682 (1947).
Kohlhoss v. Mobley. 102 Md. 199, 62 A. 236 (1905).
Kroessin v. Keller. 60 Minn. 372, 62 N.W. 438 (1895).

Kromm v. Kromm. 31 Md. App. 635 (1975).
Lee v. Hammond. 114 Wis. 550, 90 N.W. 1073 (1902).
Linck v. Voorhauer. 104 Mo. App. 368, 79 S.W. 478 (1904).
Lockwood v. Lockwood. 67 Minn. 476, 70 N.W. 784 (1897).
Long v. Booe. 106 Ala. 570, 17 S. 716 (1894).
Lonstorf v. Lonstorf. 118 Wis. 159 (1903).
Markson v. Shelton. 124 F. Supp. 206 (D. Kan. 1954).
Michael v. Dunkle. 84 Ind. 544, 43 Am. Rep. 100 (1882).
Miller v. Pearce. 86 Vt. 322 (1913).
Moelleur v. Moelleur. 55 Mont. 30 (1918).
Morgan v. Martin. 92 Me. 190 (1898).
Neville v. Gile. 174 Mass. 305, 54 N.E. 841 (1899).
Nevins v. Nevins. 68 Kan. 410, 75 P. 492 (1904).
Newsom v. Fleming. 165 Va. 89, 181 S.E. 393 (1935).
Nichols v. Nichols. 134 Mo. 187 (1896).
Nolin v. Pearson. 191 Mass. 283 (1906).
Noxon v. Remington. 78 Conn. 296 (1905).
Oppenheim v. Kridel. 236 N.Y. 156 (1923).
Palmer v. Crook. 73 Mass. 418 (1856).
Parker v. Newman. 200 Ala. 103, 75 So. 479 (1917).
Peters v. Lake. 66 Ill. 206, 16 A. Rep. 593 (1872).
Plourd v. Jarvis. 99 Me. 161, 58 A. 774 (1904).
Postlewaite v. Postlewaite. Ind. App. 473 (1891).
Powell v. Strickland. 163 N.C. 393 (1913).
Prettyman v. Williamson. 1 Pennewill (Del. Sup.) 224 (1898).
Price v. Price. 91 Iowa 693 (1894).
Puth v. Zimbleman. 99 Iowa 641, 68 N.W. 895 (1896).
Rott v. Goehring. 33 N.D. 413, 157 N.W. 294 (1916).
Rudd v. Dewey. 121 Iowa 454, 96 N.W. 973 (1903).
Sanborn v. Neilson. 4 N.H. 501 (1828).
Saunders v. Alford. 607 So. 2d 1214 (Miss. 1992).
Scates v. Nailing. 196 Tenn. 508 (1954).
Seaver v. Adams. 66 N.H. 142, 19 A. 776 (1889).
Seiber v. Pettit. 200 Pa. 58 (1901).
Shannon v. Swanson. 109 Ill. App. 274 (1903).
Sikes v. Tippins. 85 Ga. 231, 11 S.E. 662 (1890).
Sims v. Sims. 79 N.J.L. 577, 76 A. 1063 (1910).
Smith v. Hockenberry. 138 Mich. 129 (1904).
Smith v. Meyers. 52 Neb. 70, 71 N.W. 1006 (1897).
Speck v. Gray. 14 Wash. 589 (1896).
Thomas v. Siddiqui. 869 S.W. 2d 740 (Mo. 1994).

Tinker v. Colwell. 193 U.S. 473 (1904).
Tucker v. Tucker. 74 Miss. 93 (1896).
Turner v. Heavrin. 182 Ky. 65, 206 S.W. 23 (1918).
Wales v. Miner. 89 Ind. 118 (1883).
Warner v. Miller. 17 Abb. 221 (N.Y.) (1885).
Warren v. Warren. 89 Mich. 123 (1891).
Weber v. Weber. 113 Ark. 471 (1914).
Westlake v. Westlake. 34 Ohio St. 621 (1878).
Witman v. Egbert. 50 N.Y.S. 3, 27 App. Div. 374 (1898).
Wolf v. Frank. 92 Md. 138 (1900).
Woodman v. Goodrich. 234 Wis. 565 (1940).
*Yundt v. Hartrunft.*41 Ill. 9 (1866).

Index